STORY DRAMA IN THE
SPECIAL NEEDS CLASSROOM

of related interest

Social Skills, Emotional Growth and Drama Therapy
Inspiring Connection on the Autism Spectrum
Lee R. Chasen
Foreword by Robert J. Landy
ISBN 978 1 84905 840 7

Let's All Listen
Songs for Group Work in Settings that Include
Students with Learning Difficulties and Autism
Pat Lloyd
Foreword by Adam Ockelford
ISBN 978 1 84310 583 1

100 Learning Games for Special Needs with
Music, Movement, Sounds and...Silence
Johanne Hanko
ISBN 978 1 84905 247 4

Drama Therapy and Storymaking
in Special Education
Paula Crimmens
ISBN 978 1 84310 291 5

Music for Special Kids
Musical Activities, Songs, Instruments and Resources
Pamela Ott
ISBN 978 1 84905 858 2

STORY DRAMA IN THE SPECIAL NEEDS CLASSROOM

Step-by-Step Lesson Plans for Teaching through Dramatic Play

JESSICA PERICH CARLETON

Jessica Kingsley *Publishers*
London and Philadelphia

Adapted song lyrics to *We're Going on a Bear Hunt* are reproduced
by permission of Michael Carleton.

First published in 2012
by Jessica Kingsley Publishers
116 Pentonville Road
London N1 9JB, UK
and
400 Market Street, Suite 400
Philadelphia, PA 19106, USA

www.jkp.com

Library of Congress Cataloging in Publication Data
Carleton, Jessica Perich.
 Story drama in the special needs classroom : step-by-step lesson plans for
teaching through dramatic play / Jessica Perich Carleton.
  p. cm.
 Includes bibliographical references and index.
 ISBN 978-1-84905-859-9 (alk. paper)
 1. Children with disabilities--Education. 2. Drama in education. 3. Drama-
-Therapeutic use. I. Title.
 LC4025.4.C37 2012
 371.9--dc23

                                              2011031446

British Library Cataloguing in Publication Data
A CIP catalogue record for this book is available from the British Library

ISBN 978 1 84905 859 9
eISBN 978 0 85700 469 7

Printed and bound in Great Britain

To VSA/NJ for giving me the opportunity to work with such extraordinary individuals. To the participants and parents who played with me each Saturday for inspiring and challenging me.

To my parents, two of the greatest teaching experts I know, for raising the bar of teaching excellence so high while mentoring the next generation that I may aspire to.

To my husband, for supporting and believing in me, particularly when I didn't.

CONTENTS

PREFACE

I was hired by VSA/NJ*, a Kennedy Center affiliate, as the Program Outreach Coordinator creating and championing programming for individuals of all ages, backgrounds, and levels of disabilities (mental and/or physical) for the state of New Jersey in all of the arts. It was an undertaking challenging everything I had learned, experienced, and practiced in and outside the classroom. The idea of working with individuals with disabilities, particularly elementary aged children (aged 5–12), can be daunting to the point of paralysis. Before I agreed to teach these classes, I nearly convinced myself out of this extraordinary opportunity, believing I could not possibly be qualified or knowledgeable enough to provide adequate programming for this group. I agreed to teach two sessions, each session an hour in length once a week for eight weeks, to groups aged 5–14 separated according to ability. The first session would be for the younger ages and the second session for the older students. The students were generally categorized as non-verbal, non-communicative autistic spectrum. I was told that most of the students would be low functioning but not severe and sensory needy. Past programming had consisted of music and movement whereby two teachers, one specializing in music the other in movement, worked with the students to

---

* Taken from the mission statement, VSA (Very Special Arts) is an international organization on arts and disability, that was founded more than 35 years ago by Ambassador Jean Kennedy Smith to provide arts and education opportunities for people with disabilities and increase access to the arts for all. With 52 international affiliates and a network of nationwide affiliates, VSA is changing perceptions about people with disabilities around the world. Each year, seven million people of all ages and abilities participate in VSA programs, in every aspect of the arts, including visual arts, performing arts, and literary arts.

great success, but I should not let the labels or the change in artistic programming scare me. This was a great group of students and the parents would be there to be shadows and help out. No problem. I went on the internet and browsed several bookstores searching for a creative dramatics book for elementary students with autism. I found nothing, and books that looked like they might be what I wanted were priced over $100 and sealed in plastic packaging. I'm a freelance artist, who at the time couldn't even afford to have health insurance, and was not about to gamble on the hopes that after I broke the packaging this would be my dream teaching book. I couldn't believe with all the proven research on how the arts improve many aspects of daily living, learning, and social skills that there was not a specific book aiding teachers and parents in and outside the classroom. Instead, I used my first week's pay to buy books about autism and instruction methodologies for individuals with autism in the classroom.

Then I received the background sheets from the parents with answers to a series of questions about their children to help in determining their level of ability and which group would be best for them. Reading over the sheets I became very overwhelmed. The students sounded extremely low functioning and I began to feel daunted and creatively and intellectually paralyzed. So I called in the big guns—my sister-in-law, who has worked with an impressive range of disabilities and is one of the most approachable and encouraging experts I know. I gave her an overall description of the groups' backgrounds, together with some of my ideas, and advocated that any advice she could impart would be greatly appreciated. She fulfilled all my requests, and echoed my original thoughts when teaching a class—that everything in theory based on the experts may or may not actually work, so don't take it personally if it does or doesn't. Remember that they are just people who happen to be able to do this and are not able to do that and adapt accordingly—a truism for any classroom.

Here begins the journey of this book. I reflected on the research, the stories and advice of teachers in the field, and my own theatre and education training and experience and knowledge of how to structure a lesson. The lessons described in this book can later be turned into a unit plan or into a year-long program which in a fun dramatic way will help the participants to accomplish and gain skills leading into a final theatrical assessment. The activities balance the sensory and physical overload to eliminate (to the best of one's ability) outbursts, and provide steps that any teacher (whether this is your first time trying theatre-in-education techniques with your students to the veteran teacher where these techniques are consistently used in the classroom) can understand and execute in many different classrooms.

CHAPTER **1**

WHAT IS THEATRE/ DRAMA-IN-EDUCATION?

INTRODUCTION

One may hear either of these terms used interchangeably—theatre-in-education and drama-in-education. Theatre means the live performance of a theatrical piece. Theatre-in-education refers to live theatre entering the educational setting, either through a professional troupe of actors or in a student driven piece where the final result is a performance for an audience. The students themselves can be the spectators viewing a piece of theatre as a means of learning where the reflection process occurs with the actors (professionals or students) after the performance or with the teacher in the classroom. The manner in which a person or group of persons receives the information determines whether the play is a piece of drama or theatre. This simply means that when a person reads a play it is a piece of drama. However, when the text is presented (whereby actors perform the lines) to a live audience it becomes a piece of theatre.

Drama-in-education refers to using the dramatic piece of writing to be acted out by the students or as an impetus for creating a dramatic piece that results not in a performance but in the study and exploration of the drama. The students participate in multiple roles throughout the drama-in-education process. The students will take the role of a character in the story experiencing his or her journey, the role of the design expert creating the world of drama through props, costumes and set pieces, and perhaps the spectator viewing the work of the other student actors, providing new information in the drama. Other roles may emerge depending on the sophistication of the story drama.

The teacher can decide the purpose of the story dramas to be executed as a source of drama-in-education or theatre-in-education. The story dramas in this book are presented as drama-in-education where the purpose is to explore the concepts and themes in the chosen children's stories through the use of dramatic techniques. They are presented this way to eliminate pressure to perform and also to focus on the complexity of the story and what the story teaches us by engendering the role of the protagonist. Theatre requires the focus to change from the exploration of the story to mastering performance techniques such as creating a character, acting techniques for performing the text, indicating through verbal and body communication the characters' intentions and desires as well as their relationship to others. Performance techniques are another level of complicated skills that the students must learn after mastering the deconstruction of the drama. This is not to say that the teacher should avoid theatre-in-education while working with these story dramas, as the results for performing their work for their peers is a wonderful assessment and achievement outcome. When moving from drama-in-education to theatre-in-education, the teacher should accomplish two separate learning outcomes that possess two different means of assessment. Performing the drama to a live audience requires another set of learning skills that the teacher must prepare the students for in advance in order for them to share their work successfully.

KEY FIGURES IN EDUCATIONAL THEORY AND DRAMA EDUCATION

Many theorists and practitioners past and present have contributed to shaping the validation of dramatic play as a means of intellectual growth in the early stages of child development. It is during play that students take on roles and responsibility that are foreign to them in real life but in the world of play they can actualize the emotions and position of others garnering a better understanding of the world around them. Children's stories have served as a means of communicating complex messages through the journey of the main character (also known as the protagonist). Messages such as: being mindful when entering the woods as there are animals that may harm children or that interacting with strangers requires a degree of caution as not to be lead into a dangerous situation, and so forth. The Arts Education Partnership and the President's Committee on the Arts and the Humanities, funded by General Electric Corporation and the John D. and Catherine T. MacArthur Foundation detailed in their report, *Champions of Change: The Impact of the Arts on Learning* (Fiske *et al.* 1999), that the arts not only increased test scores and lower dropout rates but also succeeded in creating group camaraderie, cultural tolerance, and connections to real world situations from the new skills discovered (Jensen 2001, p.3).

There is safety in the world of play where assessing and trying new things freely advances independent learning from the information that follows. The work of Jean Piaget brought attention to the importance of play in the child's development. Piaget believed that children learn through doing versus being told how to accomplish a task. Play permits children to perform the task and therefore comprehend and reapply that learned task correctly in the future. The classic folktale *The Little Red Hen*, guides the students through the process of discovering some grains of wheat and transforming those seeds into plants that can be made into flour and then into bread to eat. The students learn through performing these tasks how seeds are cultivated and harvested, and can eventually be transformed into making bread in real life. Many of the story dramas mentioned in this book tutor the students in independent living skills such as attending a costume party, planning a walk in the woods, negotiating with friends and individuals of power, playing in the snow, etc.

Piaget's work influenced many educational theorists, most notably Lev Vygotsky. Vygotsky reexamined the importance of play as a means of understanding one's culture and language, as well as actualizing one's desires through the notion of the zone of proximal development. This means that through guided participation with a teacher, coupled with creative individuals of the same age, the student's ability to understand concepts and conduct them independently increases. Students become independent learners using props as symbols to practice the skills needed to accomplish their final goal. During the story drama students are processing information through applying possible outcomes in order to solve a task. This constant self-assessment strengthens students' ability to analyze a task by refining their thinking or their performance of the task to make it more effective. The teacher theatrics listed in this book serve as vehicles for student self-assessment. Students interview other characters in the story researching new information by collaborating among peers before making a decision (hot-seating), by physically portraying character emotions determining where the character is and where the character would like to go (tableau), and by vocalizing character sentiments with a sound, word or phrase evaluating and connecting with the other characters present to prevent isolation and encourage discussion and organization (thought tracking). The teacher theatrics are fun to lead and participate in but they are also enormously influential in the student's emotional and intellectual development. Judith Burton conducted a study at Columbia University of more than 2000 children and found that the students who engaged in arts curriculum were far superior in creative thinking, self-concept, problem-solving, self-expression, risk-taking, and cooperation than those who did not (Jensen 2001, p.5).

HOW TO USE DRAMA/THEATRE-IN-EDUCATION WITH THE SPECIAL NEEDS CLASSROOM

Following these titans' philosophies on education, everyone has the ability to learn, particularly through the use of dramatic play as a means of learning new concepts. Dramatic play is a form of kinesthetic learning, actively engaging the body to learn, analyze, and develop new skills. Howard Gardner's (1993) theory of multiple intelligences enhances a student's bodily kinesthetic intelligence where the application of the body and one's hands are the means by which an individual solves a problem. The body knows how to solve a problem even if the learner is unable to describe and/or write the necessary steps. Concepts attained through kinesthetic learning bear long-term application, like the ability to ride a bicycle after five years versus when asked to remember and give the name for what the capital of Peru is (Jensen 2001, p.74).

Children need to get up and move and engage in dramatic play. Children learn better through kinesthetic learning as seen in the arts than sitting through a class lecture and taking notes. Children develop higher critical thinking and emotion skills through dramatic play. And nowhere is it more keenly apparent than with children with special needs, particularly autism, where the arts conjure an immediate response to learning and where clearly these individuals excel. Time and time again, we hear stories of a savant with autism who drew a picture similar to one by Leonardo da Vinci or a student with attention deficit disorder dancing with clean lines and form like that of Martha Graham.

The arts serve as an entry point for individuals with special needs to learn information. As detailed in this book, the balance of activity and inactivity when dealing with dramatic play are of the utmost importance. Hence the teacher will note that all the arts—not just theatre—are integrated into the lessons to ensure a balanced learning environment. The strength of the story dramas derives from integrating each artistic aspect into a complex final outcome. Each artistic aspect prepares the student with a skill that will be executed within the drama revealing how each skill is applied to a sophisticated final performance of those skills. Improvement, particularly over an extended period of time, is undoubtedly noted. In a short period of time, students begin to make eye contact, say the next line in the story during the drama, and the number of breakdowns decreases significantly.

Albert Einstein once said that the value of an education in a liberal arts college is not the learning of many facts, but the training of the mind to think of something that cannot be learned from textbooks. Perhaps following this credo from an individual whose name now is synonymous with genius and who battled his own learning difficulties during his education resonates a valid point in favor for the arts and dramatic play. When students enter into dramatic play they learn the most important intellectual and emotional skills to usher forth the next generation of contributors engaging in dialogue and making decisions based on empathy for another—a coveted skill reaped kinesthetically.

CHAPTER **2**

GETTING STARTED

Before beginning a lesson, the facilitator must determine what the goals are for the lesson and the best way to present them to the class. It is also important to consider the number and type of students in the class, the time period in which to achieve these goals, and the space one is working with in order to set realistic goals for each lesson. I began by outlining the weekly goals for the program and preparing my materials for the classroom based on the research I had done. These key classroom structure techniques circumvented problems that had a strong possibility of arising, and were instrumental in encouraging the children to feel safe. The effective classroom and lesson structure was presented in a way they could understand, permitting them to trust their teacher. This structure facilitated the weekly lesson regardless of the number of students who attended. Particularly when dealing with autism, many things may occur that might prevent a child from consistently attending each week. Therefore, it was imperative that the lesson be consistent without any spontaneous changes that may occur based on the number of students who are in the classroom any particular week. Some weeks I had 14 students and then other weeks there were three, but by following these classroom structure techniques, the number of attending students was inconsequential to fulfilling the lesson's objective.

And—rather more importantly when reflecting on a teacher's salary—my budget for materials (which includes all props for each week, the classroom structure techniques, etc.) was $100. These materials can be recycled from year to year or shared among several class sections for under $100.

Here is a description of how the lesson was structured for each week and each lesson.

VISUAL STORYBOARD AND SCHEDULE

The visual storyboard was composed of a poster board numbering the order of activities for the day and a corresponding picture with a word for the activity, which the students could see immediately upon entering the session. This structure was followed in *every* class section. Again, consistency is key:

1. **Hello song** was written below a picture of a group of students sitting listening to their teacher.

2. **Sing** was written below a person singing. This is where we sang a warm-up song, for example, "Head, Shoulders, Knees, and Toes."

3. **Group** was written under a group of individuals standing together. Here, we did our character walks.

4. **Art** was written under three crayons. Students sat and colored their props that they would use in the drama that day.

5. **Free dance** was written under stick figures dancing. Students would take their prop and would dance, play and move with their prop so that they would not be distracted by it during the drama.

6. **Act** was written under the tragedy and comedy masks. This was when we began the story drama.

7. **Read** was written under a person holding an open book. This is when we sat down and I read the story to them that we had just acted out.

8. **Goodbye song**: Like the Hello song at the beginning of the lesson and where the same image can be used to call students together and close out the lesson.

It was incredible how helpful this was. From the very first class, the students came up and looked at the order of events as their parents read and showed them when everything was happening. It was at this moment my mentor teacher leaned over and said, "This is brilliant." Every week students would come up and read the board and a feeling of contentment came over them because there were no surprises, therefore they were not overwhelmed.

POINTER

You can use a storyboard for disciplining in the classroom. For example, pictures with text showing the first warning, second warning, and so forth explaining that the first warning is a spoken warning and explanation why. The second is sitting out, and so forth. I sometimes used a storyboard for movements with the songs, for example, "Head, Shoulders, Knees, and Toes." There was a stick figure with his hands on his head as I pointed from picture to picture so the children could understand the movements that went with the song.

SINGING

In much of my research, singing and music were mentioned as helpful tools when working with children with autism. The first day of my class my mentor had advised, seeing my lack of transitions from activity to activity, that I sing a song between each activity incorporating directions, bringing the group together, and focusing them in order to move on to the next task. What I wasn't aware of (and what was completely understated in the research I read) was that singing was like a magic wand that waved over the class and ameliorated any chaos or catastrophe that may have been occurring.

POINTER

When in doubt or overwhelmed, *sing*—sing and all will be at peace. Whenever I sang, the students would freeze and look at me with a calm I had not seen before. The singing calmed and focused them. You do not need to sing like you are on *American Idol* or have a composer write up complicated music and lyrics for the classroom. I picked melodies and songs I already knew so that I wouldn't forget the songs from week to week (consistency, again) and made up words as I went along, usually repeating the same sentences over and over again. For example, our goodbye song after reading the book was the melody of "Good Night Ladies" with the made-up lyrics: goodbye students, goodbye students, goodbye students, we'll meet again next week. Bum, bum, bum…

CLASSROOM STRUCTURE

Your students spend their entire day in the same room— your classroom. Creating the world of believability for the classroom drama that is occurring in the same room must be at the forefront for the teacher. Changing the room can help: try moving a few desks or using another area of the classroom reserved for special subjects or activities.

DETERMINING THE THEATRICAL SET-UP

The level of artistic sophistication when determining the set and playing space is entirely up to the teacher. The teacher can choose to represent the characters in the story drama in a variety of ways. Characters can be portrayed through teacher-in-role or puppets. I portrayed many of my characters by printing out copies of the animals from a coloring book, coloring them, and taping them to a stick. And in some cases (when I couldn't afford the stick or was too tired) I simply held up the piece of paper. Puppets can come in a variety of forms: stuffed animals, sock puppets, paper origami, found objects, etc. Working with children with autism while creating a new lesson every week and gathering and preparing all my materials, I went for "the simple is best" approach. The point is you can use a piece of paper, set up the given circumstances ("This is a duck who lives by himself") and the children will believe this is the duck who lives on a farm and has no friends.

DESIGNATING THE PLAYING AREAS

When setting up your story dramas, it is best to keep the playing places and identification of the playing areas consistent within the story but also from new drama to new drama. There are number of ways of doing this. The major way the teacher can set the stage for story drama time is to arrange the room indicating to the students that we are entering this imaginative creative play world. During another class, the students could plan out the set for the drama and indicate where all the places are located, props needed, and so forth. Desks can be used as part of the design creating pathways, bridges, or general obstacles.

USING THE SPACE

The space I conducted my workshops in was massive to the point where my mentor told me this may not be a great space for children with autism and I might want the other smaller room. But I loved this room. It was clearly the game room where students could come to play pool (as there were several tables), a number of sofas for sitting areas to converse or play games, and foosball tables. Yes, all of this was certainly a distraction but in the center of the room were three long pillars on the right and left sides with different colored tile flooring shaping a box, and for the purpose of this class became the activity area where we learned the key elements in preparation for the drama. When we engaged in activity outside of the colored tile area, we were entering the story drama where we were exploring new uncharted and imaginative areas. The pool tables served as supports for brown paper to lay above them, creating a cave to crawl through and encounter new characters in the drama. No space is perfect. You can make it as perfect as possible for what you are trying to achieve.

SUPPLIES

One of my greatest necessities regarding supplies for the story drama was something that many teachers can get from the art room, and that was long reams of colored paper. I bought brown, white, red, green, black, and yellow. These colors served as locations for the story drama. For example, in *The Little Red Hen* I used the brown paper for the garden to plant the seeds. In *We're Going on a Bear Hunt* the blue paper with big black dots was the creek with the stepping stones to get across, the green for the waving grass, and so forth. The students would walk from paper to paper knowing that each paper represented where they were and how to return to a certain location in the drama. Especially in *We're Going on a Bear Hunt* there are multiple locations and the drama requires the student actors to return to the many locations over and over again. Because of this repetition, the students start to become the leaders pointing to the proper location of the creek, the fields, etc. I created the character representations through printouts derived from searching the internet and finding the images that I had in mind.

VISUAL STORYBOARD

Here is a great website to get you started on your visual storyboard: Do2Learn at www.dotolearn.com. Click on the Picture Cards box and you can select any of the highlighted categories to seize your desired visual aid and then click print. You can also find some of your animal characters for the story dramas. The best part is that everything is free.

PROPS

Props are any objects mentioned or implied in the story drama. Particularly when working with students with disabilities, the more tactile the prop, the more they engage the students in the world of the drama, enhancing believability. Students are more focused using the props available versus trying to imagine size, shape, weight, and usage. Again, many times I cut out pictures from a website. These cut-outs at times were used for the art section in the dramatic formula (see Chapter 4 for an explanation of this term). Ideas are provided in the specific lesson plans for props.

SHADOWS IN THE CLASSROOM

One of the benefits of being part of a non-profit organization that offered these classes outside of the classroom on a Saturday was that we could set the expectations from parents and students in advance on how the class would be most successful. One of the stipulations was that the parents served as "shadows" throughout the lesson, guiding the students through certain activities or disruptive behavior. This was tremendously helpful and necessary as it would have been impossible for the teacher to attend to all the distractions of student discontent and/or any special assistance to complete a task.

The purpose of this role is to literally shadow the student who needs extra help or attention throughout the lesson. The shadow is to stay behind and in the dark, allowing the student in need to independently try to complete the task. The shadow would emerge if tasks required an assistant to equalize the student's ability with the rest of the class. The shadows were also there to help in student outbursts that may occur during the class or provide dexterous assistance peeling off sticker backings to attach to a prop. Students, particularly those with autism, experience amplified emotions whereby they sometimes need to remove themselves from the experience. A shadow is imperative at these moments because these outbursts can spread to the other students in the class. The shadow can defuse the outburst and involve the student again later in the lesson.

Because of the necessity of having shadows in the class, I have provided a few creative ways for the elementary teacher to secure help with a little organizing on the teacher's part.

GUIDANCE COUNSELORS AND IEP SPECIALISTS

The primary function of guidance counselors and IEP specialists is to provide the teacher and students with the resources and adaptations to allow the students to thrive in the classroom as well as with their fellow classmates. These specialists can either be the shadows themselves or engage in the organization of scheduling outside shadows to be in attendance. IEP stands for Individualized Education Program which develops and describes specific goals set during the student's school year while providing special support for the student to achieve them. The IEP specialist works with a team of professionals (usually the classroom teacher, the student, and the guidance counselor, if the guidance counselor isn't the IEP specialist him- or herself) to set realistic goals for the student.

HIGH SCHOOL STUDENTS

The trend in many U.S. states for high school students (aged 14–18) as a graduation requirement is to complete a determined number of hours of volunteer community service. These student shadows would require more planning on the teacher's part with the high school in order for the student to leave and attend the elementary class. Honor students, who could leave during a study hall or be exempt from class every so often or once a week, would be reliable and mature individuals to honor the expectations of the elementary school teacher and the story drama. Honor students are those students who maintain a grade point average of an A or higher. Each school determines what percentage constitutes an A, however the percentage for an A would not be lower than 90. The teacher can also set up a rotation of high school students so that one student is not missing a plethora of classes.

STUDENTS WITHIN THE CLASS

Depending on the specific age group of the class and level of disability, the students within the class can serve as shadows assisting during specific sections like the walks where the shadow could model the behavior or help to construct a prop. This could also encourage the class to treat each other as an ensemble, working together and caring for each other while trying to complete a common goal.

PARENT TEACHER ASSOCIATION (PTA)

The PTA will have a greater networking system within the community to locate and identify outside the school possibly experienced helpers to enter the classroom as shadows. The PTA can also organize the parents who are available and appropriate for the classroom as shadows.

PRO-SEM (PRO-SEMESTER)

Professional-semester, also known as student teaching and includes the mandated observation hours conducted by the college students, is an appointed year for college students, usually their second or third year of college, where the students must complete a designated number of hours as determined by the Department of Education for each state in the United States. These requirements determined by the state for college students before entering their professional semester include but are not limited to: a completion of specified courses in their major, successful passing the Praxis exam (examinations required in order to receive teacher certification), completion of classroom observation hours, and criminal and child abuse background checks. These students (ideally special education majors) would be perfect shadows as they desire to be teachers in the classroom coupled with the fact that in order for them to pass and continue on to student teaching doing well as a shadow is at stake.

CHAPTER **3**

TEACHER THEATRICS

Many teachers cringe at the idea of performing, far more so than being outnumbered in the classroom. The theatrics required by the teacher in these lessons can easily be executed by the debutante to the skilled thespian and require no formal training in advance. The fear that arises from either teaching a class of children with autism or portraying the bear in a children's story stems from our unpreparedness to perform the task. It is something that is foreign to us; something that is unknown. Perhaps we have never pretended to be a bear before or maybe we did for our nieces and nephews and they thought we were not very believable. And so the "not knowing" how to begin or be convincing can be immobilizing. Teachers should feel free to try each of these separately before they enter the drama with their class. The teacher can explain to the class they are going to do some theatre today and, for example, can have the students create a still-image (tableau) of playing baseball. Each student can participate in creating all the parts that make up playing a baseball game. Some could be players, fans, hot-dog sellers, referees, etc. Below are a series of teacher theatrics that can be utilized by the teacher to instill further learning in the story drama. Each of the teacher theatrics enrich the drama by drawing on mastered knowledge from other subjects. They promote dialogue among the students by discovering alternative outcomes and consequences, encouraging decision-making, and sequencing among a large group.

POINTER

Throughout this book I will provide many examples clarifying drama-in-education techniques and concepts. Examples will be selected from the story, *The Little Red Hen.*

STORY DRAMA

This book and the dramas detailed for the classroom focus around story drama. Story drama consists of actively engaging in a chosen story through the use of dramatic techniques. Story drama sticks with the narration and plot of the chosen story unraveling the beginning, middle, and end. Story drama brings to life the activity of the characters in the story through the eyes of the student actors engendering a specific role. The student actors empathize with a specific character's journey (usually the protagonist) to fulfill a quest whereby a lesson is learned. The level of complexity of the story drama is at the discretion of the teacher. The teacher can read the narration in the story and then engage in the dramatic activity outlined in the book (e.g. the Little Red Hen finds some grains of wheat and plants them) or the teacher can incorporate a number of teacher theatrics (listed later) to discover a richness in the plot, characters, message, etc. The teacher would then resume the drama by returning to the narration dictated in the book. Story drama does not stray from the story but rather develops and amplifies the information buried in the story. Story drama is an excellent methodology to introduce a class for the first time to drama-in-education. The structure is comforting to the teacher and the class is aware of each individual's responsibility before, after, and during the drama.

PROCESS DRAMA

Process drama, which is more advanced than story drama, is the action of an evolved idea that changes and grows and has no finished, predetermined ending. The purpose of the drama is to guide the students through a series of drama-in-education techniques that enhance and provide greater depth in the learning process. While embarking on this dramatic process, the teacher should be flexible to what is being offered by the students that may prove fruitful to the drama. The students may want to speak with a character, which is an activity that was not on the original list of dramatic techniques. However, by allowing this interview, the students are synthesizing the teacher's objective for the lesson, researching and gathering more information about the learning lesson presented in the drama. Process drama is an advanced form of drama-in-education where a dramatic catalyst instigates the drama. These catalysts could derive from a newspaper clipping, a picture, a story, etc. These catalysts raise an issue to be discussed and explored such as bullying or cliques.

DRAMA-IN-EDUCATION TECHNIQUES FOR PROCESS DRAMA

Drama-in-education techniques the teacher can organize into a process drama include tableaux, thought tracking, hot-seating, and narration.

TABLEAUX

In a tableau, groups or individuals "devise an image [pose or shape] using their own bodies to crystallize a moment, idea or theme; or an individual acts as sculptor to a group" (Neelands and Goode 2000, p.25). (A tableau is also known as still-image.) There are five basic elements that make up an effective tableau: levels, eye contact, facial expressions, use of space, and dynamic.

Levels

Are there different levels in the picture or is everyone at the same height? This means there should be highs and lows in the alignment of the bodies. Chairs or stools or perhaps other actors are needed in order to make someone higher than the others. This can transition into reflection where the teacher can ask the students what the image says based upon who is the highest and who is the lowest? These answers can be transferred to the story discussing themes and plot developments.

Eye contact

Where are the actors in the image looking? Are they all looking at the same person or at different actors or not at anyone at all? What does this say about the image? If eyes are the window to the soul, the choices the actors make in where and how they are looking at someone communicates volumes about the mood and purpose of the image. Eye contact also determines the *point of focus*. The point of focus is whom or what in the tableau is drawing the eye immediately.

Opportunity for Further Learning

If all the students are kneeling on the ground and looking up to another student standing on a chair looking up, we can immediately conjure the meaning(s) behind the image. Now, if the teacher asks the student on the chair to look down at the students, what message is being conveyed and how has the image changed from its original intent?

Facial expressions

The expression on the students' faces communicates internally and externally what is happening within and to the character in the image as well as to whom and what those sentiments are directed towards. By reflecting on the facial expressions of the students in the image, the viewer can determine the overall mood of the image, their individual intentions for themselves or towards another character in the image, and the internal feeling(s) of each character in the image.

Use of space

How did the students in the tableau use space to communicate a message? Are the characters close together or are they very far apart? Are some characters closer than others? The use of space communicates the relationships between the characters in the image. Are the characters united or divided? Looking back at the other elements that make up an effective tableau, the question what is dividing them or uniting them can be determined through their facial expressions, eye contact, and levels communicating the internal and/or external conflicts within the characters.

Dynamic

Dynamic refers to the energy frozen in the bodies of the characters in the tableau. If we were to pause a video of a character running away from a burning building we could still see the dynamic energy in the body and face of the character frozen in mid-action. By looking at that image, we can tell the emotions of the character and the extremes of those emotions or the objective of the character and what he or she is willing to do to achieve it. In order to dynamize the tableau the teacher can ask the students the following questions: What is at stake for these character(s) in the tableau? What is it that they desperately need and why? How might they go about fulfilling their intention? And at what lengths are they willing to go in order to fulfill that intention? At the end of *The Little Red Hen*, the other animals discover that in order to eat bread they need to do the preliminary work as well. Because they really want that bread, they are willing to do something they don't like.

Ask your students to keep the position, intention, etc. just as it is but now show how they are looking and feeling bigger times ten. As the spectators, we should see the energy in their body and how that energy is directed. If the characters are to appear as if they were frozen in the middle of a sprinting race, we should see the energy in the body mid-sprint. The teacher should feel free to ask the students how would it look in real life? Have them physically do the image—if it is a mid-sprint, have the students sprint and when the teacher says "Freeze," there is the image.

THOUGHT TRACKING

The technique of thought tracking can be used at multiple places in the drama, either through tableau or freezing a moment in the drama. To thought track the teacher taps the student actor, to give a word, phrase, or sound describing how they are feeling in a particular moment.

The teacher can execute this technique in the "Walking the room" section of the dramatic formula before entering into the drama to prepare the students for making sounds, a word, or phrase dependent upon the activity and/or what their character is thinking and/or feeling. For example, if the students are told to walk around the room as if they are walking down a muddy path in the woods, the teacher could say "Freeze" and then use the thought tracking technique. The teacher may feel that at first asking the students to give a sound that describes how they are feeling is challenging. Therefore, the technique can also be used, in order to lead into some more challenging responses, to describe something externally. With the walking down a muddy path in the woods example, the teacher could ask the students when touched to make the sound they hear when they lift their boot from the mud. These sounds can be used later in many of the selected stories for the story drama, particularly *We're Going on a Bear Hunt*.

POINTER

The method the teacher uses to thought track a student is inconsequential. You may find that tapping a student on the shoulder will not be a safe or effective way of promoting learning. Therefore, the teacher could choose a gesture, a sound, a prop piece (e.g. a magic wand when it's pointed at the student), or a physical movement that will be the student's cue to solicit a response.

HOT-SEATING

When a student, embodying a character, sits on a chair (the hot seat) whereby the other students can interrogate the character discovering his or her motivation, reasoning, feelings, etc., this is known as hot-seating. Where thought tracking helps to create mood and character development, hot-seating has the potential of delving deeper into the plot, character conflicts and relationships, ethics, themes, etc. This technique instigates dialogue perhaps with characters the students may never have spoken to before. Through this character discussion, the students develop empathy for those characters whom they may have prejudged.

POINTER

You may find as a teacher that the hot-seating technique at first is rather challenging, but students can build up to this moment throughout the year. I found the best way to first approach this technique was to treat the entire class of actors as the character and I, as the interviewer, hot-seated the character and whoever wanted to answer the questions was welcome to. Whatever answers were given, even contradictory as we contradict ourselves in real life, served as the one voice of the character. Contradictory answers can be very useful in demonstrating that all the student actors encapsulate the voice of this character by pointing out how these mixed messages can come from one character—what's the real truth? This forces the students to focus on the truth of the character and story drama where the students may need to conference internally before answering the question. As the students become more familiar with answering questions in character, it will then become easier to isolate smaller groups or individuals as a specific character.

Hot-seating can be approached in many different ways. The teacher can have one student actor portraying the character who is to be questioned or a group of student actors representing the character and answering collectively. Listed below are the simplest to the most challenging approaches to this technique of hot-seating. By following this progression from the simplest to the most challenging, the students and teachers will find transitioning to the more challenging aspects easier. This may not be true for all classes depending on the structure of the class and the ability of the students, where starting at a more challenging technique is a fine place to begin.

Going in groups: inside the story drama
PUPPET AS CHARACTER OR TEACHER-
IN-ROLE AS CHARACTER

The story dramas as depicted in this book use the method of hot-seating because it is a very simple introduction for the teacher and the students to ask challenging questions, as well as for the teacher and eventually the students answering those challenging questions. If theatre activities are new to the teacher or to the students, starting with the simple puppet technique is the best approach before moving onto more advanced approaches listed below.

Puppet technique

As explained throughout the book, puppets can take many forms. For me the puppets were paper cut-outs from a coloring book that I held and moved their head from side to side. I was the voice of the puppet, answering the students' questions while standing off to the side of the paper and always looking at the puppet when it spoke. The students followed my example, so that when these puppet characters were introduced, the students didn't look at me but at the puppet character. The teacher remains the teacher of the class with this approach, assisting the process forward with questions for the character, particularly if there is certain information the teacher wants the students to learn before moving into the next plot point or activity in the story drama.

Teacher-in-role technique

The teacher-in-role approach is described in great detail in the "Teacher-in-role" section later in this chapter. When the teacher has taken on a role in the story drama, the teacher-in-role can open up a hot-seating moment. Unlike the use of the puppet, the teacher now in role must lead the technique as that character would, perhaps asking why are they here and what do they want, encouraging the students to speak up. Teachers-in-role may need to just start sharing information about themselves and ask the student actors questions in order to instigate an interview.

PUPPET AS CHARACTER: REPRESENTED BY STUDENTS

The student serves as the voice of the character, sharing information about the character and moving the plot forward. The teacher remains the teacher facilitating the activity by asking questions and perhaps helping with answers for the student actor as the voice of the puppet. The student taking on the voice of the character needs to be decided upon in advance, otherwise the world of believability may be compromised. In

STORY DRAMA IN THE SPECIAL NEEDS CLASSROOM

the past, I have had students serve as interpreters or translators for the animal. The teacher can then speak gibberish or make the sound of the animal, say nothing and have the students invent the information, or help the students with the interpretation by asking questions as to what they think they heard the puppet character say. If the student feels comfortable, he or she can stand to the side as the teacher has in the past or put the mask in front of him- or herself, create a voice if desired, and answer the questions.

ENTIRE CLASS: REPRESENTING ONE CHARACTER

This approach is used inside of the drama where the entire class represents a specific character in the story drama. In the story dramas outlined in this book, this structure sets up the student actors as the protagonist in the story, allowing the transition into this technique to be seamless. The teacher takes on the role as the interviewer. The teacher/interviewer can be another character in the story. There are several places within the story dramas provided where the student actors on their journey to solving a problem encounter several characters along the way. Before reciting the dialogue provided in the book between the characters, the teacher (now in role) can hot-seat the protagonist, played by the student actors. The teacher (in role) can then revert back to the dialogue in the story to move the drama to the next plot point.

SMALL GROUPS: REPRESENTING DIFFERENT CHARACTERS, OUTSIDE OF THE DRAMA

Before the drama begins, small groups can be designated to represent specific character(s) in the story. For example, in the story *We're Going on a Bear Hunt*, the family is the protagonist in the story. Each small group can represent a member of that family who embarks on their journey into the woods. Each small group assigned to a character can develop their character before the implementation of this technique in a variety of ways.

The teacher can use the Mini Mantle or Mantle of the Expert techniques (described later in this chapter) where students are given a packet of information and must discover who their character is along with creating new information about their character. From this exercise, the student actors have a strong sense of their character, reducing the anxiety of "performing."

Opportunity for Further Learning

The teacher can have the other interrogating groups ask the hot-seated group questions in character. For example, reverting back to the story drama of *We're Going on a Bear Hunt*, the "brother" may be on the hot seat and the "sister" can ask him a question about their journey and what they are doing today. It could be fun for the teacher to line up the family oldest to youngest and so forth.

SMALL GROUPS: REPRESENTING DIFFERENT CHARACTERS, INSIDE THE DRAMA

The teacher will find implementing the above approach makes transitioning into this more advanced method easier. This is not to say that it is necessary to practice the above approach before executing this method in the drama. Again, the teacher knows best how to gauge everyone's comfort level and ability to achieve learning. At some point in the drama, a student actor is hot-seated either by the other student actors in various roles. *Note*: as this technique becomes more challenging, it is imperative that the students know who they are and what is expected of them in and out of role. The teacher should introduce the situation by referring to the students by their character names or clarifying that we are no longer in role and are students or outsiders asking questions to this character in order to understand the character's world.

Going solo

ONE STUDENT ACTOR: OUTSIDE OF THE DRAMA

This means that the drama has not yet started, or the drama is over, but there are more questions that the student might have where perhaps this technique may help give some insight as to why certain events happened in the story and/or drama. Because you are outside of the drama, the teacher can set up the technique as a talk show, such as Barbara Walters or Oprah Winfrey, and introduce the characters while giving character background and context helping the student to get into character. The teacher can choose the student actors by a show of hands, or if students have been assigned a character in advance to follow throughout the drama to take on the role at this time. The teacher can go into role as the interviewer or can just facilitate as an interviewer would. The teacher can take questions from the audience to ask the characters.

ONE STUDENT ACTOR: INSIDE THE DRAMA

This means that during the story drama, a student actor is placed on the hot seat to gain further information about either the character or plot development. The teacher may want to have a character piece that the student feels is appropriate. Just like how the teacher enters into role, the student can and should have the advantage of taking on a role enhancing the world of believability for the student actor taking on the role and those interrogating the character. The student actor taking on the role has the opportunity to step out of role, distinguishing for the class and the student actor him- or herself when he or she is in character and when he or she is not at any time during the drama.

NARRATION

Narration can be teacher or student driven where new information is introduced propelling the drama forward.

Narration is the dominant technique utilized in the story dramas unveiling the plot, characters, themes, etc. in a clear and complete manner. With narration, the teacher can provide information without subtext or subtlety. Narration is an excellent tool to use when the teacher may feel that the students didn't perhaps understand something or where repetition of an idea or plot development is necessary. Narration is also excellent for detailing descriptive action mirroring the "Walking the room" section in the visual storyboard how the student actors are to move from destination to destination and what obstacles may appear on their way.

With the complete story dramas and suggested stories included in this book, the story narration is very repetitive in nature where the students have the opportunity to lead the narration. This is a very simple way of turning the drama over to the students empowering them to participate in the many other techniques listed in the teacher theatrics.

TEACHER-IN-ROLE

In teacher-in-role, the teacher takes on a role in order to provide more knowledge in the drama, inspires student involvement, and stimulates the next task in the drama.

POINTER

For the story dramas listed in this book, the purpose of the roles is to fulfill a task that is to be completed by the students and to provide information and instruction for their next task. These rules also apply if the teacher chooses to use a puppet or paper cut-out for the characters the student actors meet on their journey. The teacher will not have to create a new stance, but a voice must be selected and facilitating of questions and answers needs to be prepared in advance.

The technique of teacher-in-role merits more attention because in the story drama formula expressed in this book, teacher-in-role is executed in every drama. The idea of playing a character in front of one's students can appear an off-putting task, one that seems impossible to pull off unless you're Meryl Streep or Russell Crowe. This is far from true. The truth of the matter lies in the teacher's ability to *suggest* the role he or she is trying to convey to the students. These suggestions can take several forms—a different voice or patter, a different stance, or a costume piece (hat, scarf, cane, etc.). The teacher should *not* put on a theatrical demonstration confusing the students as to their involvement and etiquette during this performance. The students may assume they are being entertained and therefore should sit and watch the performance and laugh, clap, sit, and enjoy the show. The story dramas encourage student participation throughout as actor-learners and not as audience members. In England I gave a process drama in a middle school drama classroom on George Orwell's *Animal Farm*. The teacher-in-role technique was utilized to represent multiple characters—the pig (Comrade Napoleon) and Mrs. Jones (the farmer's wife). I had another teacher present to go into role as Mr. Jones (the farmer). To represent the different characters and to indicate when I was in and out of role, I made simple yet concrete adjustments: a pashmina draped around my shoulder crossed my chest and tied at the hips like a military sash to represent Comrade Napoleon. My stance consisted of hunching over staring at the students intimidatingly and when I spoke it was in a low quiet tone. For Mrs. Jones the pashmina was worn as a shawl. The students in this process drama played the animals. They were never given costumes or new stances or different voices. The given circumstances were defined in the narration given at the top of the drama that we were animals on a particular farm who were called forth late at night for a meeting in the barn by Comrade Napoleon.

WHEN AND HOW TO TAKE ON A ROLE

When picking a role to embody, the teacher should pick a role with the intention and foreknowledge of what you want to happen. The teacher must know in advance the purpose of the role to stimulate the next task. You reveal/conceal what will initiate where the drama will go. I chose the role of Comrade Napoleon because I wanted to incite the students (like Napoleon) to believe the animals should walk on two legs, making them superior to Farmer Jones, and to organize a takeover. Later as the animals were revolting against him, Farmer Jones was introduced sitting depressed because of the animals' hatred towards him after he had cared for them all these years. Here, the role was chosen to raise awareness of how one's actions affect those around us, particularly when we are swept away by unquestioning emotions. These roles served a purpose in moving the drama forward. In order for the students to sympathize with the characters in the book, they needed to feel what those characters were feeling and the power of their mistaken actions, the consequences that follow, and learn from it.

POINTER

A wonderful video to watch that covers beautifully everything I have written, coupled with the fact you get to see the work in action, is at this website: www.teachfind.com/teachers-tv/ks12-drama-workshop-cecily-oneill. There are other videos to view as well. However, this one is led by Dr. Cecily O'Neill, a leading international practitioner in drama-in-education. She extended drama-in-education's reach with the invention of process drama and creating a methodology for teachers to implement in the classroom.

With going in and out of role, the teacher has the ability to change the tone of the drama, particularly if the emotions of the students become extreme. The teacher can step out of role and narrate the next section of the story, changing the atmosphere and releasing the dramatic tension. A friend of mine told a story where she and her elementary class were engaged in a process drama where she was in role as the bad witch and the students were on a journey to defeat the bad witch who was discriminating against certain persons in the village. At one point nearing the end of the drama, the students were empowered to confront and defeat the witch for they had successfully completed all their tasks. She said the students began charging at her, ready to throw her to the ground, and she was completely unprepared for this visceral reaction. My friend survived and so will you. There are a few lessons to learn from this episode. My friend was successful in her drama because the students were genuinely engaged in the process drama and reacted accordingly. Success. Now looking at how to deal with this reaction, the teacher should have anticipated that this reaction would occur and therefore in the beginning of the drama could have made sure to explain how the bad witch might be defeated—perhaps by a certain chant, a dance, throwing water at her, or some other imaginative non-violent action that would destroy the bad witch whereby the teacher could act accordingly. The other alternative would be to have the teacher get out of role (preferably before the students came too close) and immediately go into the narrative, so that the students are aware that the witch is gone and their teacher has returned, and so they resume proper teacher-student behavior.

POINTER: STUDENTS GETTING IN AND OUT OF ROLE

This section has discussed the importance of how the teacher is to get in and out of role. It is just as important to have the same clarity for the students. The students need to understand who they are and at what moment so as to invest in the drama sharing appropriately. The examples given in the "Teacher-in-role" section are just as applicable for the students as well. The teacher can decide if using a physical costume piece such as a hat or scarf where the students would take the piece on and off is the most clear or if an invisible means of moving in and out of character like a chant and movement is best. Some suggestions for determining when the students are in role and when they are not can be an invisible suit that the students step into and zip up like a wetsuit. Students can jump in and out of role. The teacher can possess a certain magic wand that transforms them into the character the teacher requests. The teacher needs to incorporate a "thing" that the class does to symbolize who we are. Students can then turn back into students if the teacher feels the students are distracted or overstimulated.

MANTLE OF THE EXPERT

The most advanced and involved of the process drama experiences is a technique called the Mantle of the Expert invented by the great Dorothy Heathcote*. This technique could sustain the drama over the course of a semester to the entire year crossing over several different subjects in order to complete the drama. Many teachers who use this technique select a certain time of the week (every Friday) and replace a certain class period or the last hour of the day (social studies, for example, if the drama requires a greater understanding of other cultures). It is during this time the students become imbued as experts in the area of exploration.

POINTER

Any teacher theatrics listed in this chapter can be applied to any of the story drama lesson plans. The teacher has the authority to go to whatever lengths he or she deems appropriate for the class. The teacher can use all of the teacher theatrics spread across the entire curriculum, over the entirety of the semester, or pick and choose certain theatrics that are of interest to the teacher or the class in general.

---

* Dorothy Heathcote is one of the most influential theatre education practitioners revolutionizing the field through her creation of theatre techniques in the classroom and her creation of the Mantle of the Expert. She is a retired elementary teacher and college professor who was appointed Member of the Order of the British Empire (MBE) in 2011.

MINI MANTLE

The Mini Mantle covers a shorter period of time, perhaps just one day or over the course of a week. The students take on the role as experts to complete a single task. This task can be broken up into smaller groups where each student group's work completes the overall task. For example, I conducted a Mini Mantle over the course of a week where we met for 40 minutes and the presentation was on the last day. It was a Mini Mantle on endangered species for fifth graders (10–11 years old) with special needs. The students were expert scientists with an expertise in determining uncategorized endangered species and these experts were to present their findings at the Endangered Species Conference (conveniently on the day they were to present what they learned to their parents and school). The students were given research boxes where each day the box yielded a clue as to their endangered animal, and aiding them in completing their tasks, such as filling in the animal's birth certificate, drawing or creating the food it eats and taping it to a plate, determining where the animal was in the food chain, and so forth.

SETTING UP THE DRAMA

So how do we decide to go into a drama for the first time, when this may be our first time playing characters in front of our students? What if they think we're crazy? What if they won't believe us, laugh, and not move on with the drama and then our lesson is a failure? The first step that teachers should take with their class is to explain what is about to occur— explain that the class will embark on a journey. It is the journey of the Little Red Hen, what she discovers, and how her friends respond to helping her. Explain that during the drama they will encounter many different characters that the Little Red Hen comes in contact with—the teacher will show them these characters. Then ask the students if they think they can go on the journey as the Little Red Hen. A useful tactic to include in your student preparation is to tell the students that before we enter the story drama they must put on their imagination hats. The teacher will then explain that something amazing happens when they put the imagination hats on their heads: students who are truly imaginative, can talk to animals, are accepting of all things seen and unseen, follow directions, work together with each other respectfully, and/or fulfill whatever expectations the teacher has of the students during the drama. Whether the teacher chooses to do the imagination hat technique is optional, however, the expectations of the teacher should be explained in some fashion. The teacher then has the ability to indicate what the classroom management procedure is if the students do not follow the expectations expressed for the story drama. The teacher should also explain what the classroom management will be, such as a warning system per individual. Students may be asked to sit out of the drama due to behavior, but those students can observe and participate during the reflection periods based on their perspective from the outside.

CREATING THE WORLD OF BELIEVABILITY

There are many different entry points to creating the "world of believability." It depends on the teacher, the amount of time the teacher chooses to dedicate to the dramatic process, and the experience of the students with process drama determining their ability to believe whatever the teacher deems as true in the drama. Before ever entering the story drama, there are a few simple techniques the teacher can do to create the world of believability.

Design teams

The teacher can choose all or some or just one of the following design teams, executing the tasks as a class or in small expert groups, depending on the time available.

SET DESIGN TEAM

The set design team could create a layout or map of the area as indicated in the story drama, maybe a diorama of the main playing space, which could be a house or particular part of a trail that the characters take in the drama.

COSTUME AND PROPS TEAM

The costume and props team can compile character profiles, indicating what the characters look like and are wearing. The profiles can be drawn and written out through journals or bio poems, which can be used as the puppets or characters that the class encounter on their journey.

COMMUNITY AND SOCIETAL STRUCTURE TEAM

The community and societal structure team pertains to the community or world in which the students live and the laws that govern this society. The class can create the flag for their community, motto, their pledge of allegiance, national song, and so on.

RITUAL OF THE DAY

This ritual clarifies the natural progression of the characters' days. This could be a day planner sheet where the times are filled in, revealing what a typical day is like for them from hour to hour. The ritual can also be what the farm animal community does every day. Perhaps, everyone is awakened by the cockerel at 8am and then says the pledge, sings the song, does a dance, raises the flag, etc. Whatever tasks are required of each design team can be presented as a daily ritual.

POINTER

The design team or teams have set up the given circumstances for the drama. The given circumstances contain the true information about the world of the drama. The given circumstances for *The Little Red Hen* are that there is a hen living on a farm with four other friends: the duck, the goose, the cat, and the pig (the friends may differ, depending on the version). The hen finds some grains of wheat and makes bread. This is the truth of the story that is unquestioned—needs to be on a farm, needs to have four animal friends who let her down, etc. Now, the class can go into greater detail about the farm—where things are located, what her house is made of, the proximity of the other friends' homes, etc. All of these questions and ambiguities would be fleshed out by the design teams. The ritual of the day is a wonderful way of entering the drama because the students have already taken on the role of the animals and are invested in the truth of the drama because *they* created the world of the drama.

Narration

Narration is discussed earlier in this chapter, but I would like to take narration a step further as a means of entering the world of believability. This requires more commitment to the reality of the drama from the teacher, who serves a bit like a master of ceremonies enticing the students to play. The teacher can have the book open on the first page and read aloud, indicating where in the classroom the listed places in the story are located. The students know that when they walk on the brown paper they are in the field or the garden. The right corner of the room with a chair is the hen's house where they will bake the bread. The teacher can then place the book down when action is required: the hen is walking on the farm and finds some grains of wheat. This can be an active narration where the student actors are performing the narration that is given to them simultaneously. The teacher can pick the book back up and start the next section. The story dramas in this book focus predominately on narration as means of creating the world of believability, setting up the given circumstances, and transitioning from task to task.

CHAPTER 4

DRAMATIC FORMULA

The dramatic formula is the outline of the lessons preparing the students to achieve the final goal—the story drama. The dramatic formula serves as the framework for further development of dramatic techniques, expanding opportunities for further learning. In sections of the lesson, the teacher will find *pointers* indicating which dramatic techniques would best serve a particular section and the purpose for choosing those techniques. These pointers can be omitted depending on the amount of time and commitment to the drama the teacher can afford in his or her classroom or based upon the students' readiness to engage in a longer involved drama. The teacher should approach the dramatic formula as a recipe for bread. No matter how one makes bread, there are key ingredients that are added in a particular order. The baker can jazz the bread up with raisins and cinnamon or more or less of another ingredient, but in order to make bread successfully the original framework of the recipe must be respected. The same is true for the dramatic formula. The structure of the formula prepares students with the tools they need in order to act out the drama.

The students are prepared for the story drama just as an athlete is prepared to play a game. Athletes challenge themselves by participating in a series of exercises during their practices. Basketball players will challenge themselves with dribbling exercises, lay-up drills, sprint drills, foul shot drills, passing drills, etc. All of these exercises and drills must be practiced individually and mastered for the athlete to win the game. Games are composed of a series of combined exercises creating a sophisticated assessment of the players' knowledge and ability to master the exercises. Each section is an exercise educating the students with a new dramatic tool that will be assessed in the drama. Let's examine each section and the objective for each as seen in the chosen exercises.

SONG

Song is reflected as 2. Sing on the storyboard providing the students with their first exercise. Each class starts off with a warm-up song. I always choose a song where the words or phrases would be found in the drama, the physical movements paralleling that of the drama, or depending on the mood of the class choose a song that motivates or calms down the class dynamic. I gravitated predominately between two songs— "Head, Shoulders, Knees, and Toes" (lyrics available from www. lyricszoo.com/the-wiggles/heads-shoulders-knees-and-toes) and "Shake Your Sillies Out" (lyrics available at www.lyricszoo. com/the-wriggles/shake-your-sillies-out). The latter song was always a class favorite and we wound up singing it as the warm-up song almost every week. The song was a recommendation from my mother, who teaches first grade and is known throughout the school as the queen, therefore she was the perfect expert to tap. It was a perfect song for the children to shake their sillies out, wiggle their waggles, jump their jaggles out, and yawn their sleepies out. It was fun and active and immediately prepared the students to walk around the room using their bodies to express someone or something known or foreign to them. Teachers can use any song that they desire. However, always keep in mind the skills (language, movements, emotions, etc.) the teacher wants the students to be able to accomplish during the drama and choose a song that mirrors some or all of those skills.

WALKING THE ROOM

Walking the Room, represents 3. Group Activity on the Visual Storyboard, it was the exercise I chose for every class. Teachers are not obligated to execute Walking the Room every time when engaging in a new story drama during the Group Activity section. However, whatever Group Activity the teacher chooses for this section, the skills needed by the students to succeed during the story drama need to be practiced and mastered here. The next exercise implements classroom management protocol as well as prepares the students to isolate certain moments, characters, feelings, etc. that will be found in the story drama at the culmination of the lesson. Before the students engage in any acting or characterizations of place, the teacher must implement safety for the students and ensure and assess their overall understanding of the skills addressed in the exercises to be used later in the drama. Theatre, as means of classroom management, is an extremely subtle and effective way of slowing down the drama where emotions or movement may be getting out of hand. The advantage of this kind of management is that it deters from stopping the drama and disciplining or warning a child where the blaming and shaming of the student(s) involved could invite unwanted drama and dissention in the lesson. This is really the first exercise in the dramatic formula where there are several steps the teacher must properly facilitate in order for the students to transfer those skills to the drama.

The first step, which serves as the classroom management for the story drama and for the lesson, carries an importance for mastering right from the beginning. The teacher should spend more time on the beginning and explain that the students may hear these calling words in the drama particularly if there is a need to stop. These calling words can be implemented throughout any part of the lesson to either slow down or increase the activity in the lesson.

"FREEZE, GO, JUMP, POINT" ACTIVITY

The exercise is exactly as it sounds:

- *Freeze*: when the teacher says "Freeze," the students are to freeze their bodies and mouths.

- *Go*: the students are to walk and should walk at a normal pace, with no running or talking but listening and ready for the next command.

- *Jump*: the students do one jump up in the air.

- *Point*: the teacher picks something or someone in the room for the students to point at. The teacher might say, "Point at the red chair," "Point at the floor," etc.

This whole beginning section clearly focuses the students to concentrate, pay attention, and listen for the next direction. This exercise can be applied throughout the entire dramatic technique to slow down, focus, or employ some of the teacher theatrics for further learning. This step is and should be a lot of fun. Teachers should take their time with each command, playing with the timing and the order. They can create a very fun activity just between "freeze" and "go." These two commands are very important to master because they serve as classroom management devices during the drama if the teacher feels they need to "freeze" and when the drama can "go" forward. The students will have learned this skill that can be applied at any time during the lesson.

Note: the teacher can also use the word "stop" as a substitute if "freeze" is too complicated to comprehend.

LOOKING AT A SELECTION OF EXAMPLES IN *THE LITTLE RED HEN*

Some characters found in the book to be portrayed are (depending on the version) the duck, the goose, the cat, and the pig. Some experiences in the story would be to walk in the mud, carry a heavy bag, searching for something very big, and later very small. These experiences can be a different walk when the teacher says, "Go." For example, the teacher would say, "Walk like you are looking for something very small. Go." The teacher can choose to say how they are going to walk, demonstrate how they are going to walk, say the explanation again and demonstrate. The teacher does not need to execute all three. In my classes, I only said how we were going to walk, said "Go", and off we went.

Emotions can be very difficult. It is common for students with autism and other disabilities to have difficulty expressing emotions with their faces and bodies. Therefore, when dealing with emotions during the "Walking the room" section it is important that the teacher describes and models what the face and body look like when expressing that emotion. For example, stand up very tall with head up (pride), curve one's body like there is weight on your chest pulling it down and weight on your shoulders pulling you down (sadness), like you can't stop laughing and throw your body back and forward very far (great happiness). "Walking the room" was a vital section in the dramatic formula because the teacher can isolate every moment in the drama and practice the complexity of these moments in a safe and dissected manner. When it is time for the drama the students can recognize and reproduce those moments without stress or anxiety.

Practicing and performing these character walks and emotions was always a highlight for the students, particularly coupled with the commands of freeze, go, jump, point. The teacher can also towards the end combine all these commands to reveal how these actions can tell a story. For example, walking to the bus stop very slowly because you're tired—Go; You see the bus driving past you—Freeze; You point at the bus shocked—Point; You jump up and wave your arms trying to make the bus stop—Jump and wave arms; You walk very fast towards the bus to catch—Go; You miss the bus—Freeze; You are very sad—bend over like a weight is on your back and look at the floor; You walk home very very slowly because your mom is going to be very angry—Go.

POINTER

When working with children with autism, the teacher must model emotions physically, describe how an emotion looks, and then say what the emotion is, because a child with autism often will not comprehend and demonstrate pride, sadness, or excitement. Of course this statement is dependent on the degree of disability, but modeling and a verbal description never hurt. I remember going through the walks early on and I said to the children, "Walk as if you are walking in jell-o." And every student stopped and looked at me because they had no idea how that would look, feel, or be like. Quickly, I said, "It's like your feet can't come off the ground and your legs move slowly because of this sticky substance." Trying to describe emotions is very difficult as I was at a loss at first attempting to articulate how one would move through jell-o. When choosing emotions or certain experiences, the teacher should have the physical description pre-planned.

ART

The art section is where the students will create a prop that will be used throughout the drama, or for a specific event during the drama. The art section is purposely placed here because it changes the momentum of the lesson from becoming too physically involved. In all lessons a teacher must find a balance between activity and non-activity in order for the students' concentration to stay focused. Students would mutiny if they were required to write for an eight-hour school day, as they would if they had a gym class for eight hours. Both are appropriate means of teaching, but there must be a balance. When I taught my classes, the sessions contained 45 minutes of teaching time, and from week to week the number of class participants would invariably change, so in order to accomplish all these tasks the expectations were realistic. Many times the task in art was not to build a prop but rather color a coloring sheet cut-out that would be used for the drama. Any construction of a prop was greatly simplified. During a Halloween drama based on David Steinberg's *The Witches Ball*, the students created witches' or wizards' hats to wear during the drama. I cut out and prepared the hats from black construction paper in advance before the class. For the art section, I bought from a craft store pre-made stickers containing Halloween themes that could be chosen and placed on the hat. With their parents there to help with the art section, the completion of the prop was realistic and non-stressful for the students.

FREE DANCE

After the completion of their props, the students participate in a free dance that can last for a few minutes or for the entirety of the song. Teachers should choose a song where the theme runs throughout the story drama. Suggestions are provided in the story dramas. The purpose of this section is to allow the students to play with their props freely in order for them to focus on the directions given during the drama versus playing with their prop.

THE DRAMA

The Drama, as reflected in the Visual Storyboard as 6. Act, is the story drama that will be acted out by the students. Like the Group Activity, Act can be any form of final assessment of the learned skills developed in the previous exercises performed by the students. Depending on what type of drama the teacher decides to use in the classroom, for example Mantle of the Expert, Act could be the students performing the ritual of the day as determined by the Design Team(s) in preparation for their final assessment where the ritual of the day is part of the performance of the story in its entirety at the end of the year. This is the true assessment for the teacher and the students how well the above exercises were instructed and learned. This is the basketball game where all the isolated exercises combine to create a sophisticated demonstration of advanced learning. The drama capitalizes on a learned skill set allowing other advanced levels of thinking to flourish. I remember around the fifth or sixth lesson one of the students with autism who rarely spoke not only began to anticipate the next line but also ad-libbed appropriate character dialogue with another character in the drama. I was only with these students once a week for a little less than an hour and wasn't expecting in that amount of time to witness any real change in the students. The impact of the drama reached far beyond an elementary literature class. It allowed the students to become a voice for the protagonist in the story, walking, talking, and overcoming impossible obstacles through the eyes and legs and voice of another. The barrier of "I can't" was replaced with the character's motivation of "I must." The teacher is the arbiter of the complexity of the drama by implementing Mantle of the Expert and/or the teacher theatrics (drama-in-education techniques). I choose specifically to use story drama, sticking very closely to the original text, which explains why, during the teacher narration sections after a character speaks, immediately the teacher as narrator states—"said the duck" when the duck may have spoken. Process drama would allow the drama to veer from the original story in order to investigate further a theme or issue that resonates with the students and/or an outcome of the school curriculum. Story drama can still conjure information that is not initially written in the selected story through the teacher theatrics techniques, however, the teacher through narration can always return to the selected story. Story drama can provide a great deal of comfort to a first time drama-in-education facilitator who may not feel comfortable portraying another character, or aligning the student tasks and other teacher theatrics to afford a more profound understanding of a complicated theme. The benefits of committing to the story drama are to flesh out the emotional journeys of the characters, specifically the protagonist that many times are omitted. For example, in *The Little Red Hen*, the students understand and relate to the Little Red Hen working alone on a task and her justification for eventually denying her friends the bread which she labored on. The same understanding is applied to students who complete their homework versus watching television, and deny their friends the answers who chose the latter.

READ THE STORY

Read the Story represents 7. Read on the Visual Storyboard. Like Group Activity and Act, Read can take on another form of reading depending on the type of drama chosen in the Teacher Theatrics chapter. For example, if the teacher chooses The Mantle of the Expert approach, Read might be the student scenes they have written between the characters in the story, a letter a character wrote, or a diary entry. In the context of the type of drama chosen for this book (story drama) this is where I read the book to the children. At the conclusion of the lesson, when we would sit down to read the actual story, the children were extremely attentive and fascinated with how close their interpretation of the story through the drama paralleled that of the real book. Again, like the art section, reading the story balanced the activity level in the lesson by focusing the students. The students can truly listen and appreciate the story because they know the plot, the characters, and the ending. The reading of the story is not interrupted with questions or a desire to know more about this world. But rather, the reading of the book is as the author intends, teaching the students the flow and use of language, withholding without anxiety important plot information to create climax or resolve a conflict, and the lesson the author is trying to impart.

CHAPTER 5

STEP-BY-STEP STORY DRAMAS 1

The Little Red Hen

This book revolves around two classic folktales—*The Little Red Hen* and *We're Going on a Bear Hunt*. Both of these stories are easily accessible and can be found online and the text printed out for the purposes of the story drama. Any version of the story that you can get hold of will do as they basically use the same language. Two readily available versions of these stories are the following:

- Miller, J.P. (illustrator) (2001) *The Little Red Hen*. New York: Golden Books, Random House.

- Rosen, M. and Oxenbury, H. (2009) *We're Going on a Bear Hunt*. New York: Little Simon.

These editions have particularly detailed pictures interpreting the story and nice character presentation. We discuss *The Little Red Hen* in this chapter and *We're Going on a Bear Hunt* in Chapter 6.

BACKGROUND DESCRIPTION

The Little Red Hen is a wonderful story to use early in the classroom year as a classroom management tool reminding students that the behavior they demonstrate in the classroom will echo their rewards or lack thereof in the future. We reap what we sow. If students do not listen during math class, they will have great difficulty counting numbers, adding, and subtracting. If students do not do the penmanship homework a teacher assigned, they will not be able to write their name or write words and later sentences. However, if a student does all his or her homework and listens in class, this individual will move forward in his or her learning, advancing to the next grade or receiving a class award.

OPPORTUNITIES FOR INTERDISCIPLINARY LEARNING

- *Literary techniques*, specifically in poetry or speeches, are identifiable, for example, onomatopoeia, repetition, and dialogue.

- *Science* is found throughout detailing the processes of farming, photosynthesis, and soil testing.

- *Math* is created through counting the number of seeds to calculating the growth rate of wheat by graphing and charting the results. The class could follow a recipe and measure the ingredients to make bread. Combine this with the science of how yeast activates making bread rise and you have covered two subjects at once!

- *Art* activities arise by creating the props for the drama, creating costume renderings for the animals as well as their homes.

- *Writing class* could include making a recipe book of all the hen's favorite bread recipes (raisin bread, peanut butter bread, etc.) or a newspaper article about how the Little Red Hen wins a bread competition (students can rewrite the steps how she grows her grains that create the perfect bread taste).

The Little Red Hen is a wonderful book for exploring how hard work and preparation yields food and nourishment for the coming days, months, and years. Hard work is rewarded. The Little Red Hen spots an opportunity in the wheat grains. She recognizes that these grains coupled with other grains will make bread. This bread will carry her through the winter. Despite the time and patience that goes into cultivating the grains, the Little Red Hen recognizes that in the end she will be eating fresh baked bread. This has always been one of my favorite books as a child. I loved the ending of this story where the Little Red Hen is eating her bread and all the other animals are salivating over the very last crumb. I remembered thinking, "good for her." This book also resonated with me because the Little Red Hen, even when let down by her friends and colleagues, continued on the arduous journey of cultivating the grains, picking and grinding the grains, and then taking the flour home and making bread from scratch. Many times we compare ourselves to other people, evaluating their successes thinking, "Why is that happening to him/her? I'm smarter/ faster/funnier/[*insert adjective*] than she/he is." Why does that person get to be the leader? Well, she made bread—she demonstrated that she could follow directions and model good behavior in the hallway and in the classroom. When I asked for her help, she didn't say she didn't feel like it, or take a nap during class, or look out the window and not pay attention to the directions. She made bread. She was not distracted by the tempting attitude to just check out and relax. When other students were coloring on their desks, she was reading the assigned story and looking up words she didn't understand.

STORY BREAKDOWN

There is a great deal of activity in this story drama which also means there are a lot of potential props. The Little Red Hen goes through a series of steps to make the bread. She hoes the garden, plants the grains, reaps the wheat, carries the wheat to the mill, and finally makes the bread. Depending on what version of the story you get, the Little Red Hen sits down to eat her bread. Later the other animals (having watched her eat the delicious bread) help her clean the house and tend to the fields so they too can eat the next batch of bread. In this version, the animals learned a valuable lesson of reaping what they sow.

I bought this book in France (*La Petite Poule Rousse*) where the story ended in this fashion, and one can imagine how well reading this story in French would have gone. I had a very difficult time finding this story in the United States. The version I finally found ended with the hen eating her bread. I'm sure online you can find other versions. And any version will work. The version I picked up was written much more simply than my French edition. Each started with the Little Red Hen moving onto the next activity—she found the wheat. Next page, she planted the wheat. Very simple, easy to memorize, easy to follow directions with very little description in between. Sometimes in my classes I added in some description to make the activity more real. For example, when it came time for us to plant the wheat, we grabbed our shovels and rakes (pieces of paper) and I would tell the students how the lines had to be very straight and the ground was very hard so they had to really concentrate on what they were doing. If I was a science teacher, I could go on about how plants grow and the process of photosynthesis during this section.

This book serves as a reminder throughout the year about paying attention in class, completing homework, and how each step of the process must be completed before the final result is revealed.

Opportunity for Further Learning

There are opportunities to distribute "The Little Red Hen Awards" to students who are modeling good behavior. Recipe cards made for each subject can warrant bread when completed.

For example, in math: Recipe for Writing an Equation = Step 1—counting to 20. Step 2—Ability to count placed objects and giving a group of objects a numerical value. Step 3—Understands the difference between a single digit number and a double digit number. Step 4—Ability to add single digit numbers. Here students also see what all this learning is for, addressing my favorite student complaint, "Why are we learning this?" Looking at the recipe card, students can see how each task is important to reap the benefits of solving an equation, reading a sentence, writing their names, etc.

Or an equation can be placed on the bulletin board and explained that at some point during the year in their math classes, they will learn and be able to solve this equation. They will be that smart. When students can answer the equation correctly and show how they solved it to the teacher, they will receive a "bread" prize (i.e. sticker, extra point in math, etc.). The teacher will give them the recipe for acquiring the proper knowledge to solve the equation. As they complete each step in the recipe, they can check it off their recipe card. The following is an example of a recipe card, the teacher can adapt the list of objectives based upon the needs and abilities of her class.

RECIPE CARD FOR MATH

SOLVING AN EQUATION

$$4 + 10 = ?$$

1st   Counting to 20.

2nd   Ability to count placed objects and giving a group of objects a numerical value.

3rd   Understands the difference between a single digit number and a double digit number.

4th   Ability to add single digit numbers.

DRAMATIC FORMULA

SET DESIGN AND PROPS (REAL OR IMAGINED)

- *Wheat*: grown wheat, real or imagined, that will have grown from the seeds. An image of grown wheat was used as the art project to be colored by the students.
- *Seeds*: "holes" punched from brown construction paper.
- *Dough*: roll up a white or off-white sheet and place in a large bowl for the students to knead.

- *Brown paper*: the garden or field* where the wheat is planted.

- *Bag*: carry the wheat to the mill.

- *Oven*: box with lid to put the bread in to be baked.

- *Recipe cards*: master recipe sheet with boxes drawn and a number written inside. Each box corresponds with a picture showing the correct order (as detailed in the book) in which to make bread. Pictures include: planting seeds, hoeing the garden/field*, watering the seeds, cutting the wheat, etc.

- *Watering cans*: photocopied cut-outs that can also be the art project.

- *Hand shovel or rake*: photocopied cut-outs.

*Please choose either garden or field depending on your version.

THE DRAMA (PRE-SET)

- Grains of wheat
- Little Red Hen's home
- The garden or field
- Rakes, hoes, and shovels by the garden
- Hide grains of wheat under the brown paper garden or field
- The animal friends—duck, goose, cat, and pig (depending on the version)
- Recipe cards in Little Red Hen's house.

VISUAL STORYBOARD AND SCHEDULE

1. HELLO SONG

2. SING

- Sing "Shake Your Sillies Out" or "Head, Shoulders, Knees, and Toes."

3. WALKING THE ROOM

- Freeze, go, jump, point.
- Walking through ferns or wheat.
- Duck, goose, cat, pig: make the sounds of these animals as well.
- Walking in mud.
- Picking flowers—blow the seeds or petals off.
- Carrying a heavy bag or shovel.
- Cutting through thick vines.

4. ART

Color the wheat and/or color the pictures for the recipe card to be used later in the drama.

5. FREE DANCE

When using *The Little Red Hen* as a source for the drama I suggest "Old MacDonald had a Farm" for this "Free dance" section (see lyrics in Appendix). This is merely a suggestion (as are all the ideas for songs for the "Free dance" sections presented later in this book) and may not be the best reflection of your culture or community of learners. Teachers should choose a song that represents the story but is also familiar to the students.

6. THE DRAMA

7. READ THE STORY

8. GOODBYE SONG

POINTER

The teacher will notice in the drama section a series of abbreviations:

- *TM*: Teacher models (the teacher should model the desired behavior for the students).
- *SA*: Student actors (the students playing a role in the drama).
- *TIR*: Teacher-in-role (the teacher takes on the role of one of the characters).
- *Dramatic dialogue*: the dramatic dialogue is very repetitive where at some points in the drama the teacher may not have to model the line for the student actors. Instead, they'll know what their next line is based on the action given in the teacher narration.

THE DRAMA

Teacher narration: So the Little Red Hen on a beautiful summer day

(TM: students can feel the warmth here of the summer sun or squint at the sun's brightness—sensory connections) was walking around

(TM: indicate that the students should follow these instructions) the farmyard when she came across something very interesting. Do you know what it is? A grain of wheat. And the Little Red Hen said to herself: "I will plant this grain of wheat!"

(TM: have students repeat line.)

POINTER

Either the grains of wheat should be pre-set before the drama begins or the teacher can place the seeds on the ground as the student actors are on their hands and knees looking for the seeds.

> ## Dramatic dialogue
> TM: "I will plant this grain of wheat!"
> SA: *"I will plant this grain of wheat!"*
> Teacher narrator: said the Little Red Hen.

Teacher narration: And so she picked up the seeds and carried them back home.

(TM: *picking up the seeds and carrying them back home.*)

POINTER

If the teacher chooses to go into role, the teacher can create or take on the activity that the animal is doing in the story. For example, in my version, the goose and duck are off to a play date with swords and shields. The duck could enter first with a sword and then acknowledge the children. I also like to take a few minutes to show that I as the teacher with a costume piece am someone else, so there is no confusion that the student actors are about to engage in a conversation with someone who is not their teacher, but a character in the drama.

The Little Red Hen then thought that if these seeds were to grow and make rows of wheat she would need some help and who do you think she might ask? Her friends.

(*Teacher moves towards the duck's location.*)

So first she went to her friend the duck and asked the duck if he would help her plant the grain of wheat.

(*Teacher brings out the duck—TIR or puppet*)

Dramatic dialogue

TM: "Will you help me plant this grain of wheat?"

SA: *"Will you help me plant this grain of wheat?"*

Teacher narrator: said the Little Red Hen.

TIR *as duck*: "Not I!"

Teacher narrator: said the duck.

Opportuniy for Further Learning

The teacher can interview the duck to develop a stronger character relationship among the student actors and the friends in the story drama comprehending the themes of the story through an emotional connection to the journey of the Little Red Hen.

Teacher narration: The Little Red Hen went on her way to visit the goose and she asked the goose: "Will you help me plant this grain of wheat?"

Dramatic dialogue

TM: "Will you help me plant this grain of wheat?"

SA: *"Will you help me plant this grain of wheat?"*

Teacher narrator: said the Little Red Hen.

TIR *as goose*: "Not I!"

Teacher narrator: said the goose.

Teacher narration: And so the Little Red Hen went on her way. On her travels she found the cat and so went up to the cat, who was fishing, and asked: "Will you help me plant this grain of wheat?"

Dramatic dialogue

TM: "Will you help me plant this grain of wheat?"

SA: *"Will you help me plant this grain of wheat?"*

Teacher narrator: said the Little Red Hen.

TIR as cat: "Not I!"

Teacher narrator: said the cat.

Teacher narration: And so the Little Red Hen went on her way to visit her final friend for help. She went to the pig, who was playing the violin, and asked: "Will you help me plant this grain of wheat?"

Dramatic dialogue

TM: "Will you help me plant this grain of wheat?"

SA: *"Will you help me plant this grain of wheat?"*

Teacher narrator: said the Little Red Hen.

TIR as pig: "Not I!"

Teacher narrator: said the pig.

Teacher narration: So the Little Red Hen stood straight up and said to herself: "Then I will plant it myself!"

Dramatic dialogue

TM: "Then I will plant it myself!"

SA: *"Then I will plant it myself!"*

Teacher narrator: said the Little Red Hen.

Teacher narration: And so she did. Off she went to the garden/field, picked up her small shovel and began carving a straight deep line in the earth. She pushed back the earth and carefully placed the seeds into the hole. She then pushed the extra earth over the seeds and grabbed her watering can and watered the seeds and returned back home. For several weeks the Little Red Hen returned to the garden/field to water her seeds.

POINTER

Either the wheat is pre-set (underneath the paper garden/field) or the teacher has the wheat in her hands and after the student actors leave this last time— the teacher should place the wheat on the brown paper.

But one day, when the Little Red Hen returned to the garden/field she discovered something extraordinary—the seeds had grown into wheat stalks. And there were a lot of stalks.

Dramatic dialogue

TM: And she said to herself—"Then who will help me reap the wheat?"

SA: *"Then who will help me reap the wheat?"*

Teacher narrator: said the Little Red Hen.

Teacher narration: So she went looking for help and ventured out to visit her friends to help her reap the wheat. She met the duck playing outside and she asked him: "Will you help me reap the wheat?"

POINTER

TIR technique: while the students are walking around the room to meet the next animal friend, the teacher has the opportunity to get into the next role and when ready can continue the narration, guiding the student actors to notice the animal friend, walk over and find the animal engaging in whatever activity is listed or chosen.

Dramatic dialogue

TM: "Will you help me reap the wheat?"

SA: *"Will you help me reap the wheat?"*

Teacher narrator: said the Little Red Hen.

TIR as duck: "Not I!"

Teacher narrator: said the duck.

Teacher narration: Off she went to find the goose playing with a toy sword and asked him: "Will you help me reap the wheat?"

Dramatic dialogue

TM: "Will you help me reap the wheat?"

SA: *"Will you help me reap the wheat?"*

Teacher narrator: said the Little Red Hen.

TIR as goose: "Not I!"

Teacher narrator: said the goose.

Teacher narration: And off she went again to find the cat catching butterflies and she asked him: "Will you help me reap the wheat?"

> ### Dramatic dialogue
> TM: "Will you help me reap the wheat?"
> SA: *"Will you help me reap the wheat?"*
> Teacher narrator: said the Little Red Hen.
> TIR as cat: "Not I!"
> Teacher narrator: said the cat.

Teacher narration: And off she went to find the pig playing a clarinet and she asked him: "Will you help me reap the wheat?"

> ### Dramatic dialogue
> TM: "Will you help me reap the wheat?"
> SA: *"Will you help me reap the wheat?"*
> Teacher narrator: said the Little Red Hen.
> TIR as pig: "Not I!"
> Teacher narrator: said the pig.

Teacher narration: So the Little Red Hen stood straight up and said to herself: "Then I will reap it myself!"

> ### Dramatic dialogue
> TM: "Then I will reap it myself!"
> SA: *"Then I will reap it myself!"*
> Teacher narrator: said the Little Red Hen.

Teacher narration: And so she did. She walked back to the garden/field and took her reaper and cut the wheat where it was close to the earth. She piled up all the wheat in her arms, knowing that she would need to take the wheat to the mill where the grains would be ground into a powder making flour for baking. The Little Red Hen thought to herself: "Who will help me carry the wheat to the mill?"

> ### Dramatic dialogue
> TM: "Then who will help me carry the wheat to the mill?"
> SA: *"Then who will help me carry the wheat to the mill?"*
> Teacher narrator: said the Little Red Hen.

Teacher narration: And so she needed help and once again asked her friends. She stumbled across the duck, who was still playing around: "Will you help me carry the wheat to the mill?"

> ### Dramatic dialogue
> TM: "Will you help me carry the wheat to the mill?"
> SA: *"Will you help me carry the wheat to the mill?"*
> Teacher narrator: said the Little Red Hen.
> TIR as duck: "Not I!"
> Teacher narrator: said the duck.

Teacher narration: And off she went to find the goose playing with his sword and she asked him: "Will you help me carry the wheat to the mill?"

> ### Dramatic dialogue
> TM: "Will you help me carry the wheat to the mill?"
> SA: *"Will you help me carry the wheat to the mill?"*
> Teacher narrator: said the Little Red Hen.
> TIR as goose: "Not I!"
> Teacher narrator: said the goose.

Teacher narration: And off she went to find the cat taking a nap and she asked him: "Will you help me carry the wheat to the mill?"

> ## Dramatic dialogue
> TM: "Will you help me carry the wheat to the mill?"
> SA: *"Will you help me carry the wheat to the mill?"*
> Teacher narrator: said the Little Red Hen.
> TIR as cat: "Not I!"
> Teacher narrator: said the cat.

Teacher narration: And so she found the pig playing the guitar and she asked him: "Will you help me carry the wheat to the mill?"

> ## Dramatic dialogue
> TM: "Will you help me carry the wheat to the mill?"
> SA: *"Will you help me carry the wheat to the mill?"*
> Teacher narrator: said the Little Red Hen.
> TIR as pig: "Not I!"
> Teacher narrator: said the pig.

Teacher narration: So the Little Red Hen stood straight up and said to herself: "Then I will carry it myself!"

> ## Dramatic dialogue
> TM: "Then I will carry it myself!"
> SA: *"Then I will carry it myself!"*
> Teacher narrator: said the Little Red Hen.

Teacher narration: And so she did. She gathered up all the wheat in her arms and carried the wheat to the mill to give to the miller to be made into flour.

POINTER

The teacher has a number of options regarding the miller:

- The teacher can go into role as the miller.
- The teacher can use a puppet as the miller.
- The teacher can interview or hot-seat the miller.
- The teacher can have the student actors drop the wheat off and wait a few minutes and then carry the wheat back home.

In my classes, I had the student actors drop the wheat off in a box, which I closed and pretended to turn a crank on the outside as I, as teacher narrator, explained that the wheat would turn into flour by the next day. The student actors went home to go to bed after a long day's work and awoke the next morning to walk down to the mill to collect the flour. The Little Red Hen then carried the flour while asking her friends for help to make the dough.

Teacher narration: And so the Little Red Hen had collected the flour which could then be made into dough. She decided to ask her friends if they could help her take this heavy bag of flour along with some other ingredients to be made into dough. The Little Red Hen asked herself: "Who will help me make the flour into dough?"

Dramatic dialogue

TM: "Who will help me make the flour into dough?"

SA: *"Who will help me make the flour into dough?"*

Teacher narrator: said the Little Red Hen.

Teacher narration: And so she found the duck taking a swim and she asked him: "Will you help me make the flour into dough?"

> ### Dramatic dialogue
>
> TM: "Will you help me make the flour into dough?"
>
> SA: *"Will you help me make the flour into dough?"*
>
> *Teacher narrator*: said the Little Red Hen.
>
> *TIR as duck*: "Not I!"
>
> *Teacher narrator*: said the duck.

Teacher narration: And off she went to find the goose stretching and she asked him: "Will you help me make the flour into dough?"

> ### Dramatic dialogue
>
> TM: "Will you help me make the flour into dough?"
>
> SA: *"Will you help me make the flour into dough?"*
>
> *Teacher narrator*: said the Little Red Hen.
>
> *TIR as goose*: "Not I!"
>
> *Teacher narrator*: said the goose.

Teacher narration: And off she went to find the cat reading a book and she asked him: "Will you help me make the flour into dough?"

> **Dramatic dialogue**
> TM: "Will you help me make the flour into dough?"
> SA: *"Will you help me make the flour into dough?"*
> Teacher narrator: said the Little Red Hen.
> TIR as cat: "Not I!"
> Teacher narrator: said the cat.

Teacher narration: And so she went to find the pig taking a mud bath and she asked him: "Will you help me make the flour into dough?"

> **Dramatic dialogue**
> TM: "Will you help me make the flour into dough?"
> SA: *"Will you help me make the flour into dough?"*
> Teacher narrator: said the Little Red Hen.
> TIR as pig: "Not I!"
> Teacher narrator: said the pig.

Teacher narration: So the Little Red Hen stood straight up and said to herself: "Then I will make it myself!"

> **Dramatic dialogue**
> TM: "Then I will make myself!"
> SA: *"Then I will make it myself!"*
> Teacher narrator: said the Little Red Hen.

Teacher narration: And so she did. She took the flour into her home so that she could make bread. The Little Red Hen entered her home, put the flour down on the table, and began searching for her recipe to make bread.

POINTER

The teacher can either have the recipe card and pieces hidden in the area of the home (i.e. pre-set) or the teacher can have the pieces nearby and then set the recipe pieces down in the hen house when the student actors are sleeping or when they walk down to the miller to collect the flour.

Teacher narration: When the Little Red Hen found all the pieces for her recipe for making bread, she studied each section and put the pieces in the correct order on the recipe card.

POINTER

The teacher can make the recipe cards as detailed or as short as desired depending on the length of time and the amount of student involvement. The recipe cards could include the steps already achieved by the Little Red Hen as dictated by the story—find a seed, plant it, water it, etc. and then they can continue onto how to make bread—add ⅓ cup honey to the flour, amount of water, beat the dough, etc. The students can see how far they have come in achieving their goal and how much more they need to do, giving them some perspective on how hard the Little Red Hen worked and why she is entitled not to share the bread in the end if she doesn't feel like it. The teacher can choose to make bread in class or after the lesson for the students to enjoy the fruits of their labor.

RECIPE FROM SEEDS TO FLOUR

- Find the seeds
- Hoe the garden
- Plant the seeds
- Water the seeds
- Reap the wheat
- Take the wheat to the miller
- Carry the flour home

RECIPE FOR MAKING BREAD

- 3 cups warm water (110 °F/45 °C)
- 2 packages (¼ ounce) active dry yeast
- ⅓ cup honey
- 5 cups bread flour
- 3 tablespoons butter, melted
- ⅓ cup honey
- 1 tablespoon salt
- 3½ cups whole wheat flour
- 2 tablespoons butter, melted

Directions

1. In a large bowl, mix warm water, yeast, and ⅓ cup honey. Add 5 cups white bread flour, and stir to combine. Let set for 30 minutes, or until big and bubbly.

2. Mix in 3 tablespoons melted butter, ⅓ cup honey, and salt. Stir in 2 cups whole wheat flour. Flour a flat surface and knead with whole wheat flour until not real sticky— just pulling away from the counter, but still sticky to touch. This may take an additional 2 to 4 cups of whole wheat flour. Place in a greased bowl, turning once to coat the surface of the dough. Cover with a dishtowel. Let rise in a warm place until doubled.

3. Punch down, and divide into 3 loaves. Place in greased 9 x 5 inch loaf pans, and allow to rise until dough has topped the pans by one inch.

4. Bake at 350°F (175°C) for 25 to 30 minutes; do not over-bake. Lightly brush the tops of loaves with 2 tablespoons melted butter or margarine when done to prevent crust from getting hard. Cool completely.

> *Note: this recipe is taken from http://allrecipes.com, Simple Wheat Bread. You can use whatever bread recipe you wish for your class to make (or pretend to make).*

Teacher narration: Soon the bread was ready to go into the oven and the Little Red Hen thought to herself: "Who will help me bake the bread?"

> *Dramatic dialogue*
> TM: "Who will help me bake the bread?"
> SA: *"Who will help me bake the bread?"*
> *Teacher narrator*: said the Little Red Hen.

Teacher narration: And off she went in search of her friends. She walked around outside and found the duck making a soldier's hat and she asked him: "Will you help me bake the bread?"

> *Dramatic dialogue*
> TM: "Will you help me bake the bread?"
> SA: *"Will you help me bake the bread?"*
> *Teacher narrator*: said the Little Red Hen.
> TIR as duck: "Not I!"
> *Teacher narrator*: said the duck.

Teacher narration: And off she went. She walked around and found the goose sharpening his pretend sword and she asked him: "Will you help me bake the bread?"

> *Dramatic dialogue*
> TM: "Will you help me bake the bread?"
> SA: *"Will you help me bake the bread?"*
> *Teacher narrator*: said the Little Red Hen.
> TIR as goose: "Not I!"
> *Teacher narrator*: said the goose.

Teacher narration: And off she went. She walked around outside and found the cat knitting a scarf and she asked him: "Will you help me bake the bread?"

> **Dramatic dialogue**
> TM: "Will you help me bake the bread?"
> SA: *"Will you help me bake the bread?"*
> *Teacher narrator*: said the Little Red Hen.
> TIR as cat: "Not I!"
> *Teacher narrator*: said the cat.

Teacher narration: And off she went. She walked around outside and found the pig again playing his violin and she asked him: "Will you help me bake the bread?"

> **Dramatic dialogue**
> TM: "Will you help me bake the bread?"
> SA: *"Will you help me bake the bread?"*
> *Teacher narrator*: said the Little Red Hen.
> TIR as pig: "Not I!"
> *Teacher narrator*: said the pig.

Teacher narration: So the Little Red Hen stood straight up and said to herself: "Then I will bake it myself!"

> **Dramatic dialogue**
> TM: "Then I will bake it myself!"
> SA: *"Then I will bake it myself!"*
> *Teacher narrator*: said the Little Red Hen.

Teacher narration: And so she did. The Little Red Hen returned home to put the bread dough into the oven to bake. The bread began to rise and when the top of the bread was golden, the Little Red Hen knew the bread was ready. She took the bread out of the oven to cool and placed it on the windowsill.

The smell of the bread made the animals stop what they were doing and walk towards the Little Red Hen's house. The Little Red Hen, noticing the duck was approaching, asked: "And now who will help me eat the bread?"

Dramatic dialogue

TM: "And now who will help me eat the bread?"

SA: *"And now who will help me eat the bread?"*

Teacher narrator: said the Little Red Hen.

TIR as duck: "I will!"

Teacher narrator: said the duck.

TIR as goose: "I will!"

Teacher narrator: said the goose.

TIR as cat: "I will!"

Teacher narrator: said the cat.

TIR as pig: "I will!"

Teacher narrator: said the pig.

TM: "No, I will eat it myself!"

SA: *"No, I will eat it myself!"*

Teacher narrator: said the Little Red Hen.

Teacher narration: And so she did.

(Student actors playing the Little Red Hen gobble down the bread.)
The end!

CHAPTER 6

STEP-BY-STEP STORY DRAMAS 2

We're Going on a Bear Hunt

BACKGROUND DESCRIPTION

We're Going on a Bear Hunt is a wonderful classic tale for the elementary classroom of journey and adventure. There are many educational and creative possibilities based upon the use of language describing sounds and experiences. The students understand how flexible language can be to create new words through sound known as onomatopoeia. The repetition of the text pacifies students, who may be uneasy and engaging in a drama for the first time. They have a map to follow the narration that can be used as a reference tool to look at when journeying from place to place. Particularly at the end when the stakes for the student actors are at their zenith, students have the ability to see, remember, and retrace their steps back to their home escaping the bear chase.

SCRIPT

The words used in the following story drama have been adapted by Michael Carleton and are available in full in the Appendix at the end of the book. The teacher should change the language in their story to reflect the language used in either the listed story drama or whatever version the teacher is using in the classroom to reflect the language in that story for the narration, character dialogue, character names, etc.

OPPORTUNITIES FOR INTERDISCIPLINARY LEARNING

- *Literary techniques*, specifically in poetry or speeches, are identifiable, for example, onomatopoeia, repetition, and dialogue.

- *Science* is found throughout detailing the process of hibernation for animals. The family walks through several different ecosystems to research and learn more about.

- *Math* is created through counting the number of steps from the starting point to the ending point of the student actors' journey until the end in order to calculate the number of "feet" (literal and/or figurative) to complete the expedition.

- *Art* activities arise by creating the props for the drama, creating costume renderings for the children as well as their homes.

- *Writing class* could include making a journal by each of the children and how they experienced each place. For younger learners a drawing of the place and a word that describes how the place felt for them when they were there.

We're Going on a Bear Hunt was successful for me because it allowed the students to really experience what it was like to be a character within a story. With each page the student actors explored a new place, and coupled with the paper on the floor as the set, the students believed they were truly in those places, jumping from rock to rock, fighting through the snow, and tripping over logs in the woods. All this activity focused the students to work together to prepare for these experiences and to check that everyone had successfully completed the task. The students recognized through the map and visualizing all the locations how much they had accomplished and how far away they were from finding or escaping from the bear.

STORY BREAKDOWN

This classic tale chronicles a family outing through nature in the hopes of finding a bear. The family is going on a bear hunt. It is a story of a family working together to overcome the difficult terrain and an enraged bear. The story repeats how they are unafraid because they are together, and together all things are possible. And from their arduous journey they learn a valuable lesson not to disturb a bear ever again.

There are many main events that occur in this story—every page is an event filled with movements and sounds. These movements and sounds require attention and patience to fulfill. This story is constructed with very little descriptive narrative between each place and therefore every place mentioned was utilized in the story drama. The narration is always the same, which is perfect for beginning learners. The story makes up this literary deficit in the plethora of physical and oral encounters. These main events were all executed on long reams of colored paper.

DRAMATIC FORMULA

SET DESIGN AND PROPS (REAL OR IMAGINED)

- *Green paper*: the long and wavy grass.

- *Blue paper with black round circles*: the blue paper represents the creek the students must cross and the black dots (attach construction paper or use a marker to color the circles on) represent the stepping stones.

- *White paper*: snow storm where the students trudge through the snow.

- *Brown paper*: the mud path on their journey.

- *Tree forest*: photocopies of tree cut-outs randomly taped to the floor or pillars in the room that one can walk around.

- *Snowflakes*: strewn on top of the white paper to drop over the students' heads for a storm effect.

- *Map*: a map indicating the path from where the students' journey begins, all the places they will walk through, and where the bear cave is.

- *Map places*: from place to place I drew a line that connected to a box that the students colored and then placed in the correct box.

- *Brown and black paper over two desks or chairs*: this served as the narrow dark cave where the students will meet the bear.

- *The bear*: photocopy cut-outs, stuffed animal, TIR.

THE DRAMA (PRE-SET)

- The bear in the cave
- Snowflakes on the white paper.

VISUAL STORYBOARD AND SCHEDULE

1. HELLO SONG

2. SING

    • Sing "Head, Shoulders, Knees, and Toes."

3. WALKING THE ROOM

    • Walking through long and wavy grass: hands can glide over the top of the grass.

    • Cold, wet snow: can make snow angels, throw snowballs, etc.

    • Walking in mud: feet sink and get stuck—pull feet out of the mud.

    • Walking the woods: trees are in their path, stepping over logs, ferns at their feet, pushing back vines, etc.

4. ART

    Color the places to be placed on the bear hunt map and/or make snowflakes.

5. FREE DANCE

    When using *We're Going on a Bear Hunt* as a source for the drama I suggest "A Hunting We Will Go" for this "Free dance" section (see lyrics in Appendix).

6. THE DRAMA

7. READ THE STORY

8. GOODBYE SONG

THE DRAMA

Setting up the world of believability (TIR as parent): Alright everyone, today we are going on a special journey. We are going on a bear hunt. Have you ever gone on a bear hunt before? Well, today we are, hopefully, going to find a bear at the end of our journey. Now in order to find this bear, we need some supplies. We need to put on our hiking boots, and our jackets for the outside, and we need a map telling us where to go.

POINTER

The teacher can take this opportunity to develop the world of believability more, and ask the students if there is anything else they may need and then either put on or grab those imagined/real objects.

Teacher narration: We're going on a bear hunt, hunting for bears. We're going to catch a big one, we're not scared! It's a beautiful day.

> *Activity: Can you feel the sun? How nice. It's such a nice day. We can see for miles, etc.*

Teacher narration: And we're not scared!

> *(Teacher and students should be at the green paper for the wavy grass: green paper with possible grass paper taped up.)*

Teacher narration: Oh no, what's that ahead? Long wavy grass, taller than our heads! Can't go over it—no, no, no! Can't go under it—oh, oh, oh! We'll have to go through it!

POINTER

Just like in the walks, it is imperative that the teacher model this behavior. Feel the grass and run one's hand over it—let the student actors do the same. The teacher should show how one cannot go over or under it—have the student actors see and try modeling teacher behavior as this repetitive movement will prove useful throughout the drama.

Dramatic dialogue

TIR (parent): "We'll have to go through it!"

SA: "We'll have to go through it!"

Teacher narrator: said the children.

TIR (parent): "Swishy, swashy, swish! Swishy, swashy, swish! Swishy, swashy, swish!"

SA: "Swishy, swashy, swish! Swishy, swashy, swish! Swishy, swashy, swish!"

Activity: Student actors follow the teacher through the long and wavy grass.

POINTER

The teacher has the opportunity to mimic the behavior occurring in the actual book. In my version, the parents and the children are reaching back and pulling each other up the hill of wavy grass. Ad-libbed lines can occur such as—"Hold on" and "Billy, help your sister/friend/fellow explorer up the hill."

POINTER

The teacher should take liberties with viewing the map to determine the path they need to take in order to get to the next place. Here, the students have the opportunity to become guides taking on responsibility and investing in the world of believability.

Activity: Begin walking towards the next place, the river: blue paper with black dots on floor.

Teacher narration: We're going on a bear hunt, hunting for bears. We're going to catch a big one, we're not scared! It's a beautiful day, and we're not scared!

TIR : Oh no, what's in our way? A cold and rushing river, wet and grey! Can't go over it—no, no, no! Can't go under it—oh, oh, oh! We'll have to go through it!

(Possible dialogue) SA: Can't go over it—no, no, no! Can't go under it—oh, oh, oh! We'll have to go through it!

Dramatic dialogue

TIR (parent): "We'll have to go through it!"

SA: *"We'll have to go through it!"*

Teacher narrator: said the children.

TIR (parent): "Splash, splosh, splish! Splash, splosh, splish! Splash, splosh, splish!"

SA: *"Splash, splosh, splish! Splash, splosh, splish! Splash, splosh, splish!"*

Activity: Student actors follow the teacher across the river, taking big steps and pulling their legs out of the mud on the brown paper. Splash, splosh, splish! Splash, splosh, splish! Splash, splosh, splish!

Teacher narration: We're going on a bear hunt, hunting for bears. We're going to catch a big one, we're not scared! It's a beautiful day, and we're not scared!

TIR : Oh no, what's that below? Thick, oozy mud, squishy and slow! Can't go over it—no, no, no! Can't go under it—oh, oh, oh! We'll have to go through it!

(Possible dialogue) SA: Can't go over it—no, no, no! Can't go under it—oh, oh, oh! We'll have to go through it!

Dramatic dialogue

TIR (parent): "We'll have to go through it!"

SA: *"We'll have to go through it!"*

Teacher narrator: said the children.

TIR (parent): "Squelch, squerch, squish! Squelch, squerch, squish! Squelch, squerch, squish!"

SA: *"Squelch, squerch, squish! Squelch, squerch, squish! Squelch, squerch, squish!"*

Activity: Student actors follow the teacher through the oozy mud, taking big steps and pulling their legs out of the mud on the brown paper.

Activity: Begin walking towards the next place, the dark forest: trees randomly taped to the floor or pillars.

Teacher narration: We're going on a bear hunt, hunting for bears. We're going to catch a big one, we're not scared! It's a beautiful day, and we're not scared!

TIR: Oh no, what do we see? A big, dark forest, full of big, dark trees! Can't go over it—no, no, no! Can't go under it—oh, oh, oh! We'll have to go through it!

(Possible dialogue) SA: *Can't go over it—no, no, no! Can't go under it—oh, oh, oh! We'll have to go through it!*

Dramatic dialogue

TIR (parent): "We'll have to go through it!"

SA: *"We'll have to go through it!"*

Teacher narrator: said the children.

TIR (parent): "Stumble, trip, bump, crash! Stumble, trip, bump, crash! Stumble, trip, bump, crash!"

SA: *"Stumble, trip, bump, crash! Stumble, trip, bump, crash! Stumble, trip, bump, crash!"*

Activity: Student actors follow the teacher through the forest, navigating through the vines, around the trees, and over the logs. Stumble, trip, bump, crash! Stumble, trip, bump, crash! Stumble, trip, bump, crash!

Activity: Begin walking towards the next place, the snowstorm: white paper on the floor with snowflakes scattered on top.

Teacher narration: We're going on a bear hunt, hunting for bears. We're going to catch a big one, we're not scared! It's a beautiful day, and we're not scared!

TIR : Oh no, what's coming in? A swirling, whirling snowstorm, with icy wind! Can't go over it—no, no, no! Can't go under it—oh, oh, oh! We'll have to go through it!

(Possible dialogue) SA: Can't go over it—no, no, no! Can't go under it—oh, oh, oh! We'll have to go through it!

Dramatic dialogue

TIR (parent): "We'll have to go through it!"

SA: "We'll have to go through it!"

Teacher narrator: said the children.

TIR (parent): "Brr, stomp, swoosh! Brr, stomp, swoosh! Brr, stomp, swoosh!"

SA: "Brr, stomp, swoosh! Brr, stomp, swoosh! Brr, stomp, swosoh!"

Activity: Student actors follow the teacher through the snowstorm where the teacher can pick up and drop the snowflakes above them as the student actors cover themselves with their coats and shield their eyes from the prickling flakes.

Activity: Begin walking towards the next place, the cave: brown paper taped on top of two chairs or desks.

Teacher narration: We're going on a bear hunt, hunting for bears. We're going to catch a big one, we're not scared! It's a beautiful day, and we're not scared!

TIR : Oh no, what's over there? A narrow, dark cave, perfect for a bear! Can't go over it—no, no, no! Can't go under it—oh, oh, oh! We'll have to go through it!

(Possible dialogue) SA: Can't go over it—no, no, no! Can't go under it—oh, oh, oh! We'll have to go through it!

Dramatic dialogue

TIR *(parent)*: "We'll have to go through it!"

SA: *"We'll have to go through it!"*

Teacher narrator: said the children.

TIR *(parent)*: "Tiptoe, whisper, shush! Tiptoe, whisper, shush! Tiptoe, whisper, shush!"

SA: *"Tiptoe, whisper, shush! Tiptoe, whisper, shush! Tiptoe, whisper, shush!"*

Activity: Student actors follow the teacher through the narrow dark cave. The teacher should lead so that she can obtain the bear to reveal himself.

TIR hears a noise!

TIR *(parent)*: What's that?!

SA: *What's that?!*

TIR: *(Slowly teacher should start bringing out the bear.)* One shiny wet nose! Thick furry hair! Two big goggly eyes! *(Reveal bear.)* YIKES! IT'S A BEAR!

QUICK! Back through the cave! Tiptoe, whisper, shush!

Activity: Exit cave and head towards the snow.

TIR: Back through the snowstorm! Brr, stomp, swoosh!

Activity: Exit snowstorm and head towards the forest.

TIR: Back through the forest! Stumble, trip, bump, crash!

Activity: Exit forest and head towards the mud.

TIR: Back through the mud! Squelch, squerch, squish!

Activity: Exit mud and head towards the river.

TIR: Back through the river! Splash, splosh, splish!

Activity: Exit river and head towards the grass.

TIR : Back through the grass! Swishy, swashy, swish!

Activity: Exit grass and head towards the house.

TIR : Get back to our house, open up the door. Rush up the staircase, run down the hall!

OH NO! We forgot to shut the door!

Back down the staircase, shut the door tight. Back up the staircase, turn off all the lights!

Into our bedroom, climb into bed. Pull all the covers over our heads.

We're never, ever, ever going on a bear hunt again!

The end!

CHAPTER **7**

FURTHER SUGGESTIONS FOR STORY DRAMAS

The stories presented in this chapter are not complete story dramas but ideas and suggestions are given for the dramatic formula and/or for Mantle of the Expert. You will need to obtain a copy of the original story and follow the guidelines below. Also read Chapter 8 "How to Write Your Own Story Drama" to develop these ideas into full story dramas.

DRAMATIC FORMULA 1: *CLICK, CLACK, MOO: COWS THAT TYPE* BY DOREEN CRONIN AND ILLUSTRATED BY BETSY LEWIN

GIVEN CIRCUMSTANCES

Click, Clack, Moo Cows That Type by Doreen Cronin and illustrated by Betsy Lewin follows the farmyard animals demanding better living conditions (electric heating blankets for the cold nights) or they would not produce milk and eggs. The cows, who love to type on the typewriter, send notes to Farmer Brown dictating their demands. The cows inspire the hens to join the cause and demand electric blankets too. The seemingly neutral party, the ducks, serve as the messenger between the parties. After witnessing the success of the cows and hens, the ducks decide to type a note to the farmer asking for a diving board since the pond requires some fun accessories.

THE DRAMA: BREAKDOWN OF MAIN EVENTS

- *Click, clack, moo*: the cows are typing away in the barn all day long. Farmer Brown cannot believe that his cows love to type. All he hears all day long are the sounds of the cows typing on the keys making the *click, clack, moo* sound.

- *First note on the barnyard door*: the cows place a note on the barnyard door explaining that because it gets rather cold at night, the cows would like to have electric blankets.

- *Farmer's refusal*: Farmer Brown is outraged and refuses to give the cows heating blankets.

- *Second note on the barnyard door*: the cows place a second note on the barnyard door explaining that they will not provide the farmer with any milk.

- *Third note on the barnyard door*: the third note states that the hens are cold as well and would also like electric blankets.

- *Fourth note on the barnyard door*: the cows and hens post another note claiming that they will not produce any eggs or milk.

- *Farmer Brown's reaction*: Farmer Brown is outraged and screaming the words on the note outside the barnyard door.

- *Farmer Brown's note*: his note states that he will not give them electric blankets and they are to produce eggs and milk.

- *Duck gives note from Farmer Brown to animals.*

- *Barnyard meeting*: all the animals lock the barn to have a meeting as to what to do, however, none of the animals could understand *moo*.

- *Duck gives Farmer Brown their answer (fifth note)*: the cows and hens create a deal that they will hand over their typewriter to the ducks in exchange for the electric blankets.

- *The deal is made*: the exchange is made. All are happy.

- *The ducks' dilemma*: the ducks feel that they too need something. They learn to type, and demand a diving board for the pond. A diving board is granted.

VISUAL STORYBOARD AND SCHEDULE

1. HELLO SONG

2. SING

- Sing "Shake Your Sillies Out" or "Head, Shoulders, Knees, and Toes."

3. WALKING THE ROOM

- Freeze, go, jump, point.

- Walking down a long path in a hurry.

- Ducks, cows, hens—make the sounds of these animals as well.

- Walking in mud—try to lift legs up in the air one-by-one like they are glued to the floor.

- Cold night—arms crossed, hands on shoulders and rub up and down for warmth.

- Locking up every inch of the room so that no one can enter.

- Walking in the complete dark—slowly and looking around.

4. ART

Here is a list of ideas for art activities. The teacher can choose to implement some or all of them in the "Art" section prior to the "The drama" section, or perhaps select specific ones to implement at appropriate times during "The drama."

Typewriters

Color them so that the students each have their very own and then can create the place by setting up their station in the barn where they type. This can also be a designated space set up by the teacher so that the students know that when they enter this area they are in the barn. This could be an extended activity in "Creating the World of Believability (set design)."

Letters

Students can write or type out letters that will be posted on the barnyard door.

Creating the map of the environment

See set design in "Mantle of the Expert." Where all the characters live, the space between all the locations and what resides among and between these environments. Are there paths leading from area to another? What path does Farmer Brown take to get from the barnyard to his house? A floor plan could indicate where each animal sleeps, and character profiles can be created as well.

5. FREE DANCE

When using *Click Clack Moo: Cows That Type* as a source for the drama I suggest "Old MacDonald had a Farm" for this "Free dance" section (see lyrics in Appendix).

6. THE DRAMA

The Breakdown of Main Events lists the actions that occur in the story drama. The teacher with the help of this outline can write the narrative transitions as seen in the earlier examples linking these main events. The chapter entitled "How to Write Your Own Story Drama" details how to write these transitions and suggests how the teacher can implement a teacher theatric within the drama as well.

TEACHER THEATRICS

TEACHER-IN-ROLE

In this drama, the students are consistently the animals, that is the hens, the cows, and possibly the ducks. The teacher will take on the role of Farmer Brown. The teacher should determine what represents Farmer Brown, for example, a straw hat, a pitchfork (can be a photocopy of a real pitchfork), a bandana or kerchief tied around the neck, a piece of straw to put in the mouth, etc. The purpose of going into role as Farmer Brown is to stimulate the next action. Narration coupled with teacher-in-role will direct the students as to what is happening and should happen next. If Farmer Brown refuses to give them electric blankets and sits in his house, what will the animals do? How will they respond in order to get what they want? This will motivate the student animals to type another letter.

NARRATION

The book itself moves from one event to another with very little description in between. Here is an area where the teacher can incorporate more of the further learning opportunities that were accomplished throughout the year or in a previous day session. Here, the narration indicates what happens next in the drama so that the student actors have orally heard their stage directions and therefore can set up the next task. For example, Farmer Brown returned to his home outraged stomping his feet all the way home. The animals in the barn sat down at their typewriters and begin to type a second note. The student actors will take their cue, sit down at their typewriters, and begin to type.

TABLEAUX

Here is a list of possible tableaux the teacher can implement throughout the story drama.

Character typing

Students can place their typewriters in the barn and either sit or stand in the position as their character showing how their cow or later their duck would type. Here students can discover the differences between the size, mass, and mobility of the two animals. Teachers can take time in science class discussing these attributes through the elements of creating a good tableau (levels, eye contact, facial expressions, use of space, and dynamic) for the students to gain a better understanding of animals whereby the actors can use that information to create a character.

Soundscape

Onomatopeic language is featured throughout the book. When the students have created their above listed tableau (character typing), the teacher can designate certain parts of the tableau as either click, clack, or the moo sound that occurs in the book. The teacher can point to each section (where a gesture of typing can occur) and say their designated sound.

HOT-SEATING

Hot-seating can occur either through tableau or through *freezing* a moment in time and then asking the student actors questions. The purpose of hot-seating is to *reflect* on what is happening in the drama for further critical thinking skills and/or to *assess* what the students have learned and/or to evaluate their understanding of the story. The teacher can choose, depending on the group, to hot-seat a particular animal, the animal of the student actors one at a time, or the collective student actors as the single voice of the character.

After each teacher-in-role technique

Whenever the teacher discontinues being in role (through disrobing a costume piece or otherwise), the teacher can move into the next piece of narration (such as, Farmer Brown slams the door of his house behind him). The teacher disrobes his or her costume piece and turns to the student actors, asking the cows questions as a group, for example, the farmer is really angry, how does that make you feel? Do you think the farmer has the right to be angry? Why or why not? Why do you think the farmer is angry? What do you think you should do next? The teacher can then return to narration to see what happens next in the drama.

Freezing a moment in the drama

Freezing can be used at any moment in the drama where the teacher feels the students need to gain more information in order to move onto the next task or where the teacher feels the student actors are lost in the drama. The teacher can address questions about past events, how those events are influencing their present situation, and what this means for their future outcome.

THOUGHT TRACKING

Where hot-seating is a series of questions like an interview or interrogation, thought tracking is comprised of a simple response that can assess or reflect on the students' learning but more so to enrich the drama through characterization, given circumstances, feelings, themes, etc.

7. READ THE STORY

8. GOODBYE SONG

DRAMATIC FORMULA 2: *THE WITCHES' BALL* BY DAVID STEINBERG AND ILLUSTRATED BY LIZ CONRAD

GIVEN CIRCUMSTANCES

The Witches' Ball by David Steinberg and illustrated by Liz Conrad revolves around a group of witches who are congregating for a witches' ball. The witches travel from all over the world to attend this yearly event. After casting their spells to bring on the night, they eat wonderful witchy treats and play wonderful party games. But the night comes to a close and all the witches must fly into the night until next year when they will meet again.

THE DRAMA: BREAKDOWN OF MAIN EVENTS

- *Bing, Bang, Boom*: the witches begin their journey, desperately trying to stay on their brooms, to their special spot where the annual witches' ball takes place.

- *Midnight falls*: as the day closes and the time for their party approaches, the witches cast a spell.

- *The party begins*: all of the activities and atmosphere are described and are acted out.

- *Party games*: let the games begin! The witches play several games all night long.

- *Party's over*: the party ends as day approaches and the witches make a promise to meet again next year and fly back home on their broomsticks.

VISUAL STORYBOARD AND SCHEDULE

1. HELLO SONG

2. SING

   - Sing "Shake Your Sillies Out" or "Head, Shoulders, Knees, and Toes."

3. WALKING THE ROOM

   - Freeze, go, jump, point.
   - Walking with wiggles.
   - Very quietly—tip toe.
   - Walking like you are so happy—laughing uncontrollably.

- Like you're flying or you're a plane—make wings with arms and bend knees to go lower in the air and stand up on tip toes to fly higher in the air.

- Like you are playing a guitar, beating a drum.

- Walking in the complete dark—slowly and looking around.

4. ART

Here is a list of possible art opporunities to be utilized before and/or during the story drama.

Hats

When I did this with my group, it was very primitive. I cut out big triangles (one-dimensional) and then cut out long strips about 2 inches in width that could tape around their head for the hat brim after they were finished decorating their hat.

Opportunity for Further Learning

With this the teacher could spend classes creating these decoration pieces (perhaps crossing curriculums in a history class learning about Indian, Egyptian, or other cultures' hieroglyphics and the meaning and purpose of using those symbols as a means a storytelling)—however, under my time restraints—I bought foam Halloween stickers from a crafts store and handed out two or three of each type of sticker to the students to place wherever they desired on their hat.

The brooms

These can be made from finding sticks from the school nature center and binding them together or cut long strips of different yellow-colored pieces of paper on taped paper towel cardboard rolls or whatever creative means imaginable. Or the very simple route as achieved in those Saturday mornings, print out a coloring book version of a broom and have the students color it.

Party games

Have the students design and create the party games that perhaps the witches might play—the rules, the game pieces or possibly game board, the purpose or goal of the game, the opponents or opposition and how they function, the number of participants, etc. The book lists a number of party games that are normally apparent at parties of all ages. For example, pin the tail on a donkey where the donkey was substituted with a newt. Students could explore what animals or otherwise would be a better substitute. They could pin the hat on the witch or tail on the cat.

Opportunity for Further Learning

The students could create their mascot or the mascot for each of the different countries the witches come from and introduce their mascots that represent their country and teach the other witches how to play a game based on their mascot. Party favors and treats from each country. Creating the candy based on which materials are most available in that country (crumpets in England, pastries in France, cupcakes and apple pie in the United States, and so on). The possibilities are endless.

5. FREE DANCE

When using The Witches' Ball as a source for the drama I suggest "Monster Mash" by Bobby Picket for this "Free dance" section.

6. THE DRAMA

The Breakdown of Main Events lists the actions that occur in the story drama. The teacher with the help of this outline can write the narrative transitions as seen in the earlier examples linking these main events. The chapter entitled "How to Write Your Own Story Drama" details how to write these transitions and suggests how the teacher can implement a teacher theatric within the drama as well.

TEACHER THEATRICS

TEACHER-IN-ROLE

In this drama, the students are consistently the witches who are planning and leaving for the night of the party. There are possibly two layers happening here—where the students are in character as witches but also as representatives of their countries. The purpose of going into role as head witch party planner is to lead the students through the activities that would occur at a party so that each country has the opportunity to share their knowledge with the rest of the group. A second purpose is to prepare the students for the journey to and from the party. The teacher can take the role of the flying instructor, who teaches the students how to ride their brooms. Here the teacher can control the movements of the students. I taped the students' brooms around the edge of the room and when the time came the students ran to their brooms and from the "Walking the room" section "flew" on their brooms to the desired location without moving from their paper. There was no movement around the room. The students stayed on their broom with their arms out like wings bending their knees following the description I provided as to what they were encountering on their flight. They bent their knees if we were flying below the tree line or had to rise up on their tippy toes to fly over the mountain ahead, etc. This helps to eliminate any anxiety that may occur as the students are more prepared for this event when it occurs in the drama. Another option is that the teacher should also feel free to step into role when the students have gotten their brooms and returned to the playing place. The teacher can put on her flying instructor hat and get her special wand and broom to instruct how this flying will take place. After the teacher puts on her costume and possible props, the flying instructor would introduce herself and give the witch student actors the instructions and rules on how to fly their broom and what will happen as a consequence if they do not follow instructions. The teacher can choose to slip out of role in two places. The teacher can slip out of role before the witch student actors fly off, that is the teacher narrates the journey the witch student actors take, *or* the teacher can stay in role and fly with the students describing what is coming next (for example, the same instructions how to fly from the top and then all the movements to fly and move around objects). The teacher can slip out of role when they arrive at the party. She can disrobe and narrate what happens when they arrive, describing each country like a sports announcer whereby other witches can join the commentary as well. All of the countries gathered together in the center of party space and waited for the head witch party planner to arrive and tell them what was the order of party games!"

Opportunity for Further Learning

Make a map of the journey. Narration coupled with teacher-in-role will direct the students as to what is happening and should happen next. When I first engaged in this drama TIR was not used and narration was the dominant means of moving the plot forward. There are many clear moments to incorporate TIR throughout the drama.

NARRATION

The book itself moves from one event to another with very little description in between. Here is an area where the teacher can incorporate more of the further learning opportunities that were accomplished throughout the year or in a previous day session. Here, the narration indicates what happens next in the drama so that the student actors have orally heard their stage directions and therefore can set up the next task. For example, "The witches and wizards flew through the sky swerving to avoid the clouds by lowering their brooms and ducking their heads down. They always flew through the air very slowly and in control because no human could see them so high in the air."

TABLEAUX

Here is a list of possible tableaux the teacher can implement throughout the story drama.

Flying on broomsticks

Students can place their broom and their bodies in relationship to their brooms demonstrating how they fly in their cultures incorporating the elements of creating a good tableau (levels, eye contact, facial expressions, use of space, and dynamic) for the students to gain a better understanding of country and can use that information to create a character.

Spell casting

Students create a spell in their language and share it with the rest of the class. They can translate it and have another student read it or interpret it on the spot or explain it themselves.

HOT-SEATING

Hot-seating can occur either through tableau or through *freezing* a moment in time and then asking the student actors questions. The purpose of hot-seating is to *reflect* on what is happening in the drama for further critical thinking skills and/or to *assess* what the students have learned and/or to evaluate their understanding of the story. The teacher can choose, depending on the group, to hot-seat a particular witch or country, the witch student actors one at a time, or the collective student actors as the single voice of the character.

After each teacher-in-role technique

Whenever the teacher discontinues being in role (through disrobing a costume piece or otherwise), the teacher can move into the next piece of narration (for example, the flying instructor flies up into the air for all the other witches and wizards to follow back home after the party). The teacher disrobes his or her costume piece and turns to the student actors, asking the sorcerers questions as a group, for example, how was the party this year compared to last year? Best or worse and why? Do you think you'll come back next year? Why or why not? What was different about this year that you will really miss? Is there anything you would like to change for next year? The teacher can then return to narration to see what happens next in the drama.

Freezing a moment in the drama

Freezing can be used at any moment in the drama where the teacher feels the students need to gain more information in order to move onto the next task or where the teacher feels the student actors are lost in the drama. The teacher can address questions about past events, how those events are influencing their present situation, and what this means for their future outcome.

THOUGHT TRACKING

Where hot-seating is a series of questions like an interview or interrogation, thought tracking is comprised of a simple response that can assess or reflect on the students' learning but more so to enrich the drama through characterization, given circumstances, feelings, themes, etc.

7. READ THE STORY

8. GOODBYE SONG

DRAMATIC FORMULA 3: *SNOWMEN AT NIGHT* BY CARALYN BUEHNER AND ILLUSTRATED BY MARK BUEHNER

GIVEN CIRCUMSTANCES

Snowmen at Night by Caralyn Buehner and illustrated by Mark Buehner revolves around a little boy who made a snowman and returns each morning to visit his snowman, only to find him disheveled. The snowman seems to fall apart in the night, making the little boy question what the snowman was doing overnight. The following pages imagine that all the snowmen get together at night engaging in numerous activities.

THE DRAMA: BREAKDOWN OF MAIN EVENTS

- *The building of the snowman*: the little boy is rolling up snow in big balls for the body and the face. When the story takes up, the boy is putting the final touches on the face.

- *Returning the next morning*: the next day the snowman is sagging and missing his accessories. The boy reflects on the night-time possibilities that the snowman experiences.

- *The snowman gathering*: all of the snowmen get themselves to the park. While they wait for everyone to arrive, they drink iced cold cocoa.

- *Snowman races*: let the games begin! They race through the park as many times as they please.

- *Ice skating*: next, they head to the frozen pond to show off their ice skating tricks.

- *Snow angels*: returning to the park, the snowmen lay down and create snow angels.

- *Snowball fight*: ducking, finding shelter, and creating snowballs dominate this next activity.

- *Sledding*: hiking up the hill to slide down is filled with great fun.

- *The evening comes to an end*: the snowmen are exhausted and it's now time to gather their things and head to bed.

- *The next morning*: the boy comes out and sees his snowman a mess knowing what he must have been doing at night.

VISUAL STORYBOARD AND SCHEDULE

1. HELLO SONG

2. SING

- Sing "Shake Your Sillies Out" or "Head, Shoulders, Knees, and Toes."

3. WALKING THE ROOM

- Freeze, go, jump, point.

- Skipping can be a difficult concept. You may need to have the children hop with one leg bent and then hop with the other leg bent up in the air and then combine the two.

- Very quietly—tip toe.

- Walking like you are so happy—laughing uncontrollably.

- Like you have something warm in your tummy—rubbing your stomach and making an "hmmm" sound like you've eaten your favorite warm cookies or hot chocolate.

- Roller skating—slide one foot on the floor with the other behind you and then switch. Close to running in slow motion but your feet slide on the floor. You can even have students do some tricks—jump and turn around in the air, turn on the ground, leap, etc.

- Walking in the complete dark—slowly and looking around.

4. ART

Here is a list of possibile art opportunities to be utilized before and/or during the story drama.

Snowflakes

There are multiple options with making the snowflakes. Students can cut out snowflakes from paper or it can be a printout that can be colored or have glitter glued onto it, etc. These snowflakes can be used to set the scene as the teacher can have the snowflakes falling on the ground and the students can head outside to make their snowman. The snowflakes can then be used to create the snowman. The snowflakes can either be rolled in a pile or placed in the circle indicating the bottom circle of the snowman where the rest of him is piled upon. Then they will know where to return to at the end of the play.

The costumes

The face of the snowmen and their accessories can be created many different ways. The teacher can have the students make masks out of paper plates or of white construction paper. Students can choose their eyes, nose, mouth, arms, and any accessories (mittens, gloves, scarf, broom, hat, bowtie, jewelry, etc.).

Opportunity for Further Learning

Science class can be dedicated to learning about different kinds of stones (minerals, quartz, gems, etc.) for the students to choose later for their eyes and buttons on the body. Different vegetables for the nose (carrots, cucumbers, zucchini, etc.). For the arms, these can be made from finding sticks from the school nature center and binding them together or by cutting up long strips of different yellow-colored pieces of paper on taped paper towel cardboard rolls or whatever creative means imaginable. Or the very simple route as achieved in those Saturday mornings, print out a coloring book version of a broom and have the students color it.

5. FREE DANCE

When using *The Snowmen's Ball* as a source for the drama I suggest "Frosty the Snowman" for this "Free dance" section (see lyrics in Appendix).

6. THE DRAMA

The Breakdown of Main Events lists the actions that occur in the story drama. The teacher with the help of this outline can write the narrative transitions as seen in the earlier examples linking these main events. The chapter entitled "How to Write Your Own Story Drama" details how to write these transitions and suggests how the teacher can implement a teacher theatric within the drama as well.

TEACHER THEATRICS

TEACHER-IN-ROLE

Depending on the teacher's intent, the story as written doesn't immediately beckon for teacher-in-role. When I used this story, I was the narrator throughout the entire drama and never went into role. I narrated the events that happened and then could ask questions for further reflection and detail. However, teacher-in-role can absolutely be a useful tool in this drama. For example, one of the purposes of going into role could be as the head snowman leading the student actors (as snowmen) and possibly modeling each activity. Another option is for the teacher to be the little boy, who walks out each morning to see the snowman and conjures all the activities that the snowmen act out. The teacher can help the students as snowmen get into their places and frozen forms in the playing area. The teacher now getting into role as the little boy can walk around and assess the physical states of the snowmen. (See *thought tracking* and *hot-seating*.)

NARRATION

The book *Snowmen at Night* is written from the perspective of the little boy and his imaginings of what his snowman is doing at night. The boy states what he thinks is happening and where the snowmen are going. Narration can be used exclusively if the teacher prefers.

TABLEAUX

Here is a list of possible tableaux the teacher can implement throughout the story drama.

Snowmen in front of their homes

Students can place themselves in front of their homes where they were originally created. How would the snowmen stand when they are playing in the park, and how would they stand when they felt tired and out-of-sorts the next day? The teacher can isolate half of the tableau and have the other students/ snowmen in character comment on the elements of creating a good tableau (levels, eye contact, facial expression, use of space, and dynamic) for the students to gain a better understanding of the different relationships present and character intentions that can be used as information to create a character.

Snowball fight

The snowball fight gives the teacher the opportunity to control this activity if he or she feels the class is overstimulated. Students can create a pose of what might be happening to them during a snowball fight. The teacher can also thought track the students in their poses. Then, the teacher can provide directions to commence the snowball fight in slow motion.

HOT-SEATING

Hot-seating can occur either through tableau or through *freezing* a moment in time and then asking the student actors questions. The purpose of hot-seating is to *reflect* on what is happening in the drama for further critical thinking skills and/or to *assess* what the students have learned and/or to evaluate their understanding of the story. The teacher can choose, depending on the group, to hot-seat a particular snowman, the snowmen student actors one at a time, or the collective student actors as the single voice of the character.

After each teacher-in-role technique

Whenever the teacher discontinues being in role (through disrobing a costume piece or otherwise), the teacher can move into the next piece of narration (for example, all the snowmen went to the table to drink some hot chocolate). The teacher disrobes his or her costume piece and turns to the student actors, asking the snowmen questions as a group, for example, so what activities are you hoping to do next? Do you think the boy will be upset that he returns to a mess in the morning? Why or why not? Do you think that anyone notices what you are doing at night? Why or why not? The teacher can then return to narration to see what happens next in the drama.

Freezing a moment in the drama

Freezing can be used at any moment in the drama where the teacher feels the students need to gain more information in order to move onto the next task or where the teacher feels the student actors are lost in the drama. The teacher can address questions about past events, how those events are influencing their present situation, and what this means for their future outcome.

Tableau of student snowmen

The students are in their places and showing a tableau of how they would look after playing game after game. The teacher could ask the students the following questions: Would their legs be tired? Would some of their snow melt from their sweat and overheating? Where would their accessories be? Would they even be on correctly or draped on the ground? (Here the boy must put these accessories back on the snowman.)

Tableau of a winter activity the students like to do

Students can reveal to the teacher either in-role or in general before the drama begins what activities or games the students/snowmen like to play. The teacher can go further with thought tracking with a sound, motion, gesture, etc. to give a clearer picture what some of the activities might be. By showing the snowmen's favorite snow time activity the teacher can next hot-seat the character(s), enriching the students' believability in the drama.

THOUGHT TRACKING

Where hot-seating is a series of questions like an interview or interrogation, thought tracking is comprised of a simple response that can assess or reflect on the students' learning but more so to enrich the drama through characterization, given circumstances, feelings, themes, etc.

Tableau of a snowball fight

When the students are in their places and showing a tableau of what would be happening to them during the fight, the teacher can ask what is happening and what the snowmen are going to do next. The teacher can also ask to have the snowmen identify who they might throw a snowball to next and what the consequences of that action might be—will the other snowmen be angry or will they laugh and keep playing? The teacher could ask the students after the snowball fight the following questions: Have they been hit by a snowball already and by whom? Which snowmen are they working with and which snowmen are they fighting against? How and why did this come about?

7. READ THE STORY

8. GOODBYE SONG

CHAPTER *8*

HOW TO WRITE YOUR OWN STORY DRAMA

Because we are working with children's stories, the task of writing your own drama is not an overwhelming task. The stories are written very simply and it is easy to identify the different parts and the overall message of the story. The text is simple and direct, which means that in order to transform the story into a drama the teacher will have to interpret certain details in order to achieve the message he or she wants the students to learn. The interpretations that the teacher and the students will create through the teacher theatrics to enrich the given circumstances may include the relationships between the characters, the characters' experiences and how those experiences affect their behavior, the difficulty of solving certain obstacles based upon previous experiences, the consequences after solving those obstacles and the effects, and the choices the character makes on how to achieve his or her goal. Children's stories dictate what happened, for example, the Little Red Hen went to the mill to change the wheat into flour. However, the story doesn't explain how far the mill is from her house or how arduous the journey is, if she has to complete the task by hand or just drop it off and negotiate with the miller to perform the task, etc. These are the details that the teacher makes clear to the students either through stating them during the narration or through the use of one or more teacher theatrics either before or during the drama whereby the given circumstances should become clear. If the teacher wants the student actors playing the Little Red Hen to work very hard in order to finally sit and enjoy her bread, the student actors will render the same response as the protagonist at the end of the story. The students outside of the drama will value the importance of hard work, which will spill over into their everyday life. The message the teacher wants the students to learn must be present in and throughout the story drama narration and the objective of the chosen teacher theatrics.

READ THE STORY

This seems like a very simple thing but it is necessary to read the story looking at and for the action that occurs in the story, the characters and their purpose, and the overall message of the story.

THE CHARACTERS

Take in all the characters in the story and what purpose they serve in the story. The teacher must first identify the protagonist in the story as this will be the character role the students will take on during the drama. The protagonist is the character that the story follows who is trying to do the right thing by achieving a specific goal. The next step is identifying the antagonist, the character that is preventing the protagonist from achieving his goal. After identifying these characters, the teacher will be able to identify the conflict in the story as well as all the obstacles that the antagonist creates thwarting the protagonist. It is the role of the antagonist and the other characters that the teacher will take on during the drama. For example, in *The Little Red Hen* the protagonist is the Little Red Hen, who is trying to grow, harvest, and make bread for nourishment. Her friends (duck, goose, cat, and pig) are the antagonists who make the process more difficult for her but then want to share in the results of her work.

It is important for the teacher when reviewing these characters to answer the following questions:

- Do they help the protagonist achieve his or her goal? How?

- Do they prevent the protagonist from achieving his or her goal? How?

- What are the characteristics or the personality of each character?

- What do those characteristics teach us as positive and/ or negative attributes that the students can try to emulate or learn from in class and in life?

By identifying the answers to these questions the teacher can create and direct the story drama with the intention of learning the desired lesson. This message will reveal itself on the journey upon which the protagonist (student actors) embarks encountering unknown personalities and challenging obstacles that in the process of overcoming them the students' critical thinking skills become augmented.

Once you have identified who the characters are and the role they play in the story and the role you want them to play in your drama, the next step is identifying the action that happens in the story.

OVERALL MESSAGE

Discovering what the overall message is of the story is the most crucial element before one begins to write a story drama. The chosen story may possess several messages that are of importance and will surface throughout the drama even when the teacher focuses on one main message. It is important that the teacher chooses one message in the story to focus on or the drama will not yield the result the teacher and the students are hoping for in the end. The point of the story drama will become clouded with a lot of unfulfilled information. Therefore narrowing the story down to one message is of the utmost importance. Keep it simple; keep it clear. The teacher can always teach another message through another story.

In *The Little Red Hen* the message found in the story drama at the end of book reiterates the importance of hard work that is consistent over a designated period of time. The journey to achieve bread at the end was arduous, therefore validating the decision that the Little Red Hen should not have to share the bread. Once the teacher has chosen that message, he or she is ready to begin outlining the story drama.

OUTLINING THE STORY DRAMA

Now that you know where you want to go, it's time to begin outlining the main plot points in the story. Children's stories are straight to the point, which means the teacher may not have to edit the work. Each page may constitute a plot point. The teacher can then number these events from first to last, mapping the journey the protagonist takes to achieve his or her goal. From this plot breakdown, the teacher can see how and why the protagonist makes the decisions he or she made learning from mistakes and making better decisions because of it. These character choices help the teacher create the narration and choose appropriate teacher theatrics bridging each plot point for the student actors to experience the same journey as their protagonist.

Let's use *The Little Red Hen* as our example text on how to begin writing the outline of events and transforming those events into a story drama. These events are listed based upon the book I used for my Saturday classes. Depending on the version you use the events may be different or there may be fewer events. However, the basic events (as listed below) will be close to the version that you are using and will serve as a sound example for you to follow in order to create your own version.

OUTLINE OF THE MAIN PLOT POINTS

Here is a list of the basic events in the story:

1. Little Red Hen finds some grains of wheat.

2. Decides to plant them.

3. Decides to ask her friends—duck, goose, cat, and pig.

   (a) Duck—Not I!

   (b) Goose—Not I!

   (c) Cat—Not I!

   (d) Pig—Not I!

4. She decides to plant them herself.

5. The wheat grows and it needs to be reaped.

6. Little Red Hen decides that she needs help.

7. She decides to ask her friends.

   (a) Duck—Not I!

   (b) Goose—Not I!

   (c) Cat—Not I!

   (d) Pig—Not I!

8. She decides to reap it herself.

9. Then, it needs to be taken to the mill.

10. She decides to ask her friends.

   (a) Duck—Not I!

   (b) Goose—Not I!

    (c) Cat—Not I!

    (d) Pig—Not I!

11. She decides to take it there herself.

12. She needs to make the flour into dough.

13. She decides to ask her friends.

    (a) Duck—Not I!

    (b) Goose—Not I!

    (c) Cat—Not I!

    (d) Pig—Not I!

14. She needs help baking the bread.

15. She decides to ask her friends.

    (a) Duck—Not I!

    (b) Goose—Not I!

    (c) Cat—Not I!

    (d) Pig—Not I!

16. She decides to bake it herself.

17. The bread needs to be eaten or it will get stale.

18. She decides to ask her friends.

    (a) Duck—I will!

    (b) Goose—I will!

    (c) Cat—I will!

    (d) Pig—I will!

19. "No," she says that she will eat it herself.

20. And so she does.

WHAT DO WE LEARN FROM THIS OUTLINE?

We begin to see a pattern where the Little Red Hen identifies what needs to be accomplished to make the seeds into bread. She realizes that in order to complete the task she will need help. She decides to employ her friends who could share in the reward of eating bread. We learn that her friends decide not to help her as they are enjoying other amusements. However, they would like to participate in eating the bread after all the work is done. This pattern is repeated six times as there are six main tasks to yield bread. The story drama contains six main plot points where the teacher and/or the students need to determine how they get from one point to another.

WHAT DO WE LEARN ABOUT THE CHARACTERS?

We learn a lot about the protagonist and her ability to make decisions independently outside the negation of others. We also learn how she values hard work and her decision that only those individuals who worked on creating the bread are permitted to eat the bread. The other animals prefer to engage in other amusements versus helping the Little Red Hen when asked. We also notice that each time (and she visits them several times) she asks for help they are also engaging in leisurely activities. She never asks them to leave their work and help her but rather to stop catching butterflies or wake up from a nap. The work ethic of the two groups is very clear.

HOW TO MAKE CHOICES IN ORDER TO GET TO THE NEXT STEP?

Teachers need to always remind themselves of the overall message they want their students to have learned when the drama is over. The second the teacher makes a choice or writes narrative that doesn't fulfill that message, the drama will not be clear and the students will not receive the desired message.

Teachers need to ask themselves these questions with each line they write and every teacher theatric chosen:

- What is it that needs to be accomplished in this task in order for the student actors to move onto the next task? What is the information they need?

- Is there an opportunity for further learning, drawing in other subjects in the curriculum?

- Is there an opportunity for a teacher theatric?

- Who's playing what role in each task? Teacher-in-role? Student-in-role? And how and when do these individuals get in and out of role?

- What, if any, props are needed in the next task? Do they need to be planted somewhere before the drama begins? Do the student actors need them at the beginning?

- Is the language in the narration active language? For example: "They went to the garden." This means nothing and gives the students nothing to do. In comparison to: "They walked very quickly in a straight line to the edge of the garden and stopped." This is active and informs the students how they are moving from point A to B and what they are to do when they arrive at point B. The language needs to inform the student actors how they went or came or entered a situation. Think of this language as verbal stage directions that might be found in italics in a play-script.

- Is there a pattern in events or language or character choices? These patterns can be repeated in each action step with the same narration or teacher theatrics as was previously performed? Or if the first action was narration, does the teacher want to incorporate a teacher theatric with the repeated action the second time?

INTRODUCING THE FIRST ACTION

The choice taken in the story drama in this book uses narration as the means for driving the drama to the first action. The teacher can take as much time with the narration and setting up the actions of the drama as quickly or as unhurriedly as he or she feels necessary. For example, the teacher can take the student actors on a long walk around the Little Red Hen's property and unexpectedly they find the seeds. Another option is to prep the garden for its first planting. The teacher and students can plan in advance what that entails and what equipment they may need. The students can plan the narration, which will lead them into the first action. Or the teacher can choose an opening that is short and simple and take the students to the garden and then begin the narration by saying, "One day the Little Red Hen was in her garden when she found some grains of wheat." Narration is the best option when introducing the story drama as it establishes the student-teacher dynamic and leads the students into the world of believability.

> Action #1: The Little Red Hen finds some grains of wheat.

TYING THE ACTIONS TOGETHER

If the students are aware of the given circumstances of the story drama before they enter into the drama, the teacher can use one of the teacher theatrics such as hot-seating, where through a series of questions the teacher can guide the students towards understanding the amount of work involved and imagine solutions for dealing with this problem to discover the next step. In order to use one of the teacher theatrics successfully the students can either engage in a Mantle of the Expert project throughout the year where they are well aware of the other characters and where they live, the process of taking some grains of wheat and transforming them into bread, etc., or if the teacher implemented the design team where the students would be well informed of the given circumstances having created them in order to leap to the next action. If the students are not aware of the given circumstances and specifically that the Little Red Hen has friends nearby who could possibly help her, teachers may find themselves in a process drama situation where the students drive the action veering from the original plot and the teacher needs to incorporate a series of teacher theatrics to yield the overall message. Of course, narration is simple and takes the student actors to the next step, where for the first time the student actors make the process more relaxed. The teacher does have the ability with narration to pad the story with information that isn't provided in the original story but supports it. For example, from reading the book, it is unclear how far away each house is or how long it takes her to find them. Do these characters play in the same areas? Are there spots where the Little Red Hen finds them? Does she immediately know where they are because they talked the day before? The teacher can get this information from the student actors and then use it in the narration or the teacher can narrate the drama providing this information as the student actors perform the actions.

MOVING TOWARDS AND SETTING UP THE NEXT ACTION

The next action entails that the Little Red Hen will visit four of her friends. The teacher needs to be aware in advance and make a note where each of the friends lives and how the friends will be revealed.

LOCATION

Whether the students construct the places where each of the friends lives or plays or the teacher takes the student actors to a specific place in the room, the location of friends needs to be consistent. The place where my classes were held had these huge square columns on the periphery of our playing space. Each column represented one of the friends' houses where a paper cut-out of one of the animals entered the scene from behind the column. I wanted the student actors as the Little Red Hen not to feel guilty eating the bread by themselves because they had done all the work. In order to achieve this, the student actors in each section visited each friend to ask for help and every time they heard "No." By visiting each friend every time, the journey of convincing the friends to help out was also work and part of the task that she needed to complete. At the end of the story, the friends are seen helping her with the housework with the hopes of eating the bread the next time. Again, the teacher must review what the message of the story is that he or she wants the children to understand at the end of the story drama. That message will determine if each friend needs to be visited separately and the length of the visit and if there needs to be a conversation trying to convince the friends to help out or if the friends could be all in the same place. This is something for which the teacher needs to revisit the purpose of the story drama, which will determine where physically the student actors are going to complete the next task.

WHO OR WHAT IS PLAYING THE ROLE?

Once the location(s) are determined the teacher needs to determine who or what will represent the friends and how that transformation or revelation will occur. Will the friends be puppets in some form? Will they be portrayed by the teacher(-in-role)? Will it be the students-in-role? Particularly if the friends are to be portrayed by the students, the story drama must prepare for this transformation to occur by cueing the student when to change into role and also when to get out of role and join the other student actors. This will eliminate confusion as to who's who and what's happening at that moment. However the teacher determines this moving into character structure, it can be repeated each time the Little Red Hen visits her friends. This way the students will more readily accept that their fellow student actor is now going into role as someone or something else. It is also very important that the teacher establishes before the drama commences that the student is fully prepared to take on the role. Review the *Student getting into Role*, discussed on pp.44–45.

Action #2: She asks her friends:
- Duck
- Goose
- Cat
- Pig

MOVING TOWARDS THE NEXT ACTION

What needs to be accomplished from the last task is that the friends will not help the Little Red Hen and now she needs to decide what to do with these seeds. Does she do nothing or does she plant the seeds herself? How the teacher gets to this decision can arrive in multiple forms. Narration is the easiest transition from one action to the next but the teacher can use one of the teacher theatrics as a means of reflection to come to this decision. The teacher can use thought tracking and have the student actors freeze right after the last friend leaves and for the students to express how the friends' refusals have made them feel. After everyone has shared their sentiments, the teacher can then dialogue with the student actors or use

131

hot-seating to identify what the next steps should be. What is it they can do with these seeds and what is the best thing for the Little Red Hen? The teacher can then move into narration to guide the children back to the Little Red Hen's house to plant the seeds in the garden.

> Action #3: She plants the seeds herself.

OPPORTUNITY FOR TEACHER THEATRICS

The teacher (or another colleague, perhaps the science teacher) can enter the scene in role and explain how the process works, also allowing the student actors to hot-seat this expert (for examples see below). Together they can prepare the garden. This will move seamlessly into the next task.

Opportunity for Further Learning

Teachers can decide if they would like to take the time during this action to incorporate the science behind planting and growing seeds. It doesn't need to be a sit-down science lecture but bits of information about a seed's life cycle and the duration of time that passes from seed to wheat, etc. The next action has the Little Red Hen asking her friends for help because the wheat needs to be reaped. The teacher can make this action more elaborate with watering the seeds (measuring the water and creating a chart of how often the wheat gets watered), if they would like to grow organic wheat and what that entails, weeding the garden, creating a scarecrow if need be, etc. The process of creating and preparing the garden can be an opportunity for further learning.

MOVING INTO THE NEXT TASK

As the teacher can see, a period of time has elapsed between the previous task and this one. The teacher can explain during the narration that a period of time has passed and the wheat had grown and grown or through narration have the students go to bed, wake up and water the wheat and perform this action several times to show the passing of time and the work that was performed during that time.

PROPS ISSUE: SHOWING THE CHANGE FROM SEEDS TO WHEAT

The teacher needs to think about how this is going to occur. When I did this story drama, I narrated the events as the student actors went to bed and then watered the wheat several times until we moved into the next task. When they were sleeping for the third time, I pulled out the wheat that they had colored during the art section and placed this wheat under the long brown paper that served as our garden. When the student actors did wake up and go to the garden, they were so pleased to see their wheat in the garden.

> Action #4: She asks her friends to help her reap the wheat as it has grown:
> - Duck
> - Goose
> - Cat
> - Pig

REPEATED ACTIONS AND MOVING INTO THE NEXT STEP

Again, we see the Little Red Hen go to ask her friends if they will help her with the wheat. The teacher can repeat the same process that happened in the previous action to demonstrate and reiterate how often the Little Red Hen asks her friends for help and how many times she is denied. This also justifies the ending of the story where she eats the bread herself, because she had given them many opportunities to participate in the process.

OPPORTUNITY FOR TEACHER THEATRICS

Each time the Little Red Hen asks her friends if they will help her and they say "No," she learns something about herself and her friends, which establishes her final decision at the end of the book. There is an opportunity for using a teacher theatric for reflection investigating the friends in the drama and how their actions affect the Little Red Hen. At some point in these repeated actions, the Little Red Hen may make the decision that if they don't help her, she isn't going to share her bread and therefore her objective is to teach her friends a lesson because she knows she makes the best bread in the area and they are going to want to eat it. The Little Red Hen has nothing to lose in asking her friends for help because if they help her that's great and if they don't she doesn't have to share her bread with them.

> Action #5: She decides to reap the wheat herself.

Opportunity for Further Learning

Like the planting of the seeds, there is an opportunity for further learning with the reaping of the wheat. Another expert (either a teacher or a colleague-in-role) can teach the students how to harvest the plant correctly in order to yield the best product. Here the expert can also guide the student actors into the next step: what to do with the wheat once it has been harvested. What purposes does wheat serve and how? When wheat is turned into flour, does that serve the Little Red Hen? A conversation based upon the student actors' previous choice of how to grow the wheat and the kind of wheat can lead into the differences between whole wheat flour, white flour, etc. and how that affects the taste and color of the bread they will be making.

MOVING INTO THE NEXT TASK

After the student actors have reaped the wheat, the next step is to take the wheat to the mill to be made into flour. Regardless of the number of wheat props that the students literally harvest (as they can and should also be harvesting imaginary ones as well) the teacher must reiterate the abundance of wheat the student actors have grown and harvested and that without help, the Little Red Hen is going to have a hard time taking all this wheat to miller. Here the teacher can hot-seat the student actors as the Little Red Hen to brainstorm ideas on what she can do to get the wheat to the miller as easily as possible. This should lead the students into the next step, as this solution of asking her friends for help should undoubtedly present itself and when it does the teacher should immediately move into narration and conclude that is exactly what the Little Red Hen did—she went off to ask her friends for help.

> Action #6: She asks her friends to help take her wheat to the mill:
> - Duck
> - Goose
> - Cat
> - Pig

REPEATED ACTIONS AND MOVING INTO THE NEXT STEP

Again, we see the Little Red Hen go to ask her friends if they will help her with the wheat. The teacher can repeat the same process that happened in the previous action to demonstrate and reiterate how often the Little Red Hen asks her friends for help and how many times she is denied their help. This also fulfills the ending of the story where she eats the bread herself as she had given them many opportunities to participate in the process.

OPPORTUNITY FOR TEACHER THEATRICS

Each time the Little Red Hen asks her friends if they will help her and they say "No," she learns something about herself and her friends, which establishes her final decision at the end of the book. There is an opportunity for using a teacher theatric for reflection investigating the friends in the drama and how their actions affect the Little Red Hen. At some point in these repeated actions, the Little Red Hen may make the decision that if they don't help her, she isn't going to share her bread and therefore her objective is to teach her friends a lesson because she knows she makes the best bread in the area and they are going to want to eat it. The Little Red Hen has nothing to lose in asking her friends for help because if they help her that's great and if they don't she doesn't have to share her bread with them.

> Action #7: She takes the wheat to the mill herself.

Opportunity for Further Learning

How the Little Red Hen gets to the mill can be facilitated in multiple ways. It can be as easy as narration taken directly from the book—and that's what she did. She took the wheat to the mill all by herself. And off the student actors go to the mill. Or the teacher can choose to reflect back upon the given circumstances obtained through a Mini Mantle where the students made the map of the area and can map out their journey to the mill. This team can explain all the obstacles that will be in the way—hills, bridges, the length from point A to

B, etc. An opportunity to incorporate math, determining the amount of wheat, the weight of each bag, the number of trips the Little Red Hen will have to take to complete the task. However the Little Red Hen takes the wheat to mill, the teacher should make clear through narration or a teacher theatric how difficult the task is requiring physical labor and hard work where her friends' help would have been greatly appreciated.

After the wheat has been given to the miller, the teacher needs then to decide if the student actors will wait at the mill until the wheat is done and then make the same journey back home with the wheat or if the student actors need to return the next day, etc.

MOVING INTO THE NEXT TASK

Now that the flour has made it back to the house, the next step is what to do with it. If an expert or teacher theatrics was implemented and the student actors have already decided that the wheat will be used for bread, the teacher can narrate or use another teacher theatric to indicate that with the amount of flour they have produced, the Little Red Hen is going to need help making all these loaves of bread. If narration has been the basis of moving the story drama from point to point, then the teacher could narrate right into this next step or can choose to incorporate a teacher theatric to develop the next point.

> Action #8: She asks her friends to help make the flour into bread:
> - Duck
> - Goose
> - Cat
> - Pig

REPEATED ACTIONS AND MOVING INTO THE NEXT STEP

Again, we see the Little Red Hen go to ask her friends if they will help her with the next step in the process, making bread. The teacher can repeat the same process that happened in the previous action to demonstrate and reiterate how often the Little Red Hen asks her friends for help and how many times she is denied their help. This also fulfills the ending of the story where she eats the bread herself as she had given them many opportunities to participate in the process.

OPPORTUNITY FOR TEACHER THEATRICS

Each time the Little Red Hen asks her friends if they will help her and they say "No." she learns something about herself and her friends, which establishes her final decision at the end of the book. There is an opportunity for using a teacher theatric for reflection investigating the friends in the drama and how their actions affect the Little Red Hen. At some point in these repeated actions, the Little Red Hen may make the decision that if they don't help her she isn't going to share her bread and therefore her objective is to teach her friends a lesson because she knows she makes the best bread in the area and they are going to want to eat it. The Little Red Hen has nothing to lose in asking her friends for help because if they help her that's great and if they don't she doesn't have to share her bread with them.

> Action #9: She makes and bakes the bread.

Opportunity for Further Learning

In the story drama presented in this book, the student actors had to complete the recipe card revealing everything they had accomplished up until this point and also reveal the steps involved in making bread. The student actors have the opportunity to be a bit creative with their bread, following the recipe and then improvising on that recipe to make their personal version. Perhaps adding a little cinnamon and raisins or whatever extra ingredients to make the bread they desire to eat.

MOVING INTO THE NEXT TASK

Now that this wonderful creation is completed, the teacher through narration can lead the student actors into this next step or incorporate a teacher theatric discussing why it might be a good idea to show her friends what they are missing because in the future she is going to need their help. She can't possibly do the work she has just completed year after year after year. She is going to need their help if she is going to have bread next year. The student actors can discuss how best to teach the friends a lesson ensuring they will help out the following year. If the next step in the book does not come up as a suggestion, the teacher can move into narration—and so the Little Red Hen decided that the best way to teach her friends a lesson and ensure they help her the following year was ask them one final time if they would help her eat the bread.

Action #10: She asks her friends who will eat the bread:
- Duck
- Goose
- Cat
- Pig

REPEATED ACTIONS AND MOVING INTO THE NEXT STEP

Again, we see the Little Red Hen go to ask her friends if they will help her with the final and best part of the entire process, eating the bread. This time the student actors have the privilege of asking the friends to engage in a task that is fun because of the work the student actors put into it. In the book, the Little Red Hen visits all of her friends and asks them to help her, but when the bread is baked and sitting in the window the friends come to her, lured by the smell and wanting to participate in the task of eating the bread. In this final task, the Little Red Hen does not go to them; they come to her.

> Action #11: She decides to eat the bread herself.

FINAL ACTION

The student actors get to sit and eat the whole bread by themselves.

FINAL REFLECTION

The teacher can incorporate a teacher theatric or just sit with the students and discuss what they liked about the drama, what they didn't like or understand, and what they learned from the story. Particularly if this the first drama with the students, reflection serves as a wonderful opportunity for the teacher and students when engaging in the next story.

A NOTE FROM THE AUTHOR

The purpose of this book is to give teachers a clear understanding of drama-in-education and theatre-in-education techniques, empowering teachers to implement these creative techniques in their classroom. If every teacher tries just one teacher theatric in the classroom, this book is a success. Many wonderfully creative teachers have not the time or the resources to plan and eventually implement the arts in their lessons despite the fact they are all too aware of its rewards. This breakdown of the techniques and complete story dramas should help the teacher to ameliorate those obstacles.

Every class is different. Teachers should feel free to change the language in the story dramas based on their personal style or choose a different art project that is better suited for their classroom. I have no doubt that each teacher will use the dramas and formulas to reflect the rhythm of their classes. Teachers may find that some of the teacher theatrics come easily to them, while others may take some time. The relationship between classroom teachers who have bonded with their students for a month to half a year is very different from the teaching artist who is meeting the participants infrequently and perhaps bonded for only 45 minutes in the previous session. These are all things that can affect how the story drama and other activities play out. The teacher should reflect after the lesson as well to determine how to approach any difficulties the next time to ensure success.

I wish every teacher the best of luck. Applying a simple methodical approach allows you to enjoy creating art with your students. As pioneered by the educational greats mentioned in the beginning of this book, these techniques incorporate the best methodology for achieving multiple higher level skill sets while maintaining student desire to learn and research more. Now, go and make bread!

APPENDIX: SONG LYRICS

A Hunting We Will Go

A hunting we will go, a hunting we will go,
Heigh ho, the dairy-o, a hunting we will go!
A hunting we will go, a hunting we will go,
We'll catch a fox and put him in a box,
And then we'll let him go!

A hunting we will go, a hunting we will go,
Heigh ho, the dairy-o, a hunting we will go!
A hunting we will go, a hunting we will go,
We'll catch a fish and put him on a dish,
And then we'll let him go!

A hunting we will go, a hunting we will go,
Heigh ho, the dairy-o, a hunting we will go!
A hunting we will go, a hunting we will go,
We'll catch a bear and cut his hair,
And then we'll let him go!

A hunting we will go, a hunting we will go,
Heigh ho, the dairy-o, a hunting we will go!
A hunting we will go, a hunting we will go,
We'll catch a pig and dance a little jig,
And then we'll let him go!

A hunting we will go, a hunting we will go,
Heigh ho, the dairy-o, a hunting we will go!
A hunting we will go, a hunting we will go,
We'll catch a giraffe and make him laugh,
And then we'll let him go!

Frosty the Snowman

Frosty the snowman was a jolly happy soul,
With a corncob pipe and a button nose
And two eyes made out of coal.
Frosty the snowman is a fairy tale, they say,
He was made of snow but the children
Know how he came to life one day.
There must have been some magic in that
Old silk hat they found.
For when they placed it on his head
He began to dance around.
O, Frosty the snowman
Was alive as he could be,
And the children say he could laugh
And play just the same as you and me.
Thumpetty thump thump,
Thumpety thump thump,
Look at Frosty go.
Thumpetty thump thump,
Thumpety thump thump,
Over the hills of snow.

Frosty the snowman knew
The sun was hot that day,
So he said, "Let's run and
We'll have some fun
Now before I melt away."
Down to the village,
With a broomstick in his hand,
Running here and there all
Around the square saying,
Catch me if you can.
He led them down the streets of town
Right to the traffic cop.
And he only paused a moment when
He heard him holler "Stop!"
For Frosty the snow man
Had to hurry on his way,

But he waved goodbye saying,
"Don't you cry,
I'll be back again some day."
Thumpetty thump thump,
Thumpety thump thump,
Look at Frosty go.
Thumpetty thump thump,
Thumpety thump thump,
Over the hills of snow

Old MacDonald

Old MacDonald had a farm, E I E I O,
And on his farm he had some chicks, E I E I O.
With a chick chick here and a chick chick there,
Here a chick, there a chick, ev'rywhere a chick chick.
Old MacDonald had a farm, E I E I O.

Old MacDonald had a farm, E I E I O,
And on his farm he had a cow, E I E I O.
With a moo moo here and a moo moo there,
Here a moo, there a moo, ev'rywhere a moo moo.
Old MacDonald had a farm, E I E I O.

Old MacDonald had a farm, E I E I O,
And on his farm he had a pig, E I E I O.
With an oink oink here and an oink oink there,
Here an oink, there an oink, ev'rywhere an oink oink.
Old MacDonald had a farm, E I E I O.

Old MacDonald had a farm, E I E I O,
And on his farm he had some geese, E I E I O.
With a honk honk here and a honk honk there,
Here a honk, there a honk, ev'rywhere a honk honk.
Old MacDonald had a farm, E I E I O.

Old MacDonald had a farm, E I E I O,
And on his farm he had a horse, E I E I O.
With a neh neh here and a neh neh there,
Here a neh, there a neh, ev'rywhere a neh neh.
Old MacDonald had a farm, E I E I O.

Old MacDonald had a farm, E I E I O,
And on his farm he had a mule, E I E I O.
With a hee haw here and a hee haw there,
Here a hee, there a hee, ev'rywhere a hee haw.
Old MacDonald had a farm, E I E I O.

Old MacDonald had a farm, E I E I O,
And on his farm he had a duck, E I E I O.
With a quack quack here and a quack quack there,
Here a quack, there a quack, ev'rywhere a quack quack.
Old MacDonald had a farm, E I E I O.

We're Going on a Bear Hunt adapted by Michael Carleton

We're going on a bear hunt,
Hunting for bears.
We're going to catch a big one,
We're not scared.
It's a beautiful day,
And we're not scared!

Oh no, what's that ahead?
Long, wavy GRASS, taller than our heads!
Can't go over it—no, no, no!
Can't go under it—oh, oh, oh!
We'll have to go through it!
Swishy, swashy, swish!
Swishy, swashy, swish!

We're going on a bear hunt,
Hunting for bears.
We're going to catch a big one,
We're not scared.
It's a beautiful day,
And we're not scared!

Oh no, what's in our way?
A cold and rushing RIVER, wet and grey!
Can't go over it—no, no, no!
Can't go under it—oh, oh, oh!
We'll have to go through it!

Splash, splosh, splish!
Splash, splosh, splish!

We're going on a bear hunt,
Hunting for bears.
We're going to catch a big one,
We're not scared.
It's a beautiful day,
And we're not scared!

Oh no, what's that below?
Thick, oozy MUD, squishy and slow!
Can't go over it—no, no, no!
Can't go under it—oh, oh, oh!
We'll have to go through it!
Squelch, squerch, squish!
Squelch, squerch, squish!

We're going on a bear hunt,
Hunting for bears.
We're going to catch a big one,
We're not scared.
It's a beautiful day,
And we're not scared!

Oh no, what do we see?
A big, dark FOREST, full of big, dark trees!
Can't go over it—no, no, no!
Can't go under it—oh, oh, oh!
We'll have to go through it!
Stumble, trip, bump, crash!
Stumble, trip, bump, crash!

We're going on a bear hunt,
Hunting for bears.
We're going to catch a big one,
We're not scared.
It's a beautiful day,
And we're not scared!

Oh no, what's coming in?
A swirling, whirling SNOWSTORM, with icy wind!
Can't go over it—no, no, no!
Can't go under it—oh, oh, oh!
We'll have to go through it!
Brrr, stomp, swoosh!
Brrr, stomp, swoosh!

We're going on a bear hunt,
Hunting for bears.
We're going to catch a big one,
We're not scared.
It's a beautiful day,
And we're not scared!

Oh no, what's over there?
A narrow, dark CAVE, perfect for a bear!
Can't go over it—no, no, no!
Can't go under it—oh, oh, oh!
We'll have to go through it!
Tiptoe, whisper, shush!
Tiptoe, whisper, shush!

One shiny wet nose!
Thick furry hair!
Two big goggly eyes!
YIKES! IT'S A BEAR!

QUICK! Back through the CAVE! Tiptoe, whisper, shush!

Back through the SNOWSTORM! Brrr, stomp, swoosh!

Back through the FOREST! Stumble, trip, bump, crash!

Back through the MUD! Squelch, squerch, squish!

Back through the RIVER! Splash, splosh, splish!

Back through the GRASS! Swishy, swashy, swish!

Get back to our house, open up the door,
Rush up the staircase, run down the hall!

OH NO! We forgot to shut the door!

Back down the staircase, shut the door tight.
Back up the staircase, turn off all the lights!

Into our bedroom, climb into bed,
Pull all the covers over our heads.

We're never, ever, ever going on a bear hunt again!

GLOSSARY OF DRAMA-IN-EDUCATION TERMINOLOGY

Drama-in-education: This refers to the use of any dramatic material accessed in the classroom to create and explore an issue in the classroom through the use of story.

Given circumstances: These are the circumstances or conditions that are given in the story or drama. For example, in *The Little Red Hen*, the protagonist is a red hen who is little. This is information that is given and taken as truth based upon the information the author has provided and deemed as true.

Hot-seating: This is when a student, embodying a character, sits on a chair (the hot seat) where the other students can interrogate the character in the hot seat.

Intention: (also known as motivation, objective, desire) Intention refers to each character in the story determining what it is that character is trying to do. Each character wants to do something, such as go to sleep, finish off homework, fall in love, etc.

Mantle of the Expert: The most advanced and involved of the process drama experience is a technique called the Mantle of the Expert, whereby the drama would play out over the course of a semester to the entire year crossing over several different subjects in order to complete the drama. Many teachers who use this technique select a certain time of the week (every Friday) and replace a certain class period or the last hour of the day (social studies if the drama requires a greater understanding of other cultures). It is during this time the students become imbued as experts in a specific area of exploration.

Narration: This can be teacher or student driven where new information is introduced propelling the drama forward.

Obstacles: These are the circumstances that prevent the character from fulfilling his or her objective.

Process drama: This is the action of an evolved idea that changes and grows and has no finished ending. The purpose of the drama is to guide the students through a series of drama-in-education techniques that enhance and provide greater depth in the learning process.

Prop: This is any item needed in the drama whether real or imagined in order to move the story forward.

Set: This is the constructed or imagined location of the drama.

Stakes: Stakes, often referred to as high stakes, are the height of emotional investment of a character who must achieve his or her goal. In order for there to be high stakes, the student actors must feel as if there is an element of failure. This element of failure must be palpable, forcing the class to work together and compose alternative outcomes in order to achieve their goal. For example, the three animal friends in *The Little Red Hen* at the end of the book clean the house and do their chores because they must have the bread to eat or they will starve.

Story drama: This is a classroom drama that follows the plot of a chosen story perhaps with some drama-in-education techniques (teacher theatrics) to enhance further learning. The purpose of the story drama is to explore character motivations and feelings, themes, relationships, and the overall message.

Student actor: I use the term student actor to indicate when the students are engaged in the drama as characters versus being students who are not engaged in dramatic activity. When the students are in this student actor role, the teacher should treat the students as the roles they are playing.

Tableau(x): Groups or individuals "devise an image [pose or shape] using their own bodies to crystallize a moment, idea or theme; or an individual acts as sculptor to a group" (Neelands and Goode 2000, p.25). Tableau is also known as still-image.

Tactics and strategies: These are the actions the character engages in to fulfill his or her objective. The character objective could be to finish off homework. A possible strategy is to go to a library to study.

Teacher-in-role: The teacher takes on a role in order to gain more knowledge in the drama, invoke student involvement, and stimulate the next task in the drama.

Theatre-in-education: This refers to a theatrical performance that occurs in an education setting, for example, a school tour show.

Thought tracking: This technique can be used at multiple places in the drama either through a tableau or freezing a moment in the drama where the teacher taps the student actor to either give a word, phrase, or sound describing how they are feeling in a particular moment.

REFERENCES

Fiske, E., Arts Education Partnership and U.S. President's Committee on the Arts and the Humanities (1999) *Champions of Change: The Impact of the Arts on Learning.* Washington, DC: Arts Education Partnership.

Gardner, H. (1993) *Frames of Mind: The Theory of Multiple Intelligences.* New York, NY: Basic Books.

Jensen, E. (2001) *Arts with the Brain in Mind.* Alexandria, VA: Association for Supervision and Curriculum Development.

Neelands, J. and Goode, T. (2000) *Structuring Drama Work: A Handbook of Available Forms in Theatre and Drama, 2nd edn.* Cambridge: Cambridge University Press.

OTHER VALUABLE RESOURCES

Brown, V. and Pleydell, S. (1999) *The Dramatic Difference: Drama in the Preschool and Kindergarten Classroom.* Portsmouth, NH: Heinemann.

Moor, J. (2002) *Playing, Laughing and Learning with Children on the Autism Spectrum: A Practical Resource of Play Ideas for Parents and Carers.* London: Jessica Kingsley Publishers.

O'Neill, C. (1995) *Drama Worlds: A Framework for Process Drama.* Portsmouth, NH: Heinemann.

O'Neill, C. and Lambert, A. (1991) *Drama Structures: A Practical Handbook for Teachers.* Portsmouth, NH: Heinemann Educational.

Seach, D. (2007) *Interactive Play for Children with Autism.* London: Routledge.

Stowe, C.M. (2005) *Understanding Special Education: A Helpful Handbook for Classroom Teachers.* New York, NY: Scholastic.

Wagner, B.J. (1999) *Dorothy Heathcote: Drama as a Learning Medium, revised edn.* Portsmouth, NH: Heinemann.

Wolfberg, P.J. (2003) *Peer Play and the Autism Spectrum: The Art of Guiding Children's Socialization and Imagination.* Shawnee Mission, KS: Autism Asperger Publishing Company.

BOOKS RECOMMENDED FOR STORY DRAMAS

Buehner, C. (2002) *Snowmen at Night*. Illustrated by M. Buehner. New York, NY: Dial Books for Young Readers, Penguin Group.

Cronin, D. (2006) *Click, Clack, Moo: Cows That Type*. Illustrated by B. Lewin. New York, NY: Simon & Schuster Books for Young Readers.

Miller, J.P. (illustrator) (2001) *The Little Red Hen*. New York, NY: Golden Books, Random House.

Rosen, M. and Oxenbury, H. (2009) *We're Going on a Bear Hunt*. New York, NY: Little Simon.

Steinberg, D. (2007) *The Witches' Ball*. Illustrated by L. Conrad. New York, NY: Price Stern Sloan, Penguin Group.

INDEX

CPI Antony Rowe
Eastbourne, UK
February 22, 2022

Many Southern countries had amassed large debts in the ambitious expansion programs of the preceding "Development Decades", on the naïve assumption that the USA would simply accommodate their needs for finance at the low rates which then prevailed. They now found themselves facing unsustainable debt burdens. The IFIs, as suppliers of dollar loans, were positioned to supply the resultant pressing need for credit but used this lever to impose "conditionalities" for debt relief, compelling sovereign governments to re-organize their economies in line with the extra-territorial requirements of the supplier of their trading currency. This policy shift was accompanied by a parallel theoretical shift which Todaro (1995) dubs the "neoclassical counterrevolution", now widely described as "neoliberalism".

The concern with international inequality was far from new, figuring in Marxist and Liberal criticisms of the "New Imperialism" from 1890 on, persisting in the postwar development literature (Prebisch 1950; Singer 1950; Kuznets 1955; Reinert and Jomo 2005), and hotly followed by the Dependency school (Gunder Frank 1966; Amin 1979, 2010). Whilst most early Developmentalists optimistically assumed the world economy would converge over some undefined historical period, their ranks divided between those who said socialist measures would be needed to bring it about, and those who, following Rostow's (1960) *Stages of Economic Growth* (subtitled a "Non-Communist Manifesto") claimed this would happen naturally under capitalism.

The new literature responded to the disturbing fact that convergence was not taking place. Pritchett showed that the gap between the richest and poorest nations systematically grew throughout the 20th Century, implying that Divergence was not a response to the neoliberal shock but an established historical trend, in which the neoliberal years were a mere episode. These concerns intersected with new debates among economic historians on "The Great Divergence", a phrase attributed to Huntington ([1996] 2011) and popularized by Pomeranz (2000), to describe the gap in living standards which emerged during the Industrial Revolution between the core nations of Europe and those of the rest of the world.

The issue of within-nation inequality was likewise not new, being for example the main concern of the interwar welfare state literature (Tawney [1931] 1983). In the aftermath of World War II, it became widely accepted that the state should cater for human and social needs that capitalism failed to address, especially in Europe, whose capitalists accepted the US view that welfarism was (in their countries) a necessary if temporary concession to stave off Communism.

The new literature responded to the shock of losing these welfarist protections. Neoliberal policies thus operated on two fronts: their principal effect was a successful assault on the postwar gains of the developmentalist global South, but they became better known in the global North for their effects on the working and popular classes in the heartlands. As the state retreated, many indicators of social wellbeing retreated with them, including public health, elderly care, homelessness, vulnerability, access to justice, and, of course, freedom from poverty.

The field then divided: inequality between nations was addressed by the IFI critics, whilst Piketty and others addressed that within nations. In fact the two are indissolubly connected; the division has hence impoverished theory.

Implications for theory

The new literature not only raised a range of new issues of economic and policy theory narrowly defined, but engaged the rest of the social sciences, especially the disciplines of sociology, political science, history and geography, over which the debate on convergence cast a particularly ominous shadow. In keeping with Rostow, many writers supposed that Divergence arose from delays in acquiring a fully capitalist internal economic system or "late development". Economic laws would, over time, obliterate this problem nation by nation. Yet, the evidence strongly suggested, this was not happening.

This shadow became yet darker when it fell on the foundations of neoclassical economics, because of the centrality within it its theories of Growth and Trade. The neoclassical counterrevolution, based on these foundations, predicted that the world market would equalize wages and profit rates as shown by Samuelson's (1948) famous theorem, supported by the Heckscher-Ohlin trade theory (Heckscher 1991) which became the neoclassical standard.

Yet more disturbingly, both theories rested on the paradigm of General Equilibrium which had come to dominate economics, including in its Marxist variants, in the postwar era (Freeman 2007, Freeman, Chick, and Kayatekin 2014). The bedrock on which the mainstream rests was, in summary, increasingly called into question by the facts.

The resulting discordance provoked Endogenous Growth theory (Romer 1994), a significant revision of neoclassical growth theory, whilst stronger dissenting voices came from the Dependency School (Gunder Frank 1966) and from protagonists of Uneven and Combined Development (Mandel 1976; Desai 2013), who rejected the neoclassical framework altogether.

This was not a purely abstract discussion about theoretical foundations; it had profound practical policy consequences, as Stiglitz noted in 2002, and again in 2017. Inequality called into question the Washington consensus, structural adjustment, deregulation, market liberalization, and shock therapy. Opposition to these policies crystallized not just among intellectual élites but on the streets, unleashing IMF riots, Jubilee 2000 and the "occupy

Wall Street" movement, and provoking state-level changes with profound consequences for the "New World Order" which the USA triumphantly but prematurely announced following the USSR's collapse: a striving among poor countries for economic independence, the Latin American Pink Tide, Putin's rise, the BRICS, and not least China's decisive commitment to an independent, state-led and avowedly socialist economic path.

As it became clear that China's success owed as much to its departure from the Washington Consensus as to "Globalization", two issues came to the fore: was China, through some hitherto-untried combination of state-led and market-based policies, breaking out of the subordinate status accorded the global South in the Great Divergence? And was its meteoric rise purchased at the expense of internal inequalities, or did it lay the basis for their future elimination?

These controversies go well beyond minor disputes on the margins of economics, to the heart of the question "how far can we trust the market?"

How do the relations between nations affect inequality within them?

The new literature as noted straddles two inquiries—but this is not all. Citizens of any nation are concerned about their relationship to *other persons*. However, their governments are also concerned about their relations with *other nations*. These are of course not the same thing; however, an obvious question arises: what is the relation between the two?

Such a relationship is certainly to be expected. The capitalist world, *strictu sensu*, remains divided between a small group of well-off former colonial powers, a large mass of their substantially poorer former colonies or semi-colonies, and the former socialist countries.

This produces profound pressures at both ends of the social and class spectrum. It generates, among the élites of the South, the aspiration to emulate the living standards of the North. But Northern countries are some twenty times better off than the South, placing an enormous distance between these élites and their fellow citizens, leading to the permanent structural instability expressed, for example, in Bolsonaro's controversial interregnum.

Conversely, a large world pool of cheap labor exerts downward pressure on the wages of the North, polarizing the Northern labor force. There are many other potential mechanisms of transmission between 'international' and 'national' inequality. These, however, are not explored in the new inequality literature.

Isidro Luna (2022) in this volume squarely confronts researchers such as Firebaugh and Gosling (2004) who ambitiously claim that inequality decreased in the 1980s and 1990s, basing themselves exclusively on PPP data. Such measures, in ignoring monetary income, unfortunately paint only half the picture, and choose the half with the rosiest tints in it, by ignoring the effect of terms of trade on development.

As Isidro Luna states

> *I believe that the dataset of the World Bank at current prices is a good source to achieve my purpose. The dataset used in this article is that of the GNIPC at current prices because it shows the effective wealth of a country and its evolution through time*

His calculations confirm the rising trend in inequality, especially in the neo-liberal decades, reported by many others (Wade 2018, Pritchett 1997, Freeman 2019b). As he concludes:

> *This article has demonstrated that inequality between countries increased from 1962 to 2019, that core countries can perform better than peripheral countries, that Latin American countries have not economically converged with core countries, that Latin American countries cannot apply some developmental policies, and that trade and capital flow are mechanisms that reproduce inequality in peripheral countries.*

The new inequality literature thus divides neatly into two narratives, neither of which addresses the above key question. The Piketty team in essence study *only* only differences within nations. They pay almost no attention to differences between nations, except insofar as to compare, for example, inequality in the USA with inequality in Africa. But this sheds no light on whether the relation *between* the USA and Africa has anything to do with inequality *within* either of them. The reduction of all forms of inequality to differences between 'individuals' became especially prominent under the impact of the 'Globalization' mania of the neoliberal years (Desai 2013).

Thus Milanovic (2005) promotes "household inequality" in no uncertain terms as *superior* to conventional concepts of international inequality. He presents three possible measures of it: "concept 1" calculates a conventional indicator, such as the Gini or Theil index, of the dispersion of GDP per capita between nations. "Concept 2" applies population weights to GDP per capita, correcting an important potential distortion.

Milanovic then, however, takes a third step. In his "concept 3" measure. differences between nations disappear altogether, and we compare only differences between the households that live in them:

> *Concept 2 [population-weighted international inequality] is perhaps the least interesting ... its main advantage is that it approximates well Concept 3 inequality [incorporating household inequality] ... once Concept 3 is available, however, Concept 2 inequality will be (as the saying goes) history. (Milanovic 2005, 10).*

Relations *between* nations are expunged. The issue of North-South relations, which rightly preoccupied the theorists of the fifties and sixties, are in the Piketty account left aside and in the household inequality approach, ruled out of court.

The effects of China's rise are likewise accorded no recognizable status. To illustrate, consider Tables 1 and 2, taken from the data page of the Piketty team's World Inequality Database (WID).[2] Table 1 summarizes the

Table 1. Share in national income of bottom 50% of the population.

	1980	2019	Change
World	5%	9%	66%
Turkey	13%	15%	19%
Nigeria	14%	16%	13%
Mexico	8%	8%	6%
Spain	20%	21%	4%
Pakistan	17%	17%	−1%
France	23%	22%	−5%
United Kingdom	22%	20%	−7%
Indonesia	18%	16%	−10%
Brazil	11%	10%	−13%
Japan	21%	18%	−16%
Germany	23%	19%	−19%
Italy	26%	21%	−21%
USA	19%	13%	−30%
India	21%	13%	−38%
Russian Federation	29%	17%	−41%
China	25%	14%	−43%
South Africa	13%	6%	−56%

Table 2. National Income per adult, US$.

	1980	2019	Change
China	$2096	$15,957	661%
Indonesia	$2410	$11,840	391%
India	$1781	$7355	313%
Turkey	$12,043	$25,954	116%
United Kingdom	$16,994	$34,315	102%
Pakistan	$3204	$5985	87%
USA	$29,153	$53,101	82%
Spain	$19,949	$31,964	60%
World	$10,488	$16,675	59%
Japan	$19,308	$30,337	57%
France	$27,028	$37,237	38%
Germany	$30,039	$39,984	33%
Russian Federation	$17,333	$22,005	27%
Nigeria	$6607	$7962	21%
Italy	$26,339	$30,329	15%
Mexico	$19,291	$18,157	−6%
Brazil	$15,213	$14,292	−6%
South Africa	$14,874	$13,102	−12%

evolution of the share in national income of the bottom 50% of the population of a country, generally taken as a good indicator of within-nation inequality.

If we pay no attention to between-nation differences, the worst performers are the Russian Federation, China and South Africa, for which this indicator has fallen by 41%, 43% and 56% respectively.

But then we encounter a puzzle. The share of the lowest 50% of the *World* has risen by a stellar 66 percent. Yet this share has fallen in all major countries except Turkey, Nigeria, Mexico and Spain, whose combined population is less than 6% of the world. Moreover, the worldwide share has risen by more than three times the largest improvement in within-nation share. Within-nation improvements cannot possibly explain the worldwide improvement.

How can this be? As Table 2 shows, the share of China's bottom 50% in *China's* national income has fallen somewhat, but their share in *world*

Figure 1. The Monetary Inequality Index (MII): GDP per capita of the North divided by that of the South. Data source for all figures: World Bank, Geopolitical Economy (2021) calculations.

national income has dramatically improved. China's national income has grown by a factor of over six. In consequence, the income of China's bottom 50%, relative to the world's income, is at least three times bigger.

The share of these 700,000,000 humans in *world* income has, in short, almost certainly trebled. By this measure, inequality has significantly fallen as a result of China's national growth. But Milanovic terms this a "concept 2" change—a "between-nation" difference. Dismissing this as a historical relic wipes out the most significant improvement in history in the income of one of the largest groups of the poorest people in the world.

And if like the Piketty team, we pay no attention to inter-nation differences, we report figures that we simply cannot explain.

Whatever happened to dependency?

This lacuna in the new inequality literature has claimed a second theoretical victim: the original concept of a fundamental North–South antagonism (Figure 1).

A simple chart illustrates the point, using an easily understood measure of between-nation inequality due to Kuznets (1966). We measure the GDP per capita,[3] loosely called average income, of two geopolitical *blocs* of nations: the global North and South. We then divide the North's GDP per capita by the South's to produce the "Monetary Inequality Index" (MII). This (Freeman 2019b) closely tracks the "Concept 2" Gini and Theil indices, so this result is not a statistical artifact.

Two points now emerge. First, the average nation of the South is now twice as badly off, compared to its Northern counterpart, as in 1950. In 2000 the MII attained a zenith three times worse than in 1950. It then fell for a decade, but this reversal bottomed out in 2012 at a worse level than

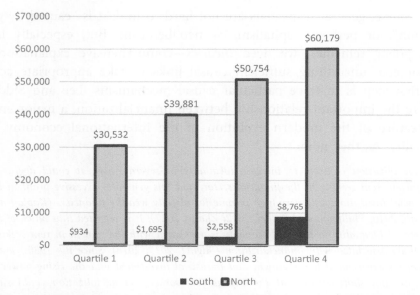

Figure 2. GDP per capita of population-weighted quartiles of the North and South in 2016.

in 1980, and all recent evidence (Chandrasekhar and Ghosh 2021) points—except for China and Vietnam—to a renewed widening of international differences.

The second point is the scale of the difference, rarely appreciated. By 2001, 2001, the average citizen of the South was 22 times worse off than her Northern counterpart. This difference is vastly greater than that within nations.

Figure 2 illustrates this point. It shows GDP per capita for each quartile of the South and the North in 2016. The average GDP of the *wealthiest* 25% in the South, at $8,765, was just over a quarter of the *poorest* quartile of the North at $30,352. Within-nation inequality does not mitigate the sheer scale of this difference: the average income of the poorest quintile in the USA,[4] at $12,937, is 30% greater than the average GDP of the richest quintile of the South at $9,860.

What causes inequality?

A singular feature of the new literature is the puzzling lack of *causal explanations* for inequality, which Lee and Siddique (2021) in this volume address.

There is no shortage of empirical data on inequality and indeed, this is one reason for the popularity of such work, which extends significantly beyond the narrow circle of cognoscenti who follow the obscure debates of the economists. Those who scan this cornucopia of numbers for policy fruit are, unfortunately, deprived of a critical piece of knowledge: *why* is this happening? As we analysts constantly repeat to our clients, data are not to be confused with information.

Of course, general scapegoats are not hard to find: it is "caused by globalization", or perhaps capitalism, or neoliberalism. But, especially if we want policy remedies, we need *theories*—comprehensive explanations of phenomena, unearthing sufficient causal links to take appropriate action. The first step is to trace particular causal mechanisms. Lee and Siddique explore the important relationship between financialization, a major empirical feature of the modern evolution of the international economy, and inequality. As they note:

> *Financialization is likely to increase inequality in several ways. It could aggravate inefficient rent-seeking in the financial sector, and this generates excessive profit in the financial institutions and very high income for already wealthy financiers (Kaplan and Rauth, 2010; Philippon and Reshef, 2012; Zhang, 2017). It is reported that much of the increased inequality in the U.S. economy is associated with the growth in rent-seeking, partially associated with financialization (Stiglitz, 2015; 2016). Since the 1980s, many countries experienced lower growth and industrial investment and the rising power of finance and short-termism at the expense of workers. Financialization could raise income inequality by depressing investment and employment.*

Financialization is one possible explanation for a feature of the recent evolution of the "industrialized" economies of the global North which contradicts the so-called "Kuznets curve" hypothesis. Kuznets (1955) hypothesized that as an economy develops, economic inequality will first rise and then fall, producing an inverted U-shaped chart of inequality against income level.

In brief, Kuznets supposed that in the early stages of development, those who already hold wealth can increase it because there are many new investment opportunities, whilst urbanization holds down wages. However, once a certain level of average income is reached (on the important assumption that industrialized societies tend to democratize and evolve welfare states), increases in per-capita income begin to decrease economic inequality.

Kuznets' reasoning concerned not the time-independent relation between income levels and inequality but their evolution over time. However, the Kuznets curve hypothesis is often cited in support of the controversial "trickle-down" claim that raising the income of the wealthy invariably raises the income of the entire nation.

Financialization clearly could act as a counter to the effects which Kuznets expected of a mature economy, because it provides an opportunity to accumulate wealth which, being essentially a form of rent, is not limited by the expansion of productive capacity. Using panel analysis, Lee and Siddique modify the Kuznets curve equation for a large sample of industrialized economies with terms to account for "financial rent", market concentration and other indicators of financialization, showing that they significantly modify the inequality-income relationship.

What does the state do? Industrialization, welfare, and inequality

We already noted that many early scholars of the relationship between inequality and development assumed, understandably in the immediate postwar years, a kind of linear progression in the social care that society would undertake as it grew wealthier. The "Kuznets curve" thus rests on the assumption that mature industrial societies almost automatically develop at least a social safety net, and evolve toward the comprehensive welfarism that characterized both Britain's post-Beveridge welfare state and the German *Sozialstaat* which evolved, with American consent, in the Adenauer years and beyond. Indeed, state-managed social welfare reached an apogee in the "Scandinavian models" of socialism, leading even to predictions of some kind of "social convergence" between capitalist and non-capitalist societies.

The state also played a critical role in the rapid growth of the "latecomer advanced economies"—South Korea, Malaysia, Taiwan, though scant few more—in a succession of "miracles" emerging as the postwar years unfolded (Page 1993, see also Krugman 1994; Bird and Milne 1999). But what, actually, is exceptional about the economic and social achievements of the so-called "advanced" industrial nations?

The Allied occupiers allowed, and even encouraged, the state to play a much more central role in the reconstruction of Germany and Japan than they found acceptable in their own countries. They had learned the lesson of Versailles: faced with the choice between the bogeys of capitalist statism and ungovernable revolutionary chaos, they opted unerringly for the lesser of the two capitalist evils.

Yet this choice was political, not economic. In the wake of the "Second Slump" of 1974 (Mandel 1979), the inflationary crises of the 1970s and the inexorable decline of dollar domination (Desai and Hudson 2021), the Reagan-Thatcher coalition opted for the withdrawal of the state from both the economy and society and the neoliberal era began.

This sudden onset of a new economic policy paradigm, accompanied by an ideological anti-state and anti-Soviet offensive of unprecedented and unanticipated scope, rudely dashed the prevailing progressivist *Weltanschauung* of a general evolution toward a benevolent welfarist or developmentalist capitalism as an automatic consequence of economic progress. Anti-Keynesian, supply-side economics sounded the retreat from the evolutionary path which the earlier developmental economists (including Rostow himself, despite his anti-communism) took for granted.

Missing was an understanding of the extent of *contingency* that affects state involvement in a capitalist economy. The state is, in technical terms we discuss later, exogenous to the economy. Its role in any given capitalist country, whether in development or welfare, is a product of class struggle, not automatic economic mechanisms. Where the capitalists were weaker or under threat—from their own workers, from other capitalist nations, or from Russia or China—the state played a correspondingly greater role, but once the capitalists felt confident of their political strength, they did not hesitate to revert to Victorian *laissez-faire* ideologies and practices.

In particular, the state's social role has no automatic connection with its economic role. We do not at all mean there is no desirable connection: the very idea of a "developed" society which cannot take care of its people is oxymoronic. The point is that capitalism does not compel capitalists to behave either morally or rationally: its political order is fundamentally irrational. Inequality, COVID, and the burgeoning ecological emergency, are just the most visible expressions of this disjuncture.

A major consequence is the "varieties of capitalism" of the nations of the global North. The most emphatically neoliberal is, of course, the USA, though outside observers often fail to recognize the diversity and creativity of combative responses—often heroically so—to be found in this vast, sprawling, failure of a nation. Neither Martin Luther King, nor Malcolm X, nor George Floyd, nor the countless indigenous peoples who perished resisting the occupier of their lands, died in vain.

Almost every combination of state social and economic involvement barring Communism itself can be found within the Northern Nations if one delves deep enough in their history. The pluripolarity of these responses (to borrow a phrase from Hugo Chavez) provides, therefore, a rich laboratory for the social scientist.

Pascal Petit (2021) in this volume enters this laboratory, scrutinizing the Piketty team's empirical material through the lens of the geographical and historical influences on specific types of the state within the global North. "[V]arious statistical and analytical studies," he writes,

> have been carried out since 2011 on the initiative of Thomas Piketty and his colleagues in Paris and Berkeley, providing an impressive statistical picture of income inequality for more than 80 countries over a period from 1980 to 2016...

> Nevertheless, these symptoms are difficult to interpret, as their impact on democracy or more precisely on the way society is made varies according to the time and the country. This does not mean that they are a kind of white noise, these signs manifest something, most often a deterioration, but in order to appreciate their lasting or reversible character and their extent, one is tempted to confront them each time with the prevailing political situations and the ideologies which structure them.

Petit analyses two sources of variation to be found in eleven industrial states which include the USA, a number of European states, Japan, and South Korea. He combines this geographical analysis with a historical study of the impact of the 'exogenous shocks' that have impacted the evolution and responses of their states.

Class: Inequality between whom and whom?

A further characteristic of the new literature is its recourse to purely Weberian income categories, which are quite different from both Marxian categories and the categories that appear in the national accounts. For Marx (Freeman 2019a) the determining characteristic of the evolution of the income of society's various component parts is society's *property* relations.

As Hashimoto (2021) in this volume notes:

> To analyze the current state of Japanese society in relation to class structure, it is necessary to establish a scheme of class structure and to develop procedures for operationalizing the concept of class and measuring the class locations of the respondents. In essence, this study is adopting an appropriate combination of several schemes of class structure and methods of empirical research that have been proposed in the 1970s and 1980s. Such methods were formulated from the perspective of structuralist and analytical Marxism.

The means to conduct a class-based analysis are fully available to scholars in the shape of the national accounts. For example, a driving force of inequality is the simple relation between employers and employees, recognized in the national accounts as sources of 'factor income'. Though they do differ from Marx (and Ricardo) they nevertheless retain a structural relation to Marx which differentiates them from Weberian categories.

Capitalists and the owners of rented property are however treated, following Adam Smith, as producers of wealth. For Marx (Freeman 2019a) and his precursors the Ricardian socialists, the workers are the sole source of new value, whilst rent and profits are deductions from it. Nevertheless, because the national accounts provide at one and the same time a measure of income and a measure of expenditure, workers' income is clearly presented.

Thus, a simple and revealing measure of inequality is the share of employment income in the social product, compared with profits, rent, and interest income. Such "property-based" measures of inequality are absent from the new literature, though they were a primary concern of the early welfare state literature of Tawney, Titmus, Beveridge and their counterparts in other countries.

Hashimoto undertakes a detailed property-based analysis of the structure of the income of the non-capitalist classes of Japan, in an attempt to account for the growth of what, in the mainstream literature, is referred to as the "underclass." "The working class is considered the lower and largest exploited class in a capitalist society," he writes.

> However, regular workers, who constitute the majority of the working class, have been ensured relatively stable employment, especially in the manufacturing industry. In contrast, the rapidly increasing non-regular workers have precarious employment, and their wages are much lower than those of regular workers. In addition, as we will see later, it is difficult for them to marry and form a family, and they are constituting a group that is different from the traditional working class. For this reason, in this study, I will refer to non-regular workers, excluding married women, as the "underclass" and regard them as a different grouping from the regular working class, even though they are included in the working class in a broad sense.

Hashimoto develops a "five-class structure" to account for the distribution of income and class structure of modern Japan, which he divides into the Capitalist class, the "new middle class", the Regular Working class, the Old Middle Class, and the underclass.
The underclass, he argues

> is fundamentally different from other classes in terms of its extremely low income, vulnerability to the risk of poverty, difficulties in marriage and family formation, and large differences from other classes in consciousness and living conditions. Therefore, from the perspective of whether or not it is possible to maintain the general standard of living, the class structure of contemporary Japan can be regarded as being divided into underclass and other classes.

Given the attention that modern inequality literature devotes to the "underclass" this class-based approach is a salutary antidote.

Labour and international inequality

The issue of class, as should be expected, leads directly to the question: what role does labor play in explaining international inequality? This constitutes another lacuna in the new literature.

In an earlier paper on international trade, Yoshihara and Kaneko (2016) explain some of the fundamental divisions in the theoretical treatment of inequality:

> Understanding why some countries in the world economy are so rich while some are so poor is one of the most important issues in economics, as there are large inequalities in income per capita and output per worker across countries, increasing since 1820. Regarding this issue, the so-called dependence school recognizes the emergence of development and underdevelopment in the capitalistic world system as a product of exploitative relations between rich and poor nations. For instance, among others, Emmanuel (1972) discusses the generation of unequal exchange (UE) between rich and poor nations due to the core-periphery structure of international economies. He argued that, in the world economy characterized by customary disparity in wage rates among developed and undeveloped nations, the international trade of commodities and capital mobility across nations cause the transfer of

surplus labor from poor nations with lower capital-labor ratios to wealthy nations with higher capital-labor ratios, which results in the impoverishment of poor nations and the enrichment of wealthy ones.

Yoshihara and Kaneko draw attention to what is arguably the greatest lacuna in the inequality literature, not to say neoclassical theory, namely that differences in wage levels are the greatest single statistical explanator of differences in income. The US minimum wage is $7.25 an hour. This is a floor, often overridden by city and state ordinances—the Washington, D.C. minimum is $13.69 per hour at the time of writing whilst activists have rallied around the "fight for the fifteen". Contrast this with India, where Unni (2005) estimates that the "predicted *daily* wage" [my emphasis — AF] of Indian workers ranges from Rs. 375.36 for "regular" urban male workers and Rs. 30.36 for rural female workers—$10 and $0.75 respectively. The vast *majority* of Indian workers could thus expect to earn less in a day—in the worst case ten times less—than the lowest-paid American worker in an hour.

The biggest prerequisite to correcting the gross inequities in international income is obviously, therefore, to raise the wage level of the average Indian worker to the level of the average American worker. Of course, this would require a substantial rise in the productivity of Indian labor. But given that China has multiplied the income level of its population by six on average, in a little under forty years, is this such an impractical suggestion? Were Indian income merely to grow at the Chinese rate of the past forty years, it would reach Korean levels by 2030 and American levels by 2040. Is that really so impractical?

Yet on productivity levels, the new inequality literature is also silent. The developmental discourse of the postwar years, when elevating productive capacity sat side by side with the eliminating inequalities of consumption, has virtually disappeared. This leads us to the greatest inequality gap of all: why is the *productivity of labor* so different, between one country and another? A variety of responses are to hand, all from outside the inequality literature.

In this respect, the comment of Yoshihara and Kaneko (op. cit.) is apposite. They note the objections to the theory of Unequal Exchange from within orthodox economics, as a result of which that theory is entirely absent from modern discussions:

> Samuelson (1976) argues that Emmanuel's theory of UE is inconsistent with the theory of comparative advantage, which implies the existence of mutual gain from trade.

Samuelson failed to comment, however, on an important difference between Ricardo's formulation of Comparative Advantage and its adaptation into neoclassical trade theory. Ricardo stated his theory in terms of the labor required to produce the output of each country. But Haberler (1930) objected on the following grounds:

> The theory of comparative costs was developed on the basis of the labor theory of value, and all theorists who accepted it have indeed assumed that it rests also logically on the labor theory of value. For the authors who reject the labor theory of value, the theory of comparative costs founders on the cliffs as the former, that is, on the fact that there simply exist no units of real cost, neither in the shape of days of labor nor in any other shape…

He then restated the theory as a factor allocation problem. This was a double switch: in place of *goods* – wine and cloth—countries now traded *factors of production*–capital and labor. And labor was no longer the source of value; capital not only contributed to value but functioned as a substitute.

A point critical to unequal exchange was thus is ignored: capital goods are *produced by means of labor*. Wine and cloth are not substitutes, nor can cloth be produced from wine, nor wine from cloth. Neoclassical theory thereby arrived at the notion, not deducible from Ricardo's original theory, that to produce in the "most efficient" way a low-wage country should substitute labor for capital domestically and acquire capital goods abroad.

But a poor country has a third option: development. By dedicating at least part of its labor force to acquire and apply technical knowledge to raise the productivity of its capital goods sector, a country can change the quantity of labor it needs to produce more capital goods – exactly as the Dependency theorists proposed and as China, to the chagrin of Presidents Trump and Biden alike, has actually done.

A very simple statistic illustrates the point: what is the actual traded price of the product of one hour of labor, in each country of the world? In terms that Marx would have understood, why does forty hours of Indian labor exchange on the world market for one hour of American labor? In particular, why do the countries of the global South require much more labor to produce capital goods than commodities and raw materials? Not because their "Comparative Advantage" lies indefinitely in producing basics and labor-intensive products, but because the market deprives them of the ability to develop a competitive capital goods sector. Their lower productivity yields a value transfer—Marx's "surplus profit" to advanced producers located in the North—with which they use to maintain a permanent monopoly of high technology.

The role of labor in production is thus a fundamental issue in understanding inequality between nations. Yoshihara (2021) in this volume returns to the issues raised in Yoshihara and Kaneko (*op. cit.*) and other papers on international trade. "Recently", he states, a vast literature has analyzed the persistent, and widening, inequalities in income and wealth observed in the vast majority of nations, while some data show inequality in per-capita income between the richer developed countries and the poorer developing ones which has been expanding since 1820. Thus, the issue of the long-run distributional feature of wealth and income in the capitalist economy should be at the heart of economic analysis, as Piketty (2014) emphasizes, and one of the central questions in economics should be to ask what the primary mechanism to generate such disparity persistently between the rich and the poor is.

However, he deals with the question at a more fundamental level: can a labor-value system serve as the basis for the analysis of international trade?

According to the standard Marxian view, the system of labor values of individual commodities can serve as the center of gravity for long-term price fluctuations in the pre-capitalist economy with simple commodity production, where no exploitative social relation emerges, while in the modern capitalist economy, the labor value system is replaced by the prices of production associated with an equal positive rate of profits as the center of gravity, in which exploitative relation between the capitalist and the working classes is a generic and persistent feature of economic inequality.

This view has been criticized because problems arise under 'joint production' in which a single capital is used to produce a multiplicity of outputs:

Some of the literature such as Morishima (1973, 1974) criticized this view by showing that the labor values of individual commodities are no longer well-defined if the capitalist economy has joint production.

Yoshihara responds to these criticisms:

Given these arguments, this paper firstly shows that the system of individual labor values can be still well-defined in the capitalist economy with joint production whenever the set of available production techniques is all-productive.

Secondly this paper shows that it is generally impossible to verify that the labor-value pricing serves as the center of gravity for price fluctuations in pre-capitalist economies characterized by the full development of simple commodity-production

This article thus underpins, theoretically, the conclusions reached in Yoshihara's other works, by arguing that the method used there is not vulnerable to Morishima's criticisms.

Shock, trend and the validity of theory

Public attention has been focused on the policy implications of inequality. It would be remiss, however, to conclude without reflecting on their implications for theory. These are not as remote from the policy as may be thought. For, if the facts stand in contradiction with the theories on which a policy is based, what grounds exist for consenting to that policy? Simply put, the conflict between the predictions of orthodox macroeconomics and the observed facts is so severe and has remained unaddressed for so long, that the economic theories which inform Northern policies can no longer be considered to rest on a scientific foundation.

This is not merely a failure of science but of democracy, uniformly recognized as founded on the informed consent of the governed. If policies are imposed based on theories inconsonant with the facts, then consent is not informed, because the theory does not justify the claim that the policies will produce the promised results. The question then posed is this: what exactly leads us to conclude that an economic theory conflicts with the facts? And how may we address the defects in the theory, and rectify the problems arising, thus addressing the adverse and harmful consequences of the theory?

The basic issue is a simple scientific matter. If the predictions of a theory conflict with the facts, which assumptions or methods lead to this conflict, what needs to be changed to open the way to theories from which the conflict is absent?

The method of science, which we characterize (Freeman 2020) as 'inductive pluralism', is quite simple: if a theory conflicts with the facts (as interpreted by the theory) we must first identify any assumptions or methods such that, if they are dropped, the conflict does not arise. Next, we must identify alternative assumptions that lead to predictions consonant with the facts.

The greatest inductive challenges facing modern economics arise from *trends*—notably historical trends. This is because economists suppose that though, observations may deviate from what a theory predicts, this does not conflict with the theory if the fluctuations remain within limits that can be plausibly explained as arising from chance.

We set aside, initially, the complex problem of distinguishing between chance and imperfect knowledge, to which both Marx and Keynes paid careful attention. We are concerned with the following inductive issue: accepting for the sake of argument the lax view that any deviation of observation from prediction may legitimately be attributed to chance, at what point does a conflict between theory and prediction oblige us to call the theory into question?

It is here that the timespan of any trend becomes paramount. It is one thing to maintain that owing to unforeseen circumstances, Convergence has been postponed for the time being. It is quite another to maintain it has been postponed indefinitely: this is just an underhand way of saying the theory does not apply. A law which never manifests itself is not a law but a doctrine. If we conclude, from the evidence, that as Pritchett suggests there is a long-term historical trend for the North to diverge from the South, or even (a more limited finding) that there is no long-term trend for them to converge, then since the theories of growth and trade predict

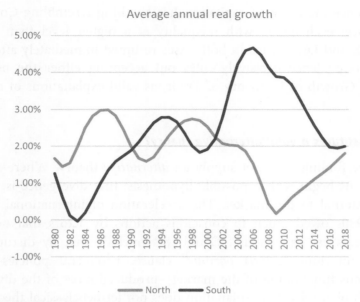

Figure 3. Growth rates and trend, outcome.

the opposite, they are false. And to the extent that neoclassical macroeconomics relies on them, it too is false.

Historical reasoning is hence vital. At certain points, inequality between nations has risen. At others—not many, any impartial observer must concede—it has declined. Generally speaking, it has risen throughout capitalist history, above all if we abandon the fiction of a continuous spectrum of national conditions and recognize the empirically confirmed distinction between the global North and South.

But it has not grown monotonically. It fell somewhat in the 1970s, and sharply from 2002 to 2012. May we still speak of a trend?

Two points are relevant. First, the 2002–2012 correction to the exceptionally high levels of the neoliberal decades did not bring international inequality back to its 1980 level. And second, this correction, mainly caused by a steep temporary rise in commodity prices, ended in 2012, when inequality resumed its upward trend.

A 2012 paper by Kemal Derviş, World Bank Vice-President for Poverty Reduction and Economic Management in 2000, and briefly in 2001 Turkey's Finance Minister, illustrates the point. Entitled 'Convergence, Interdependence, and Divergence', it proclaimed "a new convergence", boldly forecasting 4.5% growth in the global South, compared to 2.5% in the North. No such forecast was justified, as Figure 3 shows.

The 2002–2012 reversal calls for caution in supposing a permanent trend in *Divergence* but is in no wise a proof of *Convergence*. The historical evidence is completely incompatible with Derviş's claim. During only two decades since the dawn of capitalism has anything resembling Convergence taken place; each ended with inequality at a higher level than before its beginning; and Divergence in both cases resumed immediately after.

But this evidence decisively rules out accepting either the neoclassical theory of Growth or its theory of Trade, as valid explanations of reality.

What constitutes a valid alternative theory?

The above finding does not supply an *alternative* theory. Where should we look? Let us begin with a possible hypothesis: that divergence is caused by factors external to the market. The acceleration of international inequality in the 1980s owed much to conscious actions by actors that neoclassical theory treats as "exogenous". Could we conclude that by disrupting economics' notorious "*ceteris paribus*" clause, neoliberal policies—not the spontaneous functioning of the market—produced most of the divergence?

Though plausible, this explanation does not let neoclassical theory off the hook. The above measures claimed to *restore* the "free working" of a market disrupted by welfarist and developmentalist interventions. Indeed, the neoliberal years have arguably gifted economic science with the nearest to a laboratory-pure free market that the world is likely to experience. That Divergence reached world-historic highs in this period hardly confirms theories which predict that under these very conditions, the opposite should happen.

Another way to explain long-run disparities is by "endogenizing" variables previously considered exogenous such as human capital, innovation, and government policy, as in the "endogenous growth" theories associated with Romer. Their explanatory power is greater than standard theory, for sure. But there is a problem: if our endogenous variables include non-market variables like government policy, we are no longer testing whether the *market* produces Convergence or Divergence but whether it does so *in combination with appropriate government action*.

This shift in focus is of course welcome since we can study honestly and impartially study whether the optimum combination of government and market actions is to be found in India, China or the USA. It does not, however, explain the primary error in the theorems and prognostications which predict that a pure market system will produce Convergence.

In constructing an alternative, it is always essential to ask "an alternative to what?" Which *particular assumption* of any given theory is responsible for its predictive failure? This leads us to a distinction which most economic theories make but rarely scrutinize logically, between *endogenous* and *exogenous* factors.

A standard-issue economic theory assumes certain magnitudes to be given or known, externally to the theory itself. These "exogenous" magnitudes include consumer utility functions; the technological conditions of production and hence the Aggregate Production Function of neoclassical macro or the input-output relations of Linear Production Systems; and not least, the mysterious Solow residual.

In contrast, quantities of goods produced or consumed, and their prices, are "endogenous", by which economists mean that their magnitudes can be calculated once the exogenous variables are known. This gives rise to the standard-issue "problem" of high economic theory: taking the exogenous variables as given over some set of points in time, determine the values of the endogenous variables over the same set. This is the "prediction" of the theory.

Mathematically, denote the k variables of the system by a vector $Y = \{y_1, y_2, \ldots, y_k\}$. Since these variables are changing over time, let us also add a time subscript, writing $Y^t = \{y_1^t, y_2^t, \ldots, y_k^t\}$.

In general, Y^t at any one time depends on its values at previous points in time. We can write this either as a differential equation in discrete time (Goldberg 1986), or a differential equation in continuous time.[5] Engineers and natural scientists generally use continuous time, but economists, who have not deviated from period analysis since Sismondi introduced it early in the 19th Century, habitually use discrete-time.[6] The most general relation is then

$$Y^t = f(Y^{t-1}, Y^{t-2}, \ldots t) \qquad (1)$$

where f is a function encapsulating the theory. This states that Y at time t depends on whatever Y was at all previous points in time, and on time itself.

Two common simplifications, presupposed by almost all economic theories, don't affect the argument but make it clearer: the system is "autonomous", which means time doesn't enter explicitly; and there are no lags, so Y depends only on what it one period earlier. This yields

$$Y^t = f(Y^{t-1}) \qquad (2)$$

It is easy to show, as in undergraduate mathematics textbooks (e.g. Grimshaw 1990, 65) that such an equation always has a unique solution given the 'initial conditions' which specify Y at some arbitrary starting point.

The General Equilibrium paradigm that now dominates all economics makes an adaptation which constitutes a special case of (2). Y is partitioned into two groups; n endogenous variables $X = \{x_1, x_2, \ldots, x_n\}$ and m exogenous variables by $A = \{a_1, a_2, \ldots, a_m\}$, $n + m = k$. Equation (1) then becomes the slightly more complicated

$$\{A^t; X^t\} = f(\{A^{t-1}; X^{t-1}\}) \tag{3}$$

The exogenous A is supposed to be determined *independently* of the endogenous X. The technology, the accelerator, propensity to consume, psychological preferences, government spending, central bank interest rate—everything the economist considers fixed in some sense "external to the market" are "known" or "given" and treated as independent variables. This is the mathematical meaning of the term "exogenous".

There are then two possible ways to think about solving (2). The most general, the *temporal* or non-equilibrium solution, is the standard solution given by Grimshaw. This solution yields, for any A, a determinate and unique X. This method also figures in schoolbook solutions to the multi-plier-accelerator model, in Harrodian growth dynamics, and so on. It is generally adopted by the post-Keynesians (Chick 1983) and scholars of the Temporal Single System Interpretation (TSSI) of Marx (Kliman 2007; Freeman and Carchedi 1996). We designate this

$$X^t(f, \ A^t) \tag{4}$$

Since this gives X at all points in time we can drop the time superscript, giving

$$X(f, \ A) \tag{4a}$$

X here figures, technically, as a *functional*, mapping f, for any given A, to a corresponding X. In plain language, for any set of exogenous variables specified throughout time, (4a) tells us what the endogenous variables will be throughout the same time.

The General Equilibrium approach, also still adopted by many Marxists, expresses the problem in this way: suppose X does not change between $t-1$ and t, that is

$$X^t = X^{t-1} \tag{5}$$

There is then a unique solution, under the conditions expressed in the Brouwer fixed-point theorem (Sobolev 2001) for X^t in terms of A^t. This gives the different solution

$$X^*(f, \ A) \tag{6}$$

In general, the type (4) solution X does not coincide with the type (6) solution X^*. This provides an adequate means to test, empirically, which of the two solutions best explain the facts, for any particular set of phenomena. In some cases, X may be an attractor for X^*; in others, it is not.

Trends are especially relevant to any empirical test of whether this is the case, since if there is any tendency for X and X^* to diverge from each other, generally speaking, the longer the time interval considered, the more evident this tendency will be.

In at least one case—persistent long declines in the profit rate observed during capitalist history—X explains the observed historical trend (Freeman 2000, 2019c) whilst X^* does not: as Okishio (1961) proves, X^* predicts a rising historical trend. As Okishio (2001) himself notes, this is because his theorem assumes equilibrium: it is a type (6) solution.

Should we expect an analogous difference in explaining the long-run trend of rising international inequality? This is, as yet, an open question. However, since neoclassical theory rests on an equilibrium approach, we should expect it to predict decreasing inequality: if prices or technology in one location differ from those in another, the system cannot be in equilibrium. There are thus strong *a priori* grounds for supposing that the error lies in the equilibrium method.

As noted, of course, if non-market factors are made endogenous, it may be possible to explain this trend by other means. But then we no longer address the pure neoclassical theory which informs current policy, namely that *independently* of exogenous constraints, the world market will produce Convergence. In consequence, we may fail to identify the sources of error in this theory.

We, therefore, suggest a hypothesis for further research:

The endogenous divergence hypothesis:

a. if the only endogenous factors are the market variables of prices realized and quantities produced and consumed, the persistent observed long rising trend in inequality may be explained by a temporal solution.
b. under these conditions, no equilibrium solution will explain this trend.

This is a hypothesis, not a proven fact: to prove or disprove it, proponents of temporal and equilibrium approaches will have to exhibit theoretical predictions conforming to the observed long-term trends. It is, however, the most critical hypothesis to test if we wish to take seriously the central claim made by Marx himself: that the origin of capitalism's difficulties is the capitalist system itself, and that therefore, these difficulties may only be finally overcome by replacing that system by something superior.

Notes

1. All measures of income refer to GDP per capita in current US dollars at market exchange rates. The Brandt Report global North included the USSR, Yugoslavia and the Warsaw Pact countries, and China in the global South. Here, these countries are treated as distinct blocs from both the South and the North.
2. https://wid.world/data/. (Alvaredo et al. 2018, accessed 7 September 2022).

3. measured in current US dollars at market exchange rates. Technically, as Piketty notes, income is not identical to GDP. However (Freeman 2019b), the difference is small compared to that between nations; I use the most widely available data.
4. Not shown in the charts. The World Bank supplies quintiles of income for individual nations. Quartiles for the North and South are calculated using population-weighted GDP per capita for every nation in a bloc, to ensure no nation is omitted.
5. Grimshaw (1990), a classic work, illustrates using the accelerator-multiplier model, on page 5. Here the multiplier, the accelerator, and Government spending are exogenous whilst consumption and investment are endogenous.
6. Freeman (2020) shows that if price and value are *additive* (the price of two baskets of goods is equal to the price of the combined basket) and *exchange consistent* (the money paid by the purchasers of any good is equal to the money received by the sellers), any arbitrary discrete time system may be expressed in continuous time.

References

Alvaredo, F., L. Chancel, T. Piketty, E. Saez, and G. Zucman. 2018. "World Inequality Report." *World Inequality Lab* 2018.

Amin, S. 1979. *Imperialism and Unequal Development*. New York, NY: Monthly Review Press.

Amin, S. 2010. *The Law of Worldwide Value*. 2nd ed. New York, NY: NYU Press.

Bird, G., and A. Milne. 1999. "Miracle to Meltdown: A Pathology of the East Asian Financial Crisis." *Third World Quarterly*, 20 (2):421–437. doi: 10.1080/01436599913839.

Brandt, W. 1980. *North-South: A Programme for Survival: Report of the Independent Commission on International Development Issues*. London: Pan.

Chandrasekhar, C. P., and J. Ghosh. 2021. 'Is Emerging Asia in Retreat?' *Real World Economic Review*. https://rwer.wordpress.com/2021/07/13/is-emerging-asia-in-retreat/?utm_source=pocket_mylist

Chick, V. 1983. *Macroeconomics after Keynes*. Cambridge, MA: MIT Press.

Desai, R. 2013. *Geopolitical Economy: After US Hegemony, Globalization and Empire*. London: Pluto Press.

Desai, R., and M. Hudson. 2021. "Beyond the Dollar Creditocracy: A Geopolitical Economy." Valdai Discussion Club Paper 116. Accessed August 6, 2021. https://valdai-club.com/files/34879/

Freeman, A. 2000. "Marxian Debates on the Falling Rate of Profit – A Primer."ideas.repec.org/p/pra/mprapa/2588.html

Freeman, A. 2007. "Heavens above: What Equilibrium Means for Economics." In *Equilibrium in Economics: Scope and Limits*, edited by V. Mosini. London: Routledge.

Freeman, A. 2019a. "Class." In *The Oxford Handbook of Karl Marx*, edited by M. Vidal, Tomas Rotta, Tony Smith, and Paul Prew. Oxford: OUP.

Freeman, A. 2019b. *Divergence, Bigger Time: The Unexplained Persistence, Growth, and Scale of Postwar International Inequality*. Manitoba: GERG.

Freeman, A. 2019c. *The Sixty-Year Downward Trend of Economic Growth in the Industrialised Countries of the World*. Manitoba: GERG.

Freeman, A. 2020. "A General Theory of Value and Money (Part 1: Foundations of an Axiomatic Theory)." *World Review of Political Economy* 28–75. doi: 10.13169/worlrevipoliecon.11.1.0028.

Freeman, A., and G. Carchedi, eds. 1996. *Marx and Non-Equilibrium Economics*. Aldershot and London: Edward Elgar.

Freeman, A., V. Chick, and S. Kayatekin. 2014. "*Whig History and the Reinterpretation of Economic History.*" *Cambridge Journal of Economics* 38 (3):519–529. doi: 10.1093/cje/beu017.

Goldberg, S. 1986. *Introduction to Difference Equations, with Illustrative Examples from Economics, Psychology and Sociology.* New York: Dover.

Grimshaw, R. 1990. *Nonlinear Ordinary Differential Equations.* Oxford: Blackwell.

Gunder Frank, A. 1966. *The Development of Underdevelopment.* Somerville, MA: New England Free Press.

Haberler, G. 1930. "Die Theorie der komparativen Kosten und ihre Auswertung für die Begründung des Freihandels." Weltwirtschaftliches Archiv. 32 (1930):349–370. [Translated and reprinted in Anthony Y. C. Koo, ed. *Selected Essays of Gottfried Haberler.* Cambridge, MA: MIT Press.

Hashimoto, Kenji. 2021. "Transformation of the Class Structure in Contemporary Japan." *The Japanese Political Economy* doi: 10.1080/2329194X.2021.1943685.

Heckscher, E. F. 1991. "The Effects of Foreign Trade on the Distribution of Income." In *Heckscher-Ohlin Trade Theory,* edited by Harry Flam and June Flanders, p. 38. Cambridge: MIT Press.

Hickel, J. 2018. *The Divide: Global Inequality from Conquest to Free Markets.* New York and London: W. W. Norton.

Huntington, S. P. [1996]. 2011. *The Clash of Civilizations and the Remaking of World Order.* New York, NY: Simon and Schuster.

Isidro Luna, V. L. 2022. "World inequality, Latin America catching up, and the asymmetries in power", *The Japanese Political Economy.*

King, S. 2019. "Lenin's Theory of Imperialism Today: The Global Divide between Monopoly and Non-Monopoly Capital." PhD thesis. Victoria University, Melbourne.

Kliman, A. 2007. *Reclaiming Marx's Capital: A Refutation of the Myth of Inconsistency.* Lanham, MD: Lexington Books.

Krugman, P. 1994. "The Myth of Asia's Miracle." *Foreign Affairs* 73 (6):62–78. doi: 10.2307/20046929.

Kuznets, S. 1955. "Economic Growth and Income Inequality." *American Economic Review* 45 (March):1–28.

Kuznets, S. 1966. *Modern Economic Growth: Rate, Structure and Spread.* New Haven, CT. Yale University Press.

Lee, Kang-Kook, and M. Siddique. 2021. "Financialization and Income Inequality: An Empirical Analysis." *The Japanese Political Economy.* doi: 10.1080/2329194X.2021.1945465.

Mandel, E. 1976. *Late Capitalism.* London: Verso.

Mandel, E. 1979. *The Second Slump.* London: Verso.

Milanovic, B. 2005. *Worlds Apart: Measuring International and Global Inequality.* Princeton, NJ: Princeton University Press.

Milanovic, B. 2016. *Global Inequality: A New Approach for the Age of Globalization.* Cambridge, MA: Harvard University Press.

Okishio, N. 1961. "Technical Changes and the Rate of Profit." *Kobe University Economic Review* 7(1):85–99.

Okishio, N. 2001. "Competition and Production Prices." *Cambridge Journal of Economics* 25 (4):493–501. doi: 10.1093/cje/25.4.493.

Page, J. 1993. *The East Asian Miracle: Economic Growth and Public Policy.* New York, NY: World Bank/Oxford University Press.

Piketty, T. 2014. *Capital in the Twenty-First Century*. Cambridge, MA; London: Belknap Press.

Pomeranz, K. 2000. *The Great Divergence: China, Europe, and the Making of the Modern World Economy*. Princeton, MA: Princeton University Press.

Prebisch, R. 1950. *The Economic Development of Latin America and its Principal Problems*. Lake Success, NY: United Nations Economic Commission for Latin America.

Pritchett, L. 1997. "Divergence, Big Time." *The Journal of Economic Perspectives* 11 (3):14.

Petit, Pascal. 2021. "Income Inequality: Past, Present and Future in a Political Economy Perspective." *The Japanese Political Economy*.

Reinert, E., ed., 2004. *Globalization, Economic Development and Inequality: An Alternative Perspective*. Cheltenham: Edward Elgar.

Reinert, E. S., and K. S. Jomo. 2005. *The Origins of Development Economics: How Schools of Economic Thought Have Addressed Development*. London: Zed Press.

Romer, P. M. 1994. "The Origins of Endogenous Growth." *Journal of Economic Perspectives* 8 (1):3–22. doi: 10.1257/jep.8.1.3.

Rostow, W. W. 1960. *The Stages of Economic Growth: A Non-Communist Manifesto*. Cambridge, England: Cambridge University Press.

Samuelson, P. A. 1948. "International Trade and the Equalisation of Factor Prices." *The Economic Journal* 58 (230):163–184. doi: 10.2307/2225933.

Samuelson, P. A. 1976. "Illogic of Neo-Marxian Doctrine of Unequal Exchange." In *Inflation, Trade and Taxes: Essays in Honour of Alice Bourneuf*, edited by D. A. Belsley, E. J. Kane, P. A. Samuelson and R. M. Solow. Columbus: Ohio State University Press.

Singer, H. W. 1950. "The Distribution of Gains between Investing and Borrowing Countries." *American Economic Review* 15 (Reprinted in *Readings in International Economics*. London, George Allen and Unwin, 1968).

Sobolev, V. I. 2001. *Brouwer Theorem', Encyclopedia of Mathematics*. Berlin: EMS Press.

Stiglitz, J. E. 2002. *Globalization and Its Discontents*. New York and London: WW Norton.

Stiglitz, J. E. 2017. *The Great Divide: Unequal Societies and What We Can Do about Them*. New York and London: WW Norton.

Tawney, R. H. [1931]. 1983. *Equality*. London: Allen and Unwin.

Todaro, M. 1995. *Economic Development*. 5th ed. New York, NY: Longman.

Unni, J. 2005. "Wages and Incomes in Formal and Informal Sectors in India." *Indian Journal of Labour Economics* 48 (2):311–317.

Wade, R. H. 2018. "The Developmental State: Dead or Alive?" *Development and Change* 49 (2):518–546. doi: 10.1111/dech.12381.

Wade, Robert. 2020. "Rethinking the World Economics as a Two Bloc Hierarchy." *Real-World Economics Review* 92:4–29.

Wilkinson, R., and K. Pickett. 2010. *The Spirit Level: Why Equality is Better for Everyone*. London: Penguin Books.

Yoshihara, N., and S. Kaneko. 2016. "On the Existence and Characterization of Unequal Exchange in the Free Trade Equilibrium." *Metroeconomica* 67 (2):210–241. doi: 10.1111/meca.12125.

Yoshihara, Naoki. 2021. "On the Labor Theory of Value as the Basis for the Analysis of Economic Inequality in the Capitalist Economy." *The Japanese Political Economy*.

World inequality, Latin America catching up, and the asymmetries in power

Víctor Manuel Isidro Luna

ABSTRACT

Despite the increase of material wealth through time, the majority of countries throughout the world have been unable to catch up consistently with the core countries. This article shows that between-country inequality has surged, and that wealthy countries can perform better than poor countries in achieving growth in the long term. Also, it demonstrates that Latin America countries have not caught up to the leading countries, and that between the rich and Latin countries there remains "an unbridgeable gulf," using Harrod and Hirch's words. Finally, using real and financial variables, this article shows that some Latin American countries have been subjected to exclusion and exploitation and cannot apply the same developmental policies as the richest countries.

Introduction

The power of nations is related to the international command of goods and services, to sovereignty in establishing monetary and fiscal policies, and to the greater benefits that accrue to core countries than to peripheral countries in their participation in the international division of labor. As Arrighi (1990), Hicker (2018), and Wade (2020) have reported, powerful countries can maintain their wealth consistently through time, and they can use, depending on time and place, discretional policies on trade, capital movements, and the transfer of labor (Arrighi 1990). For example, even though the power of the United States appears to be in decline, the world, and peripheral countries, are worried about US policies concerning interest rates, spending (Skidelsky 2019), and migration. Following Arrighi's idea, this article demonstrates that the world distribution of income is unequal, and that core countries can perform better than peripheral countries in the command of international income. Also, this article shows that Latin America has not been catching up to the rich countries since the 1970s, that the ups and downs in Latin American development prevent these countries from being even with the core countries. Finally, this article demonstrates that powerful countries can implement developmental policies that are not available to peripheral countries, and that some variables affect core and peripheral countries in different ways. In this sense, and following Arrighi (1990), we first distinguish an exclusion mechanism such as the application of developmental policies available only to the most powerful countries, and second, mechanisms that reproduce inequality such as trade and capital flow. Two contemporary theoretical approximations exemplify this situation in Latin America: (1) one depending on the relationship between trade balance and short-term capital inflow (Harrod 1933, 1958; Shaikh 2016), and (2) one depending on the relationship between trade and income balance and the flows of foreign direct investment (FDI) (Kregel 2006, 2008).

Identifying a conceptual and spatial division between countries is one of the objectives of this article. Thus, our ideas are in line with other heterodox schools of thought such as Latin American structuralists, the dependency school, World-System theories, and theories of imperialism. Going back to Prebisch, we borrow the terminology core-periphery to refer to the duality of wealthy-poor countries. Core countries are identified in this article by their international command of goods and services, by their instrumentation of fiscal monetary policies, and by their advantage of participating in the international division of labor (trade and finance). First, this article addresses inequality between countries because such inequality illustrates whether poor countries have been able to develop and catch up to core states in terms of their command of material wealth. Rather than individuals, this analysis is centered on states because they participate in trade, pay dividends and debts, and receive remittances and foreign direct investment (FDI). Empirically, this article examines the Latin American path of convergence with case studies of Argentina, Brazil, and Mexico. These countries have different economic and political backgrounds, but, especially after the 1970s and 1980s, they have been forced to adapt restrictive policies (sound finance and structural reforms). This article also shows that the United States can establish more independent policies than Latin American countries, and it highlights the negative effect of trade and finance on Latin American countries.

After this introduction, this article proceeds as follows: First, the article defines inequality between countries based on the command of goods and services, describes the evolution of inequality, explains the dataset that is used to calculate inequality, and shows the evolution of inequality from the 1960s to the present day between core and peripheral countries. Second, Latin America's gross national income per capita (GNIPC) at current prices is compared with the level of income of different quintiles. Third, the differential degree in power between the United States and some Latin American countries is exemplified by the privilege of the US in applying an independent fiscal monetary policy and by showing that the Latin American path of development is driven by external factors such as the flows of trade and capital. Finally, the conclusion highlights new relevant issues for further discussion.

Defining inequality and measuring inequality from 1962 to 2019

The three types of economic inequality are unweighted between countries, weighted between countries, and global inequality (Milanovic 2007, 2013). In the first type, one country of the world represents one observation in the measure of inequality; in the second, it is one observation weighted by the population of the country. Finally, the third considers not only inequality weighted by the population but also the distribution of income within countries (within-countries inequality), which is called global inequality. In assessing inequality, Milanovic (2007) has noted that global inequality is the best and weighted between countries inequality is the worst. Unweighted between-countries inequality is theoretically useful because it shows "whether nations are converging (in terms of their income levels)" (Milanovic 2007, 15), and it is empirically important because, for many years, it has been the most important factor in global inequality.[1] In this article, unweighted between-countries inequality displays whether peripheral countries have been able to develop and catch up to core states in terms of the command of material wealth. Also, it shows the performance of the core and peripheral countries through time and that, globally, using Arrighi's words, "the capability of a state to appropriate the benefits of the world division of labor is determined primarily by its position ....The further up in the hierarchy of wealth a state is, the better positioned its rulers and subjects are in the struggle for benefits" (Arrighi 1990, 15). Core states can, then, implement contingent trade and monetary, fiscal, and migration policies according to their position within the world structure of wealth (refer to Arrighi 1990; Reinert 2007; Hicker 2018).

One of the problems in measuring wealth and international convergence is if income at purchasing power parity (PPP) or a current dollar metric must be used in making comparisons. Some leading scholars in inequality, such as Milanovic (2016) and Firebaugh (2000), prefer gross domestic product per capita (GDPPC) at PPP because they are worried about the well-being of people in their own country. Both Milanovic and Firebaugh focus their analyses on nontradable goods. Other scholars such as Arrighi (1990, 1991) and Korzeniewicz and Moran (1997, 2000) prefer gross national income per capita (GNIPC) at current prices because they are worried about measuring one country's population command of tradable goods and services. This article agrees with Korzeniewicz and Moran (1997, 2000) that convergence is related to the ability to buy goods and services at the actual exchange rate. Wealth and convergence are shown not only in the ability to buy a bundle of good and services at domestic prices but also in the participation of people and countries in the world market; the appreciation/depreciation of the foreign exchange has distributional effects on nations and people. For example, depreciation increases the burden of debt, and can also increase domestic prices as well as reduce salaries (see Grasso, Malic, and Ziccarelli 2017). Using Arrighi's words (1990, 15 ; see also Arrighi 1991 and Korzeniewicz and Moran 1997), GNIPC at current prices helps us observe this "hierarchy of wealth" through time between nations.

Some neoclassical authors measuring inequality, using GDP per capita at PPP, have reported that inequality increased after WWII but declined during the 1980s and 1990s (Firebaugh and Goesling 2004). Along the same lines, Shultz (1998) has claimed that inequality decreased in the 1990s, and, finally, Clark (2011) has attested that inequality was stagnant during the 1990s but declined during the 2000s. In contrast, O'Rourke (2001) has asserted that inequality declined from World War II (WWII) to the end of the 1950s, and, afterwards, inequality increased until 1992. Unlike O'Rourke, Milanovic (2007, 2013) has studied inequality using GDP per capita at PPP; like O'Rourke, he finds an increasing trend of the Gini Index in the 1980s that continued until the 1990s. For Milanovic, however, inequality was stable in the 1960–1970 period and declined from the beginnings of the 2000s to 2011. Like O'Rourke, Korzeniewicz and Moran (2009) have found an increasing trend in equality, especially during the 1980s, and similar to Milanovic, they found a decline in inequality from the beginnings of the 2000s to 2007; however, Korzeniewicz and Moran used gross national income (GNI) at current prices weighted by population, which considerers net transfer from abroad.

At the empirical as well as at the theoretical level, wealth and convergence have been broadly studied. Previous researchers have constructed more robust and broader datasets (Arrighi 1990; Korzeniewicz and Moran 1997; Firebaugh and Goesling 2004; and Milanovic 2016); however, I believe that the dataset of the World Bank at current prices is a good source to achieve my purpose. The dataset used in this article is that of the GNIPC at current prices because it shows the effective wealth of a country and its evolution through time.[2] For example, in measuring the wealth of a country, Mexico has had a historical trade deficit as well as a negative balance of income (net payments of dividends and utilities and net interest debt), but currently it receives an important amount of remittances. I emphasize that I do not utilize a consistent dataset through time; however, using a reduced consistent dataset of the GNIPC from 1982 onward and a reduced consistent dataset of the gross domestic product per capita at current prices (GDPPC) from 1970 onward produces the same trends as my broader dataset. Then, measuring inequality through the GNIPC demonstrates a world hierarchy of wealth, and in this world, hierarchy is "an unbridgeable gulf" (Hirsch 1977, 22; also, Arrighi 1994, 19) between core and peripheral countries that is manifested in the income but also in the different developmental policies that can be established.

Measuring inequality and showing its evolution

We now proceed to show the evolution of world inequality from 1962 to the present day. We focus on world inequality, its evolution, and the better performance of the core versus peripheral countries in commanding growth in the long term. To study inequality between countries, the World Bank dataset is divided in five equal parts of countries (quintiles), and the mean of the GNIPC at current prices is obtained. The quintile V is the top quintile and the quintile I is at the bottom of the distribution. This article follows the line of thinking in Arrighi (1990), Pritchett (1997), Wallerstein (1999), Reinert (2007), Hicker (2018), Chandraseknar (2017), and Wade (2020), all of whom claim that mobility from core to peripheral countries is rare, and that the wealthier countries at the end of the nineteenth century and the beginnings of the twentieth century were the same–with some exceptions– as today. Thus, in the short or even medium term, some countries may look very promising, but in the long run they are not able to catch up to the leading countries.

Inequality between countries increases if the mean of the top-quintile is divided by the mean of the bottom quintile; this indicator was reached 21.8 times in 1962 and 57.7 times in 2019 (refer to Figure 1). Inequality increased slowly from 1962 to the mid-1980s, skyrocketed from 1987 through the mid-1990s, had ups and downs in the mid-1990s-2007 period, and declined drastically after the current economic crisis, from 2013 to the present-day stagnation. The ratio of the top-quintile/bottom quintile clearly illustrates the evolution of the growth of world inequality. However, the Gini Index is a conventional tool to measure inequality (Milanovic 2007, 2016; O'Rourke 2001; Firebaugh 1999, Firebaugh and Goesling 2004). Figure 2 shows that the Gini Index was 0.5163 in 1962 and 0.5855 in 2019, a difference of 0.0692, which indicates the inequality between countries increased by nearly 1/14 of its total value. Also, this global between-country inequality is larger than the Gini Index of some domestic economies, such as Brazil (0.539),

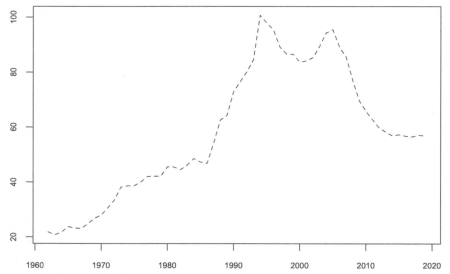

Figure 1. Top Quintile's GDP Mean Divided by Bottom Quintile's Mean. Source: Author's elaboration with data from World Bank 2020.

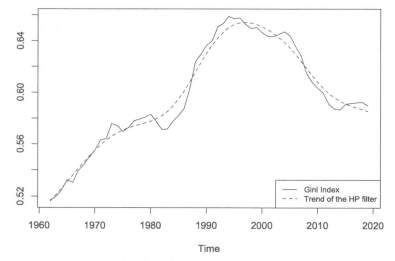

Time

Figure 2. Gini Index and the Trend of the HP Filter. Source: Author's elaboration with data from World Bank 2020.

Honduras (0.521), and Angola (0513), which were considered the most unequal in the world in 2018.

Figure 2 also shows the movement of the slope change in the trend. The six periods that can be distinguished are presented in Table 1.[3] During the Golden Age of capitalism, particularly the period of 1962–1974, all nations grew quite well. This period manifests the good performance of core countries after WWII and the process of decolonization and the establishment

Table 1. Quintiles' Mean of the Real GDP per Capita, Growth Rate.

	I	II	III	IV	V
1963–1974	6.4	7.7	8.5	11.2	11.7
1975–1982	7.2	9.3	10.4	9.5	9.2
1983–1997	0.6	−0.2	1.2	1.7	5.4
1998–2007	5.6	8.2	7.8	7.3	5.2
2008–2012	9.5	9.6	8.4	5.7	1.9
2013–2019	1.9	1.4	−0.1	1.8	1.2

Source: Author's elaboration with data from World Bank 2020

of national development projects in many poor countries. In the 1975–1982 period, the mean income of the II-IV quintiles grew faster than the top quintile, so inequality rose at a slower pace. During this period, the top quintiles were affected by the shock of oil prices, the collapse of profitability, and the abandonment of a state of confidence that promoted growth after WWII. In the 1983–1997 period, the performance of the top quintile exceeded by far the performance of the I-IV quintiles. This period reflects the establishment of neoliberalism all over the world, the adjustment of poor countries to orthodox policies such as macroeconomic stability and sound finance, and the efforts of many countries to pay back the heavy burden of external debt. Consequently, inequality skyrocketed around the world. During the period 1998–2007, the top quintile demonstrated the worst performance. This period saw the boom of commodities due to the increased demand for the commodities of China, and, for example, in Latin America, the rise of the pink tide led by some progressive governments that were supported by many organized social movements. The period after the Great Crisis continued with the poor performance of the top quintile, but during the 2013–2019 period, the I-IV quintiles were affected drastically, and the top quintile seemed to mitigate the damages. Then, we have shown some similarities with O'Rourke and Korzeniewicz and Moran in the evolution of inequality such as the increasing trend in the 1990s and the decreasing trend at the beginning of the 2000s. Despite the fluctuation of the inequality index in the short run, from 1962 to 2019 inequality increased during two periods, one with high participation of the state and the other with an increasing trend of liberalization.[4]

Power, Latin American's catching up and the relationship between trade balance and Capital inflows

According to Olin Wright (1987), the distribution of wealth between units such as people and states can be dependent or independent of other units. Wealth and power imply the existence of poor countries, and well-off countries can establish measures to perpetuate their position in the hierarchy of wealth. Harrod (1958) studied two kinds of personal wealth in capitalism. Oligarchic wealth is based on the individual's command of more goods and services than such an individual produces, and also on this individual's command of scarce goods and services. Meanwhile, democratic wealth is based on the efforts of each person. According to Hirsch (1977, 22), following Harrod, between the two kinds of wealth there is "an unbridgeable gulf"; therefore, the totality of individuals cannot achieve the same affluence in a society. Arrighi (1990) tried to extend Harrod and Hirsch's idea to nations and noted that "Opportunities for economic advance, as they present themselves serially to one state after another, do not constitute equivalent opportunities for economic advance by all the states" (1990, 16). Also, he distinguished mechanisms of exclusion that are policies not all the countries can use at the same time and mechanisms that reproduce inequality such as trade and finance whereby poor countries scarcely benefit from their participation in the international division of labor. Empirically, many scholars from a heterodox viewpoint have commented that developmental policies are relational and that core countries take advantage of their position in trade and financial activities (Reinert 2007; Ocampo 2016; Hicker 2018; Wade 2020). From a neostructuralism viewpoint, Ocampo (2016, 68 and 69) comments that developmental policies are relational,

> The first one is the persistence of large inequalities in the world economy, which arose quite early in the history of modern economic development and has tended to expand through time. Empirical studies indicate that (absolute) convergence in per capita incomes has been the exception rather than the rule .... The major implications of this fact are that economic opportunities are largely determined by the position that a particular country occupies within the world hierarchy, which makes climbing the international ladder a rather difficult task.

Furthermore, according to Wade (2020, 9), some core countries benefit the most from their higher position, and these countries establish organizations that reflect their interests, such as trade organizations:

> *Countries of the North enjoy common economic benefits from their superior position in the world hierarchy, making for common interests in protecting their position from challengers.* They translate common interests into political treaties, such as free trade agreements (eg NAFTA), political federations (eg European Union), and security agreements (eg NATO); and into common agreements linking groups of northern countries with regions of the South (eg Lome Convention, a trade and aid agreement between the European Economic Commission and 71 African, Caribbean and Pacific countries, signed in 1975). The seven leading economies of the North have concerted their actions through the G7 summits, claiming to be the top table of governance for the world (though not replacing the UN Security Council on security issues); and supported by tiers of other G7 coordination forums.

In this section, we demonstrate that Latin American countries, in the long term, do not have the same command of goods and services as the core ones. Also, mirroring the ideas of Harrod, Hirsch, Wade, Hicker and

Arrighi, this section demonstrates that some developmental policies are relational, and mostly are available to core countries. Specifically, this section shows that Latin American countries have not caught up to core countries over a long period of time (1962 to 2019); therefore, core countries can apply more independent policies contingent upon their power.

Starting with our three Latin American countries, the biggest and the most industrialized Latin American countries have been unable to catch up to the core countries from 1962 to the present day. Conversely, the most powerful country of Latin America, Brazil, is now deindustrializing (Medialdea 2012; Isidro Luna 2014a). Today, it is obvious that Argentina, Brazil, and Mexico are not catching up to the leading countries. From the 1930s through the 1970s, the years of the import-substitution model, with nationalist governments and a favorable international context to promote growth, Argentina, Brazil, and Mexico encouraged public enterprises as well as some public financial institutions. Also, the governments of these countries nationalized natural resources companies and built infrastructure to prevent bottlenecks to their industrialization process (refer to Cortes-Conde 2007). Above all, Mexico and Brazil grew steadily, around 6 percent during this period; converged incipiently to the United States; expanded domestic markets; developed basic industries with the help of development banks; improved some social indicators such as life expectancy at birth; and even benefited from the access to international loans during the 1970s, concentrating these two countries during these decades at roughly 40 percent of the total loans made to the peripheral countries, excluding the oil exporting countries (Quijano 1981).

Domestic and international conditions to promote growth changed in Latin American countries during the 1960s and afterward. Domestically, Argentina, Brazil, and Mexico's elites pressured governments during the 1950s and the 1960s to maintain the bulk of the benefits of the economic growth. For example, a coup d'état in Argentina during the 1950s established conservative measures such as nonprogressive income distribution, policies favoring agribusiness, concentration of banking, and targeting of inflation (Ferrer 1963; Peña 1974; Schvarzer 1978). The 1964 coup in Brazil resulted in policies such as no land distribution, the strengthening of the agribusiness elite, a concentration of the banks, and a curb on salaries as well as on public spending. Finally, no coup occurred in Mexico, but political dissidents were repressed, and during the 1960s, high interest rates were imposed to control inflation, income was unequally distributed, and the banking system was highly concentrated (Maxfield 1988; Isidro Luna 2014b). Thus, agribusiness, financial elites, and an industrial bourgeoise without any leadership obstructed the growth of these Latin American countries, and domestically no competitive industrial area arose.

Internationally, an increase in inflation, a decline in private profitability, and deterioration in confidence led to a slowdown in international economic growth during the 1970s. Gradually, throughout the 1970s to the 1990s, first Argentina, then Mexico, and finally Brazil, by consent or by force, implemented neoliberal policies: adjustment (sound finance) and structural macroeconomic reforms (trade and financial liberalization and labor reforms) (refer to French-Davis, Muñoz, and Palma 2000; Frenkel and Rapetti 2009). During this neoliberal period, the economic successes of Brazil and Mexico came to a standstill, and Argentina, Brazil, and Mexico had to pay a heavy burden in the service of external debt whose obligations depend on the behavior of variables determined in the international arena: exports, finance, and the exchange rate.

In Argentina, Brazil, and Mexico, the GNIPC evolved as follows since the 1970s: The three countries have transitioned between the average GNIPC of the third and fourth quintiles (refer to Figure 3), and none has persistently surpassed an income quintile. In contrast, they have experienced many crises since the 1970s. Mexico was severely hit during the 1980s and after the Great Crisis; during the 1995 Mexican crisis, the country was also drastically hit but had a fast recovery. Brazil's economy slowed down during the 1980s, at the end of the 1990s (1999), and like Mexico, after the Great Crisis. Argentina grew slowly through the 1960s and 1970s, but its growth sharply declined at the beginning of the 2000s and after the Great Crisis. However, unlike Mexico, Argentina and Brazil had remarkable growth during the commodities boom. Unfortunately, this boom was short lived, and all these countries, including Mexico, faced many problems after the Great Crisis. Thus, the "unbridgeable gulf" between the top quintile and the Latin American countries is easy to appreciate.

Alternatively, Figure 3 also displays the development path of three other countries, India, China, and South Korea. India may be an important geopolitical partner, with its important production of software and IT-enabling services (Chandraseknar 2017), but it is not catching up to the leading countries. China has been able to consistently leave behind the poorest quintiles of income. The GNIPC of China is far lower that of the rich countries, but China has quickly upgraded to other quintiles. However, China is not an example of a free market; it is an example of a country with an important public sector and domestic market, and that uses price controls (Harris 2009; Xie, Li, and Li 2012; Qi and Kotz 2020; Ye 2020; Weber 2021), with more space than other countries to carry out more discretionary trade, fiscal, and monetary policies. Finally, South Korea is a country that suffered from the 1997 and 2008 crises, but that clearly has converged to one of the leading countries. Korea was in the II quintile in 1962, but it was upgraded to the top quintile in 2019. Several scholars have

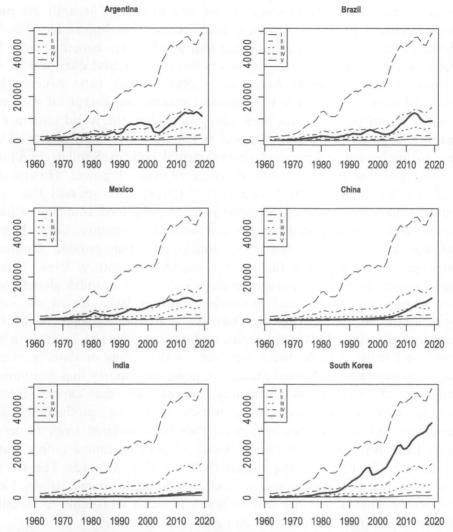

Figure 3. Latin American Catching Up, Quintiles, and Countries' GNIPC at Current Prices. Source: Author's elaboration with data from World Bank 2020.

argued that South Korea is not an example of catching up by commercial and financial liberalization. Wallerstein (1999) stated that geopolitcal reasons following World War II explain South Korea's success, and Wade (2020) reaffirmed this idea, saying that South Korea received US financial, technological, and military aid after WWII. Kvangraven (2021) reported that South Korea benefited from the Japanese-Chinese conflict at the beginning of the twentieth century when Japanese elites decided to industrialize South Korea, and that after WWII South Korea also benefited from foreign licenses and external finance. Fischer (2018) argued that Korean success has been due to its access to credit in key historical moments; for example,

South Korea had access to credit at the end of the 1970s until the mid-1980s, whereas in Latin America, such access was impossible. Finally, Chandraseknar (2017) has commented that South Korea benefited from US special interest and from the opportunity to carry out land distribution.

Unlike China and South Korea, since 1982 onward, Latin America has faced turbulent conditions in its economic growth, and except for the commodities boom period, it has been falling behind in the world structure of wealth and power. This lack of power is manifested in the inability of the state to implement independent developmental policies. Similar conditions do not apply to countries with different degrees of power. Historically, Wade (2020), Reinert (2007), and Hicker (2018) have stressed that core countries have prevented the development of peripheral countries. Chang (2002a, 2002b) commented that in the nineteenth century, Great Britain and the United States used protectionism to spur growth. Similarly, Vernengo (2016) reported that in the eighteenth century, Great Britain used a central bank to encourage development and to establish global domination over the world. Such powerful countries have denied the same opportunities to the newcomers. Thus, the tools for development are not democratic. Today, the United States is the most powerful country in the world, and it has a trade deficit but receives the inflow of short-term and long-term capital. The United States is a powerful country that combines a trade deficit with fiscal autonomy because of the capital inflow. Unfortunately, Latin American countries have low productivity and unemployment, and as has been seen, they have suffered from recurrent crises. Latin America's trade deficit is also adjusted by capital inflow, but it has more difficulty attracting capital than the United States. The United States has a trade deficit and a need for foreign capital, as do Latin American countries, but the United States is much more able to establish developmental policies than the Latin American countries.

Finally, turning to the mechanisms that reproduce inequality, peripheral countries do not benefit to the same degree as core countries in their participation in world markets. This participation reinforces unequal development. One way to participate in the international division of labor is the relationship between trade and financial flow (foreign investment and debt). For example, historically, Latin American countries have had trade deficits and have needed capital to cover these deficits in the current account. After WWII, economists such as Prebisch (1970, 1986) and Singer (1950) claimed that trade and capital flow were not mutually beneficial for all countries. There was a deterioration in terms of trade for peripheral countries and transfers of capital from the peripheral to core countries. Also, Singer (1950) clearly stated that the foreign direct investment of core countries may determine specialization and the export of commodities, and

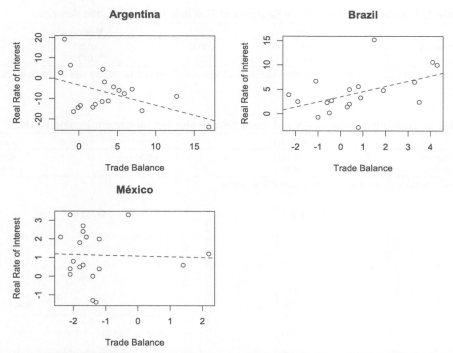

Figure 4. Relationship Between Trade Balance and Real Rate of Interest from 2002 to 2020. Source: Author's elaboration with data from International Monetary Fund (2021a, 2021b) and World Bank (2020).

then the evolution of the terms of trade may be determined by foreign investment. Using two contemporary scholars, I would like to highlight two approaches to relating trade and capital flows as mechanisms that reproduce inequality. First, according to Shaikh, following Harrod (1933, 1958), countries with a trade deficit, due to deterioration of the terms of trade, need to attract short-term capital: "If free trade leads to persistent trade imbalances, how is the balance of payments maintained? … short-term capital movements may be triggered by exchange rate movements and/or interest differentials" (Shaikh 2016, 520, 521). Second, countries with a trade deficit need to attract long-term capital. According to Kregel (2006, 2008), after the 1970s, trade deficits have been covered by long-term capital, and, furthermore, long-term capital may have totally changed the trade pattern. Currently, for Kregel, FDI may cause trade deficits in some countries; however, this new pattern of trade is not beneficial to peripheral countries since the remittances paid to home countries are huge (Figure 4).

Following Shaikh's hypotheses, trade balance is associated here with net short-term capital. Not only is competitiveness in poor countries achieved by low labor costs, but a high interest rate must be established to cover the trade deficit. We associate trade balance divided by GNI versus the real interest rate from 2002 to 2020 with data from the International Monetary

Table 2. Correlation Between Trade Balance and Real Rate of Interest, Latin America.

	Argentina	Brazil	Mexico
Correlation	−0.4867	0.4846	−0.0361
R-square	0.2400	0.2300	0.0010

Source: Author's elaboration with data from International Monetary Fund (2021a, 2021b) and World Bank (2020)

Table 3. Correlation Between FDI and Trade Balance plus Net Investment Income Balance.

	Argentina	Brazil	Mexico
Correlation	−0.5841	−0.906	−0.6938
R-square	0.34	0.82	0.48

Source: Author's elaboration with data from CEPAL 2020a

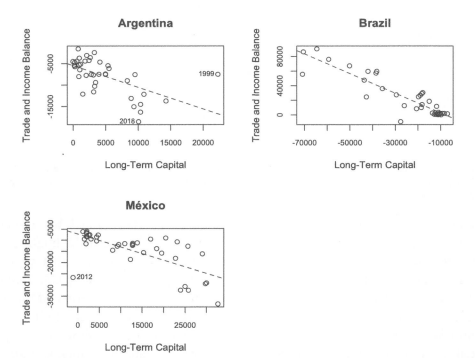

Figure 5. Relationship Between FDI and Trade Plus Net Investment Income Balance 1980–2018, Millions of Dollars. Source: Author's elaboration with data from CEPAL 2020b.

Fund and the World Bank.[5] A negative relationship is expected to occur in these two variables: a positive trade balance should be related to a low interest rate and a negative trade balance to a higher interest rate. Table 2 shows this correlation is low in Mexico; in Brazil, a positive trade balance is correlated with a higher interest rate; and, in Argentina, the theoretical prediction is fulfilled. Then, in Argentina, to cover the external constraints, short-term capital may be needed, thereby obstructing other variables such as investment and other real sectors (refer to Table 2).

Following the second idea based on Kregel, poor countries need capital, but capital does not substantially increase capital formation, and on many occasions, the outflow of capital can be significant. For example, net utilities and dividends paid to foreign countries in Argentina were 0.45 percent of GDP in the 1981–1990 period, 0.55 percent of GDP in the 1991–2000 period, 1.63 of GDP in the 2001–2010 period, and 1.5 percent of GDP in the 2011–2017 period. In Brazil, the net utilities and dividends were 0.58 percent of GDP in the 1981–1990 period, 0.49 percent of GDP in the 1991–2000 period, 1.24 of GDP in the 2001–2010 period, and 1.2 percent of GDP in the 2011–2017 period. Finally, net utilities and dividends paid to foreign countries in Mexico were 0.57 percent of GDP in the 1981–1990 period, 0.8 percent of GDP in the 1991–2000 period, .78 of GDP in the 2001–2010 period, and 1.21 percent of GDP in the 2011–2017 period. Table 3 displays the correlations between FDI and the trade balance plus net investment income balance, and Figure 5 shows the scatter plots of the trade balance plus net investment income balance (net balance of income minus compensation to employees) versus the flow of FDI. From a theoretical point of view, flows of FDI should justify the trade pattern; in this case, positive inflow of long-term capital should be associated with a negative trade balance and net investment balance. All three countries have followed this pattern, but above all Mexico and Brazil. This pattern was established during the 1990s with the commercial and financial liberalization, since, during these years, many Latin American countries used developmental tools led by the market, thus opening their economies.

Conclusion

This article has demonstrated that inequality between countries increased from 1962 to 2019, that core countries can perform better than peripheral countries, that Latin American countries have not economically converged with core countries, that Latin American countries cannot apply some developmental policies, and that trade and capital flow are mechanisms that reproduce inequality in peripheral countries. With capitalism, equality is a relational process since rich countries can use several tools to perpetuate their position at the top of the distribution of wealth, and access to developmental tools is not democratic. I suggest eight relevant issues for further discussion: (1) even though the analysis of the inequality in individuals, as Milanovic has described (2007), is relevant, the inequality between countries is also relevant because it shows the hierarchy of wealth between countries and the capability of core countries to preserve their position. (2) Inequality between countries is a relational process of development, so not all countries can converge at the same level of income and power. (3) Between-country inequality and Latin American development over the last

60 years were examined in this article. Mechanisms of plunder and exploitation that obstructed the development of Latin American countries in previous centuries persist to present day. Examples include slavery in Brazil under the Portuguese Crown from the sixteenth to nineteenth centuries, an unfair system of labor called encomienda in Mexico and savage mining exploitation in Mexico and Perú from the sixteenth century to the beginnings of the nineteenth century, foreign power intervention in Mexico during the nineteenth century, and exploitation by external debt of all Latin American countries from the nineteenth century to present day. Despite colonialism limiting the development of peripheral countries and shaping Latin American elites during the nineteenth century, its effects on contemporary between-country inequality will be reserved for a future study. (4) The state is an important unit of catching up since it can establish trade, fiscal, monetary, and migration policies, and according to its degree of wealth and power, can manage liberalization or protectionism or carry out independent policies on money. Also, as has been demonstrated in recent days, states can implement humane policies on health and migration, but not by neglecting the role of organized social movements. In the case of Latin America, I consider that states can fulfill adequate social policies when governments have pressure from below. (5) Latin America can learn from previous experiences of developmental success. Chandraseknar (2017) mentions the experiences of South Korea, China, and India, among others. South Korea combined industrialization and a high level of exports, China combined industrialization with a domestic market, and India relied on the production and export of services (software and IT-enabled services). One Latin American problem is that Argentina, Brazil, and Mexico are deindustrializing, and, furthermore, the region is prone to capital movements and the repayment of external debt. Therefore, Latin America needs reindustrialization, capital control, and other measures such as reinvestment of the profits of foreign companies, access to long-term loans with a low rate of interest, or, in some cases, cancelation of external debt. (6) Latin America has an important indigenous bourgeoise. The members of this class have not developed their home countries and have continued to accrue wealth during the neoliberal era, so, as is the case for the state, state-supported progressive movements must direct the process of development. (7) Latin America has not had the geopolitical relevance South Korea and China have; however, Latin American countries need to have a deal with core countries to access the know-how and transfer of technical progress, and to mutually transfer high skills and a low-skill labor force. (8) International cooperation is needed to deal with problems such as trade imbalances and capital movements, but also with problems of external debt. Additionally, other current problems could be solved by international cooperation: an

international organization different from the World Bank could help to renew old infrastructure in core as well as in peripheral countries and improve the conditions of life of people in their home countries as well as reduce migration caused by low salaries or threats to security. Years ago, Banco del Sur was founded in Latin America and recently the BRICS' New Development Bank was established. The future will show if these or other organizations can provide new alternatives to finance development.

Notes

1. Wade (2020) has stated that between-countries inequality is the main factor driving inequality. Also, Milanovic (2016) has stated that between-country inequality has driven global inequality since the 1950s.
2. See the Appendix for more details about the dataset
3. These trends can be also found using a reduced consistent dataset of the GNIPC or a reduced dataset of the GDPPC at current prices. Whereas using a reduced consistent dataset of the GNIPC from 1982 onward shows a more moderate increase of inequality during the 1990s, it hides the dynamic and world economy, and, for example, the impoverishment of the republics that belong to the former Soviet Union and other countries (Refer to Appendix).
4. Core countries achieved higher growth rates of GNICP than other quintiles in two of six periods; however, the only period with very poor performance compared to other quintiles was the 2008–2012. Despite some peripheral countries converging in some periods, with promising perspectives in the short run, in the long-rung, peripheral countries were not able to maintain their growth. The dynamics of capitalism are that peripheral countries cannot grow consistently in the long run and crises hit them severely. In subsequent research, I will use the Monetary Inequality Index for interbloc comparisons.
5. Real interest rate nominal interest rate minus producer prices index.

Acknowledgements

I would like to thank anonymous reviewers for all their useful comments. I would also like to thank to Tanadej Vechsuruck, Francisco Martínez-Hernández, Naphon Phumma, Christine Pickett, and Zebo Idrisova for comments and corrections to previous drafts of this paper. All mistakes are the author's responsibility.

Disclosure statement

No potential conflict of interest was reported by the author(s).

References

Arrighi, Giovanni. 1994. "The Long Twentieth Century." In *Money, Power and the Origins of Our Time*. New York: Verso.

Arrighi, Giovanni. 1990. "The Developmentalist Illusion: The Reconceptualizacion of the Semiperiphery." In *Semiperipheral States in the World-Economy*, edited by William Martin, 11–42. Westport: Greenwood Press.

Arrighi, Giovanni. 1991. "World Income Inequalities and the Future of Socialism." *New Left Review* 189:39–65.

Chang, Ha-Joon. 2002a. *Kicking Away the Ladder: Development Strategy in Historical Perspective*. London: Anthem Press.

Chang, Ha-Joon. 2002b. "Kicking Away the Ladder: An Unofficial History of Capitalism, Especially in Britain and the United States." *Challenge* 45 (5):63–97. doi:10.1080/05775132.2002.11034173.

Chandraseknar, C. P. 2017. "Alternative 'Models' of Structural Transformation in Asia and Their Implication." *Japanese Political Economy* 43 (1–4):38–60. doi:10.1080/2329194X.2018.1561189.

Comisión Económica para América Latina y el Caribe (CEPAL). 2020a. "Data from: Cuadernos estadísticos." (dataset). Accessed May 1, 2020. http://interwp.cepal.org/cuaderno_37/index.htm.

Comisión Económica para América Latina y el Caribe (CEPAL). 2020b. "Data from: Anuario estadístico de América Latina." (dataset). Accessed June 1, 2020. http://interwp.cepal.org/anuario_estadistico/anuario_2020.

Clark, Rob. 2011. "World Income Inequality in the Global Era: New Estimates, 1990–1998." *Social Problems* 58 (4):564–592. doi:10.1525/sp.2011.58.4.565.

Cortes-Conde, Roberto. 2007. "Fiscal and Monetary Regimes." In *The Cambridge Economic History of Latin America, Vol. 2: The Long Twentieth Century*, edited by Victor Bulmer-Thomas, John Coatsworth, and R. Cortes-Conde, 209–248. New York: Cambridge University Press.

Ferrer, Aldo. 1963. "Devaluación, redistribución del ingreso y el proceso de desarticulación industrial en la Argentina." *Desarrollo Económico* 2 (4):5–18. doi:10.2307/3465744.

Fischer, Andrew. 2018. "Debt and Development in historical perspective: The external constraints of late industrialisation revisited through South Korea and Brazil." *The World Economy* 41 (12):3359–3378. doi:10.1111/twec.12625.

Firebaugh, Glenn. 1999. "Empirics of World Income Inequality." *American Journal of Sociology* 104 (6):1597–1630. doi:10.1086/210218.

Firebaugh, Glenn. 2000. "Observed Trends in between-Nation Income Inequality and Two Conjectures." *American Journal of Sociology* 106 (1):215–221. doi:10.1086/303114.

Firebaugh, Glenn, and Brian Goesling. 2004. "Accounting for the Recent Decline in Global Income Inequality." *American Journal of Sociology* 110 (2):283–312. doi:10.1086/421541.

French-Davis, Ricardo, Oscar Muñoz, and Gabriel Palma. 2000. "Las economías latinoamericanas, 1950–1990." In *Historia de América Latina. Economía y sociedad desde 1930*, edited by Leslie Bethell, 83–161. Barcelona: Crítica.

Frenkel, Roberto, and Martin Rapetti. 2009. "A Developing Country View of the Current Global Crisis: What Should Not Be Forgotten and What Should Be Done." *Cambridge Journal of Economics* 33 (4):685–792. doi:10.1093/cje/bep029.

Grasso, Genaro, Estanislao Malic, and Leandro Ziccarelli. 2017. "El rol financiero del tipo de cambio en economías periféricas." In *Discusiones sobre el tipo de cambio. El retorno de lo mismo*, edited by Florencia Médici, 221–250. Buenos Aires: Universidad Nacional de Moreno.

Harris, Jerry. 2009. "Statist Globalization in China, Russia, and the Gulf States." *Science & Society* 73 (1):6–33. doi:10.1163/ej.9789004176904.i-476.12.

Harrod, Roy. 1933. *International Economics*. New York: Harcourt, Brace and Company.

Harrod, Roy. 1958. "The Possibility of Economy Satiety-Use of Economic Growth for Improving the Quality of Education and Leisure." *In Problems of United States Economic Development*, edited by Committee for Economic Development, 207–313. New York: Committee for Economic Development.

Hicker, Jason. 2018. *Divide Global, Inequality from Contest to Free Markets*. New York: W.W. Norton & Company.

Hirsch, Fred. 1977. *Social Limits to Growth*. London: Routledge.

International Monetary Fund (IMF). 2021a. "Interest Selected Indicators." https://data.imf.org/regular.aspx?key=61545855.

International Monetary Fund (IMF). 2021b. "Data from: Balance of Payments and International Investment Position Statistics." (dataset). Accessed December 3, 2021. https://data.imf.org/?sk=7A51304B-6426-40C0-83DD CA473CA1FD52&sId=15426337 11584.

Isidro Luna, Víctor. 2014a. "El BNDES y la industrialización en Brasil. Evidencia histórica y econométrica." *Panorama Económico* 9 (18):26–122. doi:10.29201/pe-ipn.v9i18.50.

Isidro Luna, Víctor. 2014b. "The Role of Development Banks in the Process in the Process of Economic Development-Two Latin American Experiences: Mexico and Brazil." *World Review of Political Economy* 5 (2):204–230. doi:10.13169/worlrevipoliecon.5.2.0204.

Korzeniewicz, Patrici, and Timothy Moran. 1997. "World-Economics Trends in the Distribution of Income, 1965-1992." *American Journal of Sociology* 102 (4):1000–1039. doi:10.1086/231038.

Korzeniewicz, PatricioRoberto, and Timothy Moran. 2009. *Unveiling Inequality: A World Historical Perspectives*. New York: Russell Sage Foundation.

Kregel, Jan. 2008. *Financial Flows and International Imbalances-The Role of Catching- by the Late Industrializing Developing Countries*. New York: Levi Institute.

Kregel, Jan. 2006. "Understanding Imbalances in a Globalised International Economic System." In *Global Imbalances and the U.S. Debt Problem—Should Developing Countries Support the U.S. Dollar?*, edited by Jan Teunisson and Age Akkerman, 149–173. The Hague: Fondad.

Kvangraven, Ingrid. 2021. "Beyond the Stereotype: Resting the Relevance of the Dependency Research Program." *Development and Change* 52 (1):76–112. doi:10.1111/dech.12593.

Maxfield, Sylvia. 1988. *International Finance, the State and Capital Accumulation: Mexico in Comparative Perspectives*. Boston: Harvard University Press.

Medialdea, Bibiana. 2012. "Límites estructurales al desarrollo económico: Brasil (1950–2005)." *Problemas del Desarrollo* 43 (171):55–81. doi:10.22201/iiec.20078951e.2012.171.33583.

Milanovic, Branco. 2007. *Worlds Apart: Measuring International and Global Inequality*. New York: Princeton University Press.

Milanovic, Branco. 2016. *Global Inequality*. Boston: Harvard University Press.

Milanovic, Branco. 2013. "Global Income Inequality in Numbers: In History and Now." *Global Policy* 4 (2):198–208. doi:10.1111/1758-5899.12032.

Ocampo, José. 2016. "Dynamic Efficiency: Structural Dynamic and Economic Growth in Developing Countries." In *Efficiency, Finance, and Varieties of Industrial Policy: Guiding Resources, Learning, and Technology for Sustained Growth*, edited by Akbar Noman and Joseph E Stiglitz, 65–102. New York: Columbia University Press.

Olin Wright, Erik. 1987. "Inequality." In *The New Palgrave: A Dictionary of Economics*, 1st ed., edited by John Eatwell, Murray Milgate, and Peter Newmanm, 1–7. London: Palgrave.

O'Rourke, Kevin. 2001. *Globalization and Inequality. Historical Trends.* Boston: NBER.

Prebish, Raúl. 1986. "El desarrollo económico de la América Latina y algunos de sus principales problemas." *Desarrollo Económico* 26 (103):479–502. doi:10.2307/3466824.

Peña, Milciades. 1974. *Industria, Burguesía industrial y liberalización nacional.* Buenos Aires: Ediciones Fichas.

Prebisch, Raúl. 1970. *Transformación y Desarrollo. La gran tarea de la América Latina.* México: FCE.

Pritchett, Lant. 1997. "Divergence, Big Time." *Journal of Economic Perspectives* 11 (3):3–17. doi:10.1257/jep.11.3.3.

Qi, Hao, and David Kotz. 2020. "The Impact of State-Owned Enterprises on Chinás Economic Growth." *Review of Radical Political Economics* 52 (1):96–114. doi:10.1177/0486613419857249.

Quijano, José. 1981. *México: Estado y Banca Privada.* México: Centro de Investigación y Docencia Económica (CIDE).

Reinert, SErik. 2007. *How Rich Countries Got Rich … and Why Poor Countries Stay Poor.* London: Constance.

Shaikh, Anwar. 2016. *Capitalism. Competition, Conflict, Crises.* New York: Oxford University Press.

Shultz, Paul. 1998. "Inequality in the Distribution of Personal Income in the World. How It is Changing and Why." *Journal of Population Economics* 11 (3):307–344. https://www.jstor.org/stable/20007589.

Singer, Paul. 1950. "The Distribution of Gains between Investing and Borrowing Countries." *The American Economic Review* 40 (2):473–485. http://www.jstor.org/stable/1818065.

Skidelsky, Robert. 2019. *Money and Government: Past and Future of Economics.* New York: Yale University Press.

Schvarzer, Jorge. 1978. "Estrategia industrial y grandes empresas: el caso argentino." *Desarrollo Económico* 18 (71):307–351. doi:10.2307/3466342.

Vernengo, Matias. 2016. "Kicking Away the Ladder, Too: Inside Central Banks." *Journal of Economic Issues* 50 (2):452–460. doi:10.1080/00213624.2016.1176509.

Xie, Fusheng, An Li, and Zhongjin Li. 2012. "Guojinmintui: A New Round of Debate in China on State versus Private Ownership." *Science & Society* 76 (3):291–318. https://www.jstor.org/stable/41510564. doi:10.1521/siso.2012.76.3.291.

Ye, Min. 2020. *The Belt Road and beyond: State-Mobilized Globalization in China 1998–2008.* New York: Cambridge University Press.

Wade, Robert. 2020. "Rethinking the World Economics as a Two Bloc Hierarchy." *Real-World Economics Review* 92:4–29.

Wallerstein, Immanuel. 1999. *The End of the World as We Know It. Social Sciences for the First Century.* Minneapolis: University of Minnesota Press.

Weber, IsabellaM. 2021. *How China Escape Shock Therapy. The Market Reform Debate.* New York: Routledge.

World Bank. 2020. Data from: World Development Indicator." (dataset). Accessed June 2, 2020. https://databank.worldbank.org/source/world-development-indicators.

Appendix

The dataset contains information for 163 countries from 1962 to 2019. It excludes the former Soviet Union, the former Yugoslavia, and the former Sudan as well as Qatar and Kuwait. By 1962, the database encompassed 65.45 percent of the world's population in 163 countries (Figure A1). Information for the GNIPC is not available for many poor countries because of national account consolidation, so the inequality indexes might be higher if this information were considered.

Contrasting our results, we plot inequality with a reduced consistent dataset of the GNIPC and the GDPC. First, we measure inequality with a 103-country dataset of the GNIPC from 1982 onward; second, we measure inequality with a 121-country dataset of the GDPPC from 1970 onward. The three ways of approaching inequality exhibit the same trends (Figure A2).

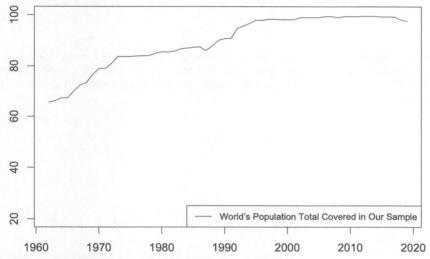

Figure A1. World's Population Total Covered in Our Sample, Percent
Source: Author's elaboration with data from World Bank 2020

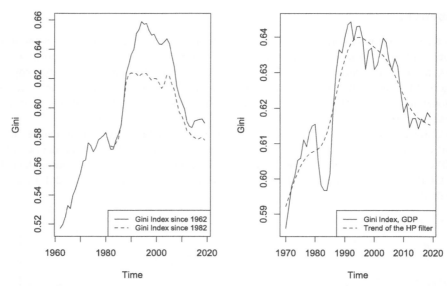

Figure A2. Gini Index, Original Dataset Versus Gini Index from 1982 Onward (Left Axis), Gini Index of Current GDP, US Dollars (Right Axis). Gini Index since 1982, 103 countries. Gini Index current GDP, 121 countries in the sample. Source: Author's elaboration with data from World Bank 2020.

Financialization and income inequality: an empirical analysis

Kang-Kook Lee and Md Abu Bakkar Siddique

ABSTRACT
This study investigates the effect of financialization and financial rent on income inequality across countries, including
advanced and emerging markets and developing countries, in
the 1998–2017 period. Employing a new measurement and
dynamic panel estimation, we find that financialization measured by financial rent increases income inequality. We also
find that the more monopolized banking sector is associated
with higher income inequality. It suggests that market concentration in the banking sector creates ample opportunities for
banks to generate excess profit and income, which leads to
higher top income concentration and overall inequality.
Commonly used variables for financialization such as bank
income, the stock trading value, stock market capitalization,
and the banking sector asset compared to the economy are
also harmful to inequality.

Introduction

Financialization became a buzzword recently because it has been one of the
most important changes in advanced capitalism after the 1980s. It is a phenomenon that the role and power of the financial sector became stronger
in the economy (Epstein 2005). Many studies in the heterodox macroeconomics tradition have paid serious attention to the development of financialization. Though there is a debate on the definition of financialization, its
bad effects on stable economic growth and income distribution have been
reported (Krippner 2005; Pollin 2007; Lapavitsas 2011; Hein 2015). Even
some mainstream economists now recognize inefficiency in the financial
sector and financialization and the harmful effect of too much finance on
growth, although most still argue that financial development is generally
good for the economy (Philippon 2012; Arcand, Berkes, and Panizza 2015).
Financialization has been studied mainly as a phenomenon of advanced
economies such as the United States. However, we can also see the

development of financialization in developing and emerging market economies (Crotty and Lee 2005; Bonizzi 2013; dos Santos 2013; Kaltenbrunner and Painceira 2015). The financial sector has grown continuously, and household debt rose in many countries recently; financial liberalization, deregulation, and financial opening played an essential role. Along with these changes, the profit of the financial sector also increased in comparison with that in the corporate sector.

Thus, there is a growing concern about financialization and its possible consequences in both advanced and developing countries, such as bad effects on investment, growth, and financial instability (Orhangazi 2008; Gutiérrez and Philippon 2017). Another important area that should be studied is income inequality. Financialization is likely to increase inequality in several ways. It could aggravate inefficient rent-seeking in the financial sector, and this generates excessive profit in the financial institutions and very high income for already wealthy financiers (Kaplan and Rauh 2010; Philippon and Reshef 2012; Zhang 2017). It is reported that much of the increased inequality in the U.S. economy is associated with the growth in rent-seeking, partially associated with financialization (Stiglitz 2015, 2016). Since the 1980s, many countries experienced lower growth and industrial investment and the rising power of finance and short-termism at the expense of workers. Financialization could raise income inequality by depressing investment and employment.

This paper empirically examines the effect of financialization on inequality employing cross-country panel regressions. Several empirical studies discuss the impact of financialization on income inequality using different variables of financialization (Kus 2012; Assa 2012; Huber, Petrova, and Stephens 2020). We complement the existing empirical literature by introducing new measures and a more sophisticated method and also by including a large number of countries. We use a new variable for financial rent-seeking measured by the difference of the return on bank capital in the banking sector and the annual deposit rate to represent excessive profit in the banking sector (Epstein and Montecino 2016; Basu, Inklaar, and Wang 2011). As a variable for income inequality, we mainly use the Gini coefficient of disposable income and use top income concentrations. Section 2 discusses financialization and rent-seeking in the financial sector and how they are measured. Section 3 presents an argument about the relationship between financialization and income inequality. It also examines stylized facts of financialization and income inequality across countries after the 1990s. Section 4 explains data and methodology and then presents empirical results about how financialization affects income inequality. Section 5 concludes with a discussion of the policy implications of our study.

Financialization, rent-seeking, and their measurement

Heterodox macroeconomics and radical political economy have examined financialization as a recent structural change of capitalism that could explain stagnant growth and rising inequality. Though there is no single definition of financialization, the popular one is "an increasing role of financial motives, financial markets, actors, and financial institutions in the operations in domestic and international economies" (Epstein 2005, 3). According to Hein (2019, 977–79), financialization has been conducive to rising gross profit share, falling labor share, increasing inequality, growing shareholders' power and short-termism, increasing rate of return on equity, rising debt-driven consumption, and liberalization of the capital market and capital account. An increase in financial income, financial globalization, and shareholders' value orientation are characteristics of the financialization process. Important aspects of financialization include massive proliferation, excessive expansion of banks and financial institutions, and financial transactions over trade and production. Financialization changes the conduct of the economy significantly. In finance-dominated capitalism, non-financial companies (NFCs) and households are more involved with financial markets for short-term gain and speculative income. It results in higher profit in the finance industry, stagnant growth, and rising inequality (Hein 2015, 2019). Financialization also tends to make the economy more unstable. The series of financial crises that occurred after the 1980s and the global financial crisis of 2008–2009 are supposed to be associated with financialization (Stockhammer 2010).

The financial system in advanced countries was heavily regulated in the golden age of capitalism based on the lessons of the Great Depression. However, the structural crisis of capitalism and the response of capital to the crisis paved the way for financialization (Kotz 2015). It was pushed for by the neoliberal change in the economy since the early 1980s, such as a series of financial deregulation and cross-border liberalization introduced by the Thatcher administration in the United Kingdom and the Reagan administration in the United States. It was not confined to Anglo-Saxon countries. European countries followed them, and many other economies also headed toward the introduction of neoliberal economic policy (Bonizzi 2013). For example, liberalization of capital flows, overvalued currency, and informal dollarization signaled a rise of financialization in Chile (Becker et al. 2010).

Though financialization is a crucial change in the current capitalist economy, it may not be easy to measure it exactly because it is a complex phenomenon taking various forms. Financialization has been measured primarily by the profit share and asset size of the financial sector compared with the whole economy and by the increased financial orientation of

NFCs (Epstein and Montecino 2016). In particular, the increase of financial profit and financial income since the 1980s is one essential feature of financialization reported by many studies (Stockhammer 2004; Dumenil and Levey 2005; Epstein and Jayadev 2005). Empirical studies employ various financialization indicators related to the finance industry, NFCs, and the household sector. For example, bank income, securities assets held by banks, stock trading value, market capitalization, credit expansion, value added, and employment in finance, insurance, and real estate are used as proxies of financialization (Kus 2012; Huber et al., 2020; Alexiou, Trachanas, and Vogiazas 2021; Assa 2012).[1] Other studies use net dividend, interest payment, and income through the financial channel of NFCs as a measurement of financialization (Lin and Tomaskovic-Devey 2013; Alvarez 2015). De Vita and Luo (2020) utilize household debt as a financialization indicator.

Some researchers emphasize that the increase in profit of the financial sector, associated with rent-seeking, is an essential aspect of financialization, in which a money lender is defined as a rentier (Pollin 2007). In this paper, we focus our discussion on excess profit from rent in the financial sector and use it as an indicator of financialization. Much of this profit is generated by extracting income from the workers, taxpayers, and debtors along with financialization. Several studies point to factors affecting the finance industry's large profits that include the degree of market concentration, asset price bubble and busts, and the bailout of banks that are "too big to fail" (Stiglitz 2016; Epstein and Montecino 2016).

Rent was originally referred to as the returns to land which is a fixed production factor, and afterward, it included monopoly profit earned through market power. It means an income not as a reward for creating wealth but from grabbing a share of the wealth produced by others. Rent-seeking is defined as unproductive, expropriating activities that bring positive returns to the individual but not society.[2] A part of income that is larger than what can be earned from competitive markets is the rent derived through an artificial scarcity, exploitation of resources, or monopoly. Rent could take a form of an excess income or abnormal profit in reality. Therefore, financial rent is the high income that the finance employees, traders, and shareholders receive and the excess profits that financial institutions make compared to normal income and profits.

The existing literature estimates financial rents using three measures: excess profits, excess incomes, and unit cost of financial intermediation.[3] The first two measures are profit- or income-based estimates from a service givers' perspective. The last one is a cost-based measure from a service takers' viewpoint. Philippon and Reshef (2012) define financial rent as the wage difference between the finance and non-finance industries with the same education and skill level. However, measuring rent in terms of excess income is a conservative approach because it only considers the average income. The lion's share of excess income is highly concentrated among a small number of the top executives, financial engineers, and traders (Epstein and Montecino 2016). For example, the top tier of finance professionals receives substantial bonuses, incentives, special allowances, and other compensation such as stock options. There are also data constraints of wages for all countries.

This paper introduces a profit-based measurement to estimate financial rent following other studies. Wang (2011) and Basu, Inklaar, and Wang (2011) argue that the capital share and internal rate of return in the banking sector are considerably higher than those in the private sector in the United States. After comparing National Income and Product Accounts data with their model, they show that banks implicitly overcharge compensation of systemic risk and hence overprice financial products and services due to mistreatment of riskiness. After examining their work extensively, Epstein and Montecino (2016) consider half of the total accumulated profit in the banking sector as financial rent in the United States because these excess profits stem from improper adjustment or mistreatment for risk. We use return on bank capital (ROC) to measure financial rent or excess profit in the banking sector.[4] The ROC is calculated by the returns on assets divided by the bank capital to assets ratio from the Global Financial Development Database (GFDD) (World Bank 2019). Next, we introduce a new measurement of financial rent by comparing the ROC of the banking sector and the return we can expect from alternative investments in financial assets. As we discussed, the return on bank capital is higher than that on capital in other industries because banks expropriate financial rent from the economy. And we may well think that the return on bank capital is excessive if it is higher than the interest rate. Therefore, we calculate our RENT variable by subtracting the saving rate from the banking sector's ROC.

$$return\ on\ capital(ROC)_{i,t} = \frac{return\ on\ assets_{i,t}}{capital\ to\ assets_{i,t}}$$

$$RENT_{i,t} = ROC_{i,t} - annual\ deposit\ rate_{i,t}$$

The rationale of this measure is that we deduct the annual deposit rate as a proxy of the next available opportunities of returns on financial claims. We assume that if bank capital is invested in any market debt securities, it may have earned a certain amount of interest, dividends, or yield. This measure is indeed a simple proxy that may suffer from measurement errors associated with heterogeneity across countries. Ideally, we may well estimate financial rent using the methodology used by Basu, Inklaar, and

Wang (2011), or we may compare the return on capital of banks and that of other sectors. However, it is not feasible to use these methods for a cross-country investigation because of limited data availability. Therefore, we follow the argument by Epstein and Montecino (2016) and use this simple method using bank balance sheet data to estimate financial rent. Though this measure may not calculate the exact size of excess profit associated with rent-seeking, this could be a proxy for financial rent in the cross-country empirical analysis. We use this financial rent variable as an alternative measurement of financialization to complement other indicators of financialization.

Financialization and inequality

How financialization increases inequality

The performance of the real economy became poor after the 1980s in advanced economies because financialization altered industrial firms' structure and motives and magnified their rentier motivations. The reemergence of rentiers fostered financial profits at the expense of industrial profits, depressing industrial investment in the neoliberal period. Financial rent and financialization could also be associated with rising inequality through the following mechanisms. First, financialization strengthens the power of capital, especially that of finance, and weakens workers' bargaining power and trade unions. This, in turn, lowers the overall wage share and increases the profit share, the financial profit in particular and inequality in general. Second, lower wages and higher inequality due to financialization reduce aggregate demand, which does harm to real investment and equity. Financialization could also be harmful to industrial investment and employment because of short-termism in shareholder capitalism and the rising power of rentiers (Onaran, Stockhammer, and Grafl 2011; Lavoie and Stockhammer 2013). Third, higher financial rent increases the financial industry's income excessively high, leading to the rise in the top 1 percent income share of the total income (Stiglitz 2016).

Hein argues that financialization and neoliberalism have contributed to a fall in the labor share and aggregate demand, resulting in rising inequality through three channels: (1) increasing relevance of the financial sector over non-financial sector investment, (2) increasing management salaries and thus rising overhead cost, and (3) weakening unionism (Hein 2015, 925–929). Empirical studies find that finance-oriented management under financialization lowers real investment (Stockhammer 2004). For example, the U.S. economy has experienced underinvestment despite high Tobin's Q, driven by the rising role of funds that brought about the change in corporate governance along with financialization (Gutiérrez and Philippon 2017).

Lower aggregate demand could decrease real investment, productivity, and profitability in the real economy.[5] As a result, capital has moved to the financial markets largely. NFCs increase insider trading, and financial institutions explore derivatives to maximize financial profitability with a proliferation of financialization. Finally, financialization greatly increases the profit and income of the finance industry while it reduces wages in the real economy, as empirical studies report (Philippon and Reshef 2012; Zhang 2017). All these bring about rising inequality.

This study attempts to shed new light on the role of financial rent in rising inequality from the perspective that inequality is positively associated with rentier capitalism (Pollin 2007). The rentiers, such as money lenders, extract a large profit at the expense of workers, customers, and taxpayers with short-termism (Epstein 2018). Their strong power tends to cut labor costs and raise top executives' compensation. Most of all, increasing incomes at the top percentile through higher financial rent in rentier capitalism is a plausible channel through which financialization raises inequality. More concentration in financial markets along with financial deregulation creates ample opportunities to create excess financial profits. Anti-competitive practices in debit and credit cards have strengthened preexisting market power to generate higher financial income. Lack of transparency in derivative markets such as credit default swaps produces a large amount of rent. It is not surprising that financial rent derived in this way is translated into higher incomes for their managers and shareholders, thus increasing inequality (Stiglitz 2016).

Several studies support the rent-seeking theory as an explanation for increasing top income concentration. Philippon and Reshef (2012) argue that the salary of workers in the financial sector, including that of financiers in the top percentile, is much higher than that of workers in other sectors with similar education even though there was no increase in efficiency in the financial sector (Philippon 2012).[6] Higher earnings in the finance industry are reported to be an essential driver for rising top income concentration (Zhang 2017). The bank employees and owners are the direct and firsthand beneficiaries of excess profits. Khan (2000) claims that excess income from financial rent continues to be available for banks, particularly for their owners. Kaplan and Rauh (2010) find that the top-percentile income group includes investment bankers and institutional investors in the United States. Pursuing shareholders' value orientation along with financialization and financial rent-seeking has also contributed to rising earnings disparity between CEOs and employees. For instance, the CEOs of publicly listed companies are paid higher remuneration than the non-listed companies. It is well documented that CEOs' annual compensation at the top 350 firms in the U.S. economy increased by 876 percent from 1978 to

2012, while the labor compensation in the whole economy stagnated (Bivens and Mishel 2013).

Cross-country empirical studies using various measures report that financialization exerts a negative effect on income equality and the labor income share. Assa (2012) finds that the value added and employment in the finance industry are positively associated with income inequality using a fixed effects model for 33 OECD countries. Kus (2012) reports that financialization measured by several variables increases income inequality, using the GMM (generalized method of moments) methodology for 20 Organisation for Economic Co-operation and Development (OECD) countries. De Vita and Luo (2020) use a similar model and find that household debt positively affects inequality. An empirical finding of Huber, Petrova, and Stephens (2020), with an error correction model for 18 countries, also shows that financialization increases inequality. Shin and Lee (2019) report that a high dividend of NFCs contributes to rising inequality, using a panel cointegration model for 17 OECD economies. Alexiou, Trachanas, and Vogiazas (2021) find that financialization increases inequality in OECD countries, although its significance depends on measurements using the fixed effects model.[7] Pariboni and Tridico (2019) report that financialization, primarily measured by stock market capitalization, results in a negative consequence for the labor income share using the fixed effects model for 28 OECD countries. Other empirical studies investigate the inequality effect of rent-seeking specifically. An empirical study of 22 developed economies reports that the higher wages in the financial sector contribute to the rise in income inequality (Boustanifar, Grant, and Reshef 2018). High wages of skilled workers in the finance industry account for increased skill premiums in the whole economy. Angelopoulos et al. (2019) use financial friction as a proxy of rent-seeking to examine its impact on wealth inequality using U.S. data. Their calibration results demonstrate that rent-seeking reduces aggregate welfare and increases wealth inequality. However, most empirical studies on the inequality effect of financialization and financial rent are limited to advanced countries.

Rising inequality and financialization: Stylized facts

Let us first examine the trend of income inequality using disposable income Gini coefficients from the Standardized World Income Inequality Database (SWIID) (Solt 2020).[8] Inequality has continued to rise in most advanced countries, including the United States, Germany, and Sweden, after the 1980s, along with the conservative political change, while it has not in France as we can see in Figure 1. Inequality is generally higher in low-income countries than in high-income ones. However, the change in

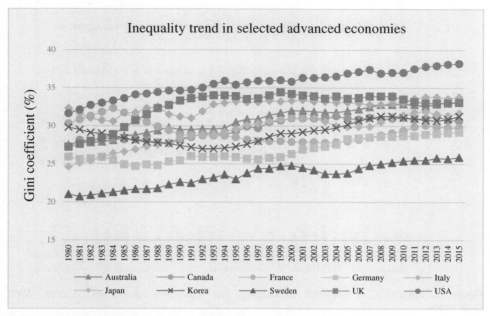

Figure 1. Inequality in selected advanced economies. Source: SWIID (Solt 2020).

income inequality in developing countries is more complicated, showing variations depending on regions and countries. It should be noted that inequality has fallen in Latin America and the Middle East, while other developing countries saw a rise in inequality. Inequality was very high in Latin American countries such as Brazil and Mexico. However, it fell after the 1990s in this region, when the leftist government took power. Among others, Eastern European countries experienced a large and rapid increase in inequality after the transition toward capitalism. Within the same income group and the region, countries also have different trajectories, as shown in Figure 2. India shows an upward trend of inequality, but other countries in South Asia are different. Inequality rose in most East Asian countries, including China and Indonesia, while Malaysia experienced a fall in inequality. Inequality has changed differently, country by country, in Sub-Saharan Africa.

Many empirical studies argue that globalization, technical changes, and policy or institutions explain rising income inequality (Milanovic 2015). Jaumotte, Lall, and Papageorgiou (2013) find that international trade reduces inequality, while foreign direct investment increases it. Globalization and technological progress could increase the return of human capital while reducing job opportunities for unskilled workers. In particular, the skill-biased technological change due to the progress of information and communication technology contributes to rising inequality (Pi and Zhang 2018). It is reported that the effect of technology is even

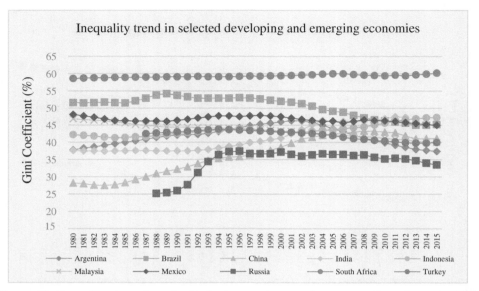

Figure 2. Inequality in selected developing and emerging economies. Source: SWIID (Solt 2020).

larger than that of globalization (Jaumotte, Lall, and Papageorgiou 2013). Financial globalization and capital account liberalization increase inequality, but trade openness, specifically with better education, reduces it (Furceri and Loungani 2018; Lee 2014). The unemployment rate is positively associated with inequality in OECD countries (Maestri and Roventini 2012). Political and institutional change is also crucial to rising inequality, as history demonstrates (Piketty 2020). Inequality has increased along with weakening unionism and workers' bargaining power as well as a conservative change in politics that led to a tax cut after the 1980s (Pontusson 2013).

In this study, we examine the role of financialization in rising inequality in developed and developing economies besides these factors. Financialization has been expanded in advanced economies since financial deregulation in the 1980s, as many studies report. This was not only confined to developed countries but also witnessed in emerging and developing economies since the 1990s. Several studies report the development of financialization in diverse dimensions in developing countries. They include asset price bubble in the stock market, an increase of institutional investors, expansion of foreign bank assets, banks' involvement in securitization, and short-termism of financial investments (Bonizzi 2013; dos Santos 2013). Another common aspect of financialization in developing countries is the aggressive involvement of NFCs in financial investment and the expansion of household credit (Demir 2007; Lapavitsas and dos Santos 2008).

Figure 3 demonstrates that financial rent as we defined above and bank income out of GDP rose since 1998, fell during the global financial crisis,

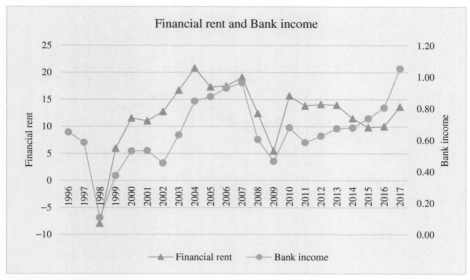

Figure 3. Financial rent and bank income out of GDP. Source: GFDD (World Bank 2019).

and recovered after it. Though the trend of financial rent is somewhat mixed, there is a positive association between the Gini coefficient and financial rent measures. A simple average of financial rent in 102 countries increased from 5.94 in 1999 to 13.65 in 2017, by about 130 percent. Bank income also increased by some 62 percent during 1996–2017 for 150 countries. There was likely an upward trend of banking and financial sector assets and financialization index after the 1980s for more than 100 countries, as Figure 4 shows. Banking and financial sectors' assets and stock trading value increased substantially over the world. Furthermore, the banking sector became more concentrated in many countries. As of a simple average of 137 countries, the Lerner index rose to 0.3196 in 2014 from 0.2094 in 1996. In 2014, an average H-statistic of 131 countries was 0.5650.[9] This suggests that banks came to operate under monopolistic competition recently, which is an important source of rent and indicative of financial rent-seeking.

The above analysis implies that financialization has developed not only in advanced economies but also in many other economies. The finance industry has become more profitable than the real industry; the NFCs have turned to financial investment and bond markets to raise funds; and households have increased their debt and consumption based on it. Along with financialization, financial rent increased in many countries, as measured by excess profit in the banking sector. This could result in the rise in inequality across countries, and we empirically examine it in the next section.

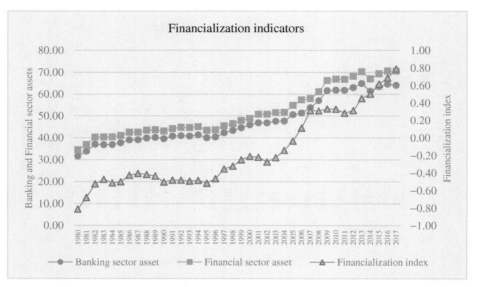

Figure 4. Banking and financial sector assets out of GDP and financialization index. Source: GFDD (World Bank 2019).

Empirical analysis

Model specification, data, and method

We conducted a dynamic panel data estimation using annual data and the two-step system GMM methodology (Arellano and Bond 1991; Blundell and Bond 1998). We use the dynamic panel regressions because current inequality could be strongly affected by income distribution in the former period. The GMM estimator is apt for addressing an endogeneity bias, serial correlation of idiosyncratic errors, and heteroscedasticity, producing efficient and consistent estimates in dynamic panel estimations. It is also fit for panel data when the number of panel countries is larger than time like in our sample.[10] The GMM methodology is the most commonly used in dynamic panel regressions because it could demonstrate the causal relationship. Therefore, we employ the following equation:

$$GINI_{i,t} = \beta_1 GINI_{i,t-1} + \beta_2 RENT_{i,t} + \beta_3 Z_{i,t} + u_{i,t} \qquad (1)$$

GINI is the Gini coefficient of disposable income; *RENT* is financial rent, our new financialization indicator; and Z_i represents control variables. First, we include GDP per capita and its square term to take the Kuznets curve into account (Kuznets 1955). Education, measured by the secondary school enrollment ratio, government consumption spending, foreign direct investment measured by stock, and trade openness are included as additional control variables in the benchmark model. Later, we complement the results of this model by using an alternative model and different variables for financialization and inequality. It should be noted that the benchmark specification with the Kuznets curve may suffer from the endo-geneity bias because economic growth and inequality could interact with each other. Thus, in an alternative specification, we control for the unemployment rate, union density, and GDP growth without the Kuznets curve relationship, similar to Kus (2012).

Gini coefficient data are collected from SWIID by Solt (2020). It has a broad country coverage and comparability, using the Luxembourg Income Study (LIS) as the basis of consistent comparison to include as many countries and years as possible.[11] Other empirical studies commonly use this income inequal-ity variable for that reason. As an alternative to the Gini coefficient of dispos-able income, the top income concentration from the World Inequality Database, including the top 1 percent income share or the top 10 percent income share, is also used as a dependent variable in subsequent analysis (WID, 2020).

Financial rent is our key explanatory variable for financialization. It is measured by a difference between returns on bank capital and the annual deposit rate, as we discussed in the previous section. Further, bank income, the value of stock traded, banking sector assets, and the financialization index to incorporate these are also tested instead of financial rent, following Kus (2012).[12] Finally, we examine the inequality effect of market concentra-tion in the banking sector that is closely associated with financial rent. Financialization variables such as financial rent and others to generate financialization index are from the Global Financial Development Database (GFDD) by the World Bank (World Bank 2019). Foreign direct investment is a stock measure of liabilities from Lane and Milesi-Ferretti (2017). For trade openness, GDP per capita, GDP growth, education, government con-sumption spending, and unemployment rate, we use the World Development Indicators (WDI) in 2020 by the World Bank (World Bank 2020). We collect union density from the International Labor Organization (ILO) in 2020. Overall, our sample includes up to 128 countries including advanced economies and developing and emerging market economies (DEEs) over the period after the 1980s, although the exact number of countries and the period is different depending on specifications. A brief definition of variables and descriptive statistics are reported in Tables 1 and 2, respectively.[13]

Empirical results

Table 3 reports the empirical findings of the two-step system GMM estima-tions in our baseline model, which covers 89 countries for the 1998–2017 period. We find that financial rent makes a positive and significant effect on the Gini coefficient of disposable income. This suggests that rent-

Table 1. A definition of variables and data sources.

Variables	Definition	Sources
Gini	Disposable income Gini coefficient	Solt (2020)
Top1	Top 1% income share	WID (2020)
Top10	Top 10% income share	WID (2020)
Return on capital	Return on regulatory capital of banks (%)	Authors' own calculation
Annual deposit rate	The rate paid by bank to its depositors	WB (2019)
Financial rent	Difference between return on bank capital and annual deposit rate	Authors' calculation
Financialization index	Average of standardized z-score of bank income, stock trading value and banking sector assets	Authors' calculation
Bank income	Bank income before tax over GDP	WB (2019)
Stock trading value	Value of stock traded in market over GDP	WB (2019)
Banking sector assets	Banking sector assets over GDP	WB (2019)
Financial sector assets	Financial sector assets over GDP	WB (2019)
Lerner index	A measure of market concentration	WB (2019)
Asset concentration	Asset concentration held by top 3 banks	WB (2019)
Market capitalization	Stock market capitalization ratio to GDP	WB (2019)
GDP per capita	Log of GDP per capita (constant 2010 US$)	WB (2020)
GDP Growth rate	Annual growth rate of GDP	WB (2020)
Education	Net secondary school attainment	WB (2020)
Government consumption spending	Government share of total expenditure as a percentage of GDP	WB (2020)
Trade openness	Export plus import over GDP	WB (2020)
Unemployment rate	Unemployment of labor force (International Labor Organization estimate)	WB (2020)
Foreign direct investment	Stock measure of FDI liabilities	Lane and Milesi-Ferretti (2017)
Union density	Trade union density rate	ILO (2020)

seeking in the financial sector, along with financialization, results in a rise in income inequality. The positive effect of financial rent remains significant and unchanged over the subsequent regressions after controlling for several more control variables. The coefficient of financial rent does not appear to be large, but we should consider that our specification uses annual data of the Gini coefficient that usually changes small in reality. In terms of the size, when there is an increase in financial rent by one standard deviation, 22.78 percent of capital, the Gini coefficient will increase by around 0.1139. The coefficients of GDP per capita and its square term indicate the inverted U shape of the Kuznets curve between the level of growth and inequality. Education and government consumption enter significantly in the model. However, globalization variables such as trade openness and foreign direct investment are not significant to inequality. The diagnostic tests, including serial correlation tests and the overidentification test, suggest that our specification using the GMM methodology is well established. We also investigate the effect of financial rent on inequality for a

Table 2. Descriptive statistics.

Variables	Observations	Mean	SD	Min.	Max.
Gini	4642	38.15	8.476	17.4	62.4
Top1	4866	15.003	6.038	1.94	63.76
Top10	3490	42.331	12.789	13.28	79.874
Return on capital	1990	16.00	26.32	−463.785	314.038
Annual deposit rate	3807	6.696	4.342	0.01	20
Financial rent	1326	12.76	22.78	−381.165	220.332
Financialization index	6160	−0.111	0.840	−3.184	4.346
Bank income	2606	0.666	1.087	−14.424	6.536
Stock trading value	2811	23.449	52.711	0	822.317
Banking sector assets	6075	48.32	45.421	0.004	892.896
Financial sector assets	6103	52.475	50.367	0.02	892.900
Lerner index	2338	0.265	0.157	−1.609	1.534
Asset concentration	3265	70.286	19.969	17.16	100
Market capitalization	2763	49.572	79.548	.012	1098.94
GDP per capita	7008	8.435	1.546	5.101	12.185
GDP Growth rate	7093	3.461	6.222	−64.047	149.973
Education	2479	68.56	25.588	0.22	99.91
Government consumption spending	5871	16.432	7.556	0	135.809
Trade openness	6380	84.245	54.396	0.021	861.177
Foreign direct investment	5845	27.33	43.46	−5.155	786.199
Unemployment rate	5180	7.891	5.853	0.11	37.98
Union density	832	26.643	19.2	0.2	91.6

Table 3. Financial rent and inequality.

EXPLANATORY VARIABLES Time period	(1) GINI 1998–2017	(2) GINI 1998–2017	(3) GINI 1998–2017	(4) GINI 1998–2017	(5) GINI 1998–2015
Lagged dependent variable	0.830***	0.898***	0.815***	0.810***	0.883***
	(0.025)	(0.018)	(0.039)	(0.039)	(0.015)
Financial rent	*0.005****	*0.003****	*0.005****	*0.005****	*0.003****
	(0.001)	(0.001)	(0.002)	(0.002)	(0.001)
Log of GDP per capita	3.214***	2.458***	5.493***	5.483***	2.865***
	(0.874)	(0.588)	(1.150)	(1.151)	(0.760)
Square of a log of GDP per capita	−0.207***	−0.138***	−0.306***	−0.305***	−0.162***
	(0.053)	(0.035)	(0.067)	(0.067)	(0.044)
Education		−0.021***	−0.043***	−0.044***	−0.019***
		(0.005)	(0.010)	(0.009)	(0.004)
Government consumption spending			−0.015	−0.015	−0.021**
			(0.010)	(0.010)	(0.010)
Trade openness				0.001	−0.001
				(0.001)	(0.001)
Foreign direct investment				0.000	
				(0.001)	
Observations	1121	622	609	609	530
No. of countries	89	73	70	70	65
Diagnostic test					
No. of instruments	60	60	62	63	59
AR(1)	0.0405	0.0213	0.0622	0.0746	0.0702
AR(2)	0.114	0.373	0.830	0.826	0.327
Hansen test	0.550	0.383	0.563	0.552	0.537

Standard errors in parentheses. ***$p < 0.01$, **$p < 0.05$, *$p < 0.1$; intercept is not reported.

subsample of advanced economies and DEEs. Though results are not reported, we find that the effect of financial rent and financialization remain qualitatively the same for both groups of countries including developed and developing countries. We also test conditional effects by

Table 4. Financialization indicators and inequality.

EXPLANATORY VARIABLES Time period	(1) GINI 2000–2016	(2) GINI 2000–2016	(3) GINI 2000–2016	(4) GINI 2000–2016	(5) GINI 2000–2016
Lagged dependent variable	0.944***	0.855***	0.858***	0.827***	0.874***
	(0.008)	(0.011)	(0.016)	(0.010)	(0.011)
Unemployment rate	0.058***	0.044***	0.027***	0.037***	0.040***
	(0.009)	(0.007)	(0.006)	(0.006)	(0.007)
GDP growth rate	0.011*	−0.005	−0.020***	−0.004	0.001
	(0.006)	(0.003)	(0.004)	(0.004)	(0.003)
Union density	−0.011***	−0.014***	−0.011***	−0.011***	−0.012***
	(0.003)	(0.002)	(0.002)	(0.002)	(0.002)
Education	−0.006**	−0.026***	−0.015***	−0.045***	−0.020***
	(0.002)	(0.005)	(0.004)	(0.007)	(0.005)
Government consumption spending	−0.031***	−0.075***	−0.105***	−0.099***	−0.085***
	(0.009)	(0.014)	(0.013)	(0.014)	(0.011)
Trade openness	0.001**	−0.001	−0.002***	−0.003***	−0.001
	(0.000)	(0.001)	(0.001)	(0.000)	(0.001)
Financial rent	*0.003****				
	(0.001)				
Financialization index		*0.162****			
		(0.029)			
Bank income			*0.077****		
			(0.009)		
Stock trading value				*0.002****	
				(0.000)	
Banking sector assets					*0.003****
					(0.001)
Observations	231	582	549	506	575
No. of countries	43	73	66	64	72
Diagnostic test					
No. of instruments	59	60	60	60	60
AR(1)	0.0446	0.000776	0.00157	0.00238	0.00152
AR(2)	0.777	0.0325	0.104	0.0309	0.0939
Hansen test	0.974	0.347	0.191	0.294	0.520

Standard errors in parentheses, ***$p < 0.01$, **$p < 0.05$, *$p < 0.1$; intercept is not reported.
Note. The result of Hansen test in column 1 suggest that this model may suffer from an over-identification problem, which can be explained by the smaller number of sample countries. This problem disappears when we
   exclude time-dummy from the regression of Column 1. However, AR(1) and AR(2) diagnostic suggest that our
   model is valid in terms of serial correlation tests.

including interaction terms, but we do not find any significant conditional effects of financial rent on inequality.[14]

We may well think that the Kuznets curve relationship between inequality and GDP per capita could be endogenous because inequality could also affect growth. Therefore, we also examine the inequality effect of financial rent without the Kuznets curve relationship. In an alternative specification, we include other control variables such as the unemployment rate, union density, education, government consumption, and globalization without GDP per capita, following Kus (2012). Column 1 in Table 4 reports that financial rent affects inequality significantly in this specification, too, although the number of sample countries is smaller than our benchmarking model. Besides, we test the financialization index and its components used by Kus (2012) to check out the robustness of our findings in other columns. The financialization index in Column 2 in Table 4 exerts a

Table 5. Market concentration in the banking sector, other financialization indicators, and inequality.

EXPLANATORY VARIABLES	(1) GINI	(2) GINI	(3) GINI	(4) GINI	(5) GINI
Time period	1998–2015	1996–2014	1996–2015	1980–2015	1980–2015
Lagged dependent variable	0.883***	0.773***	0.780***	0.934***	0.773***
	(0.015)	(0.029)	(0.029)	(0.046)	(0.055)
Log of GDP per capita	2.865***	6.242***	6.436***	2.641*	8.183***
	(0.760)	(0.992)	(1.063)	(1.498)	(2.437)
Square of a log of GDP per capita	−0.162***	−0.350***	−0.364***	−0.143	−0.459***
	(0.044)	(0.055)	(0.059)	(0.087)	(0.138)
Education	−0.019***	−0.047***	−0.044***	−0.024**	−0.061***
	(0.004)	(0.009)	(0.009)	(0.010)	(0.018)
Government consumption spending	−0.021**	−0.051**	−0.048**	−0.010	−0.047**
	(0.010)	(0.022)	(0.022)	(0.024)	(0.022)
Trade openness	−0.001	−0.006**	−0.004*	−0.003	−0.010***
	(0.001)	(0.003)	(0.002)	(0.002)	(0.003)
Foreign direct investment	0.000	0.001	0.000	0.001	0.001*
	(0.001)	(0.001)	(0.001)	(0.001)	(0.001)
Financial rent	*0.003****				
	(0.001)				
Lerner index		*0.548***			
		(0.234)			
Asset concentration			*0.007***		
			(0.003)		
Financial sector asset				*0.005***	
				(0.002)	
Stock market capitalization					*0.007****
					(0.003)
Observations	530	969	1147	1412	1045
No. of countries	65	101	115	121	82
Diagnostic test					
No. of instruments	59	60	62	77	77
AR(1)	0.0702	0.111	0.0164	0.00150	0.166
AR(2)	0.327	0.119	0.212	0.0403	0.207
Hansen test	0.537	0.612	0.799	0.963	0.778

Standard errors in parentheses, ***$p < 0.01$, **$p < 0.05$, *$p < 0.1$; intercept is not reported.

significant positive effect on the Gini coefficient of disposable income. All three components of this index are also positively and significantly associated with it.[15] This suggests that the oversized banking sector because of financialization is detrimental to income distribution. Among control variables, the unemployment rate increases inequality, while union density, trade openness, government spending and education, and GDP growth reduce it.

In Table 5, we test the effect of market concentration in the banking sector by employing the Lerner index and asset concentration of the banking sector in our benchmarking specification with all control variables. The Lerner index is a measure of market power in the banking market, defined as the difference between output prices and marginal costs. The asset concentration is the share of bank assets held by the top three banks (World Bank 2019). The market concentration in the banking industry is an essential source for excess profit and financial rent for banks, which could increase income inequality. The significant result of the Lerner index and market concentration in Columns 2 and 3 suggests that the banking

Table 6. Financial rent and financialization and top income concentration.

EXPLANATORY VARIABLES Time period	(1) TOP1 1998–2015	(2) TOP1 1996–2015	(3) TOP1 1996–2014	(4) TOP1 1980–2015	(5) TOP1 1980–2015
Lagged dependent variable	0.484***	0.649***	0.741***	0.600***	0.605***
	(0.056)	(0.044)	(0.041)	(0.046)	(0.055)
Log of GDP per capita	7.886***	4.969***	3.052***	4.474***	6.605***
	(1.997)	(1.046)	(0.589)	(1.049)	(1.672)
Square of a log of GDP per capita	−0.415***	−0.263***	−0.164***	−0.244***	−0.347***
	(0.107)	(0.055)	(0.032)	(0.058)	(0.091)
Education	−0.079***	−0.048***	−0.029***	−0.048***	−0.075***
	(0.017)	(0.011)	(0.006)	(0.008)	(0.020)
Government consumption spending	−0.028	−0.059**	−0.055***	−0.046***	−0.061
	(0.037)	(0.026)	(0.016)	(0.015)	(0.040)
Trade openness	−0.008	−0.007**	−0.005**	−0.005**	−0.004
	(0.006)	(0.003)	(0.002)	(0.003)	(0.005)
Foreign direct investment	−0.005**	−0.001*	−0.001***	−0.001**	−0.002***
	(0.002)	(0.001)	(0.000)	(0.001)	(0.001)
Financial rent	0.017***				
	(0.005)				
Bank income		0.190***			
		(0.040)			
Lerner index			0.985***		
			(0.202)		
Financialization index				0.050	
				(0.068)	
Stock trading value					0.001
					(0.002)
Observations	525	1031	973	1407	1003
No. of countries	69	110	105	128	82
Diagnostic test					
No. of instruments	60	62	60	77	77
AR(1)	0.155	0.0888	0.0699	0.0698	0.0778
AR(2)	0.286	0.246	0.167	0.213	0.239
Hansen test	0.138	0.182	0.434	0.0479	0.198

Standard errors in parentheses, ***$p < 0.01$, **$p < 0.05$, *$p < 0.1$; intercept is not reported.

sector's monopoly raises income inequality by creating opportunities for financial rent-seeking. The correlations between financial rent and the Lerner index and asset concentration are indeed positive, with 0.2026 and 0.1782, respectively. Our finding demonstrates that larger rent-seeking due to less competition in the financial sector is associated with higher inequality.[16] Columns 4 and 5 in Table 5 also test the effects of alternative measures of financialization such as financial sector asset and stock market capitalization, covering a much longer period starting from 1980. These variables exert significant positive effects on inequality, and this is broadly consistent with the findings of other empirical studies. Education has a consistently negative and significant effect on inequality in all models. Trade openness and foreign direct investment become significant with opposite signs in Column 5 to cover the longer period.

Finally, we replace the net Gini coefficient with the top 1 percent income share as a dependent variable to investigate the effect of financial rent and other financialization indicators on top income concentration. The results in Table 6 are qualitatively similar to those for the Gini coefficient.

Financial rent, bank income, and the Lerner index significantly affect the top 1 percent income share, while the financialization index and stock trading value have insignificant but positive effects on it. We find that most indicators used in this paper as proxies of financialization are significant to top income concentration, while financial sector assets are not. The effect of financial rent, bank income, and financialization index also remains positive and significant for the top 1 percent income share when we employ the alternative specification without the Kuznets curve relationship in Table 4. When using the top 10 percent share as the top income concentration, we find that most variables for financialization and market concentration have a significant effect, while financial rent was not significant, although results are not reported in the table. This implies that financial rent appears to specifically play an important role in worsening income inequality by affecting the very top of the income distribution. This is consistent with the findings of other studies (Bivens and Mishel 2013; Angelopoulos et al. 2019). The regression results suggest that financial rent-seeking along with financialization is good for top-earning groups only and bad for the entire population's income distribution.

Furthermore, we have conducted the cross-country ordinary least squares regressions and the system GMM regressions using 5-year average panel data to examine the long-run and the medium-run effects with the same specifications. Overall, the positive effects of financial rent and other variables for financialization on inequality remain unchanged. Our empirical findings implicate that rent-seeking in the banking sector and the development of financialization are closely associated with income inequality because they result in excessive income and profit in the financial sector. It should be noted that the empirical results demonstrate that the positive effect of financialization on inequality is not only in developed countries but in all countries. The government should make efforts to limit the financialization process with more effective regulation to reduce monopoly power and promote competition to reduce inequality. Other policies, such as the development of public education, could help decrease income inequality.

Conclusions

Rising inequality is one of the most serious concerns to policymakers and economists. The existing literature points to globalization, technologies, and political and institutional factors as causes of rising income inequality. Recently, financialization and rent-seeking in the financial sector have been considered by many researchers as one important determinant of rising inequality. Many studies argue that financialization depresses wages of the non-financial industries with the strong power of rentiers who want to cut labor costs and weaken unionism. It reduces consumption and investment, resulting in lower aggregate demand and unequal income distribution. Most of all, financialization and financial rent-seeking contribute to excessive income and profit in the banking sector and high remuneration for top executives. These are major causes of the rapid increase of income in the top income group, which exacerbates overall income inequality.

This study empirically examines the effect of financialization on income inequality, employing dynamic cross-country panel regressions. We introduce financial rent, a new measurement of financialization, and also use market concentration in the banking sector together with other commonly used financialization variables. The empirical analysis finds that financial rent-seeking and market concentration in the banking sector have been significantly associated with income inequality since the 1990s. The result holds for inequality measured by the Gini coefficient of disposable income and top income concentration as well. This study makes a contribution to current research by complementing current empirical studies with a new measure of financialization. It should be also noted that this study covers not only advanced countries but also emerging and developing economies, which is different from current studies.

Our empirical findings are generally consistent with those of other empirical studies that report the significant inequality effect of financialization. In particular, they suggest that monopoly profit and excess income in the banking sector through rent-seeking worsen income distribution. Financial rent-seeking along with financialization extract excess profit at the expense of customers, taxpayers, and workers most of all. This leads to rising inequality and top-level income concentration. The government should regulate the banking sector and promote competition so that banks cannot generate excess profit from rent-seeking and market concentration.

Disclosure statement

No potential conflict of interest was reported by the author(s).

Notes

1. More recent studies that use these measures include Pariboni and Tridico (2019), De vita and Luo (2020). Huber et al. (2020) and Alexiou et al. (2021).
2. More precisely, one gets rent if he earns an income higher than the minimum that person would have accepted, defined as the income in the next opportunity (Khan, 2000).
3. The unit cost is more precisely a measure of the efficiency of the financial sector. Philippon (2012) finds that the annual cost of financial intermediation has increased in the U.S. along with the development of the financial sector over the past 30 years.

It suggests that the efficiency of the finance fell because of rising rent. The unit cost is measured by value added in the financial sector as a share of GDP divided by total intermediated assets.

4. Though the deposit rate is deducted as the cost of the fund during the final accounting of ROC, we may consider deposit money as input resources of intermediation in the banking sector and subtract the deposit rate as a proxy of the next possible returns from other financial assets.

5. There is a debate regarding the causality between financialization and lower profitability. Although the decline in the profit rate could promote financialization, as some Marxist political economists argue (Lapavitsas, 2011), empirical evidence suggests that higher dividend and interest payment have an adverse effect on profitability and capital accumulation (Stockhammer, 2004; Tori and Onaran, 2018). There could be interactions between them as financialization lowered real investment, aggregate demand, and profitability, which further deepened financialization.

6. It should be noted that an increase in tax at top income does not result in a decrease in the growth rate, and thus its source is mainly rent. If these incomes were a result of their efforts, those at the top would respond by working less hard, with adverse effects on GDP growth (Philippon and Reshef, 2012).

7. There are also country-level studies using various methodologies that find that financialization increases income inequality. They include Lin and Tomaskovic-Devey (2013) on the US, Alvarez (2015) on France, and Stockhammer (2004) on the U.S., UK, France, and Germany.

8. We derive the Gini coefficient data from version 8.1 of the SWIID dataset, which covers 187 countries for the 1981-2017 period.

9. The H-statistic is a measure of the degree of competition in the banking industry. It measures the elasticity of banks' revenues relative to input prices. Under perfect competition, the H-statistic equals 1. Under a monopoly, H-statistic is less than or equal to 0. When H-statistic is between 0 and 1, the system operates under monopolistic competition (World Bank, 2019)

10. Our sample covers a country-year observation unit. The number of countries ranges from 43 to 128, and the time varies between 1980–2017 and 1998–2017, depending on model specifications.

11. The SWIID presents the Gini data, based on an estimation of the relationship between LIS GINI and all other GINI data available for the same country and year that are not included in LIS but available in other sources. These sources are income distribution data from the OECD, the socio-economic database for Latin America and the Caribbean, Eurostat, PovcalNet, and national statistical offices around the World (Solt, 2020).

12. Kus (2012) makes a financialization index using the z-score of these variables. Considering data constraints, we take banking sector assets as one component of the composite index by replacing banks' securities.

13. In the regression analysis, we remove very few extreme values or outliers of deposit rates to reduce measurement error, using the interquartile range (IQR) method. However, the regression results without excluding these do not change qualitatively.

14. We have considered a possible conditional relationship and have tested several interactions of financial rent and condition variables such as GDP per

capita and others. However, we do not find any significant result of the interaction variable.

15. We also find that bank income and stock trading value are significant and positive to disposable income Gini in our benchmarking specification including the Kuznets curve.
16. The effect of the Lerner index remains positive and significant when we use this index as an alternative proxy of rent-seeking in the alternative specification without the Kuznets curve relationship, similar to table 4.

References

Alexiou, C., E. Trachanas, and S. Vogiazas. 2021. "Income Inequality and Financialization: A Not so Straightforward Relationship." *Journal of Economic Studies*. doi: 10.1108/JES-05-2020-0202.

Alvarez, I. 2015. "Financialization, Non-Financial Corporations and Income Inequality: The Case of France." *Socio-Economic Review* 13 (3):449–475. doi: 10.1093/ser/mwv007.

Angelopoulos, A., K. Angelopoulos, S. Lazarakis, and A. Philippopoulos. 2019. "The Distributional Consequences of Rent Seeking." CESifo Working Papers No. 7835.

Arcand, J., E. Berkes, and U. Panizza. 2015. "Too Much Finance?" *Journal of Economic Growth* 20 (2):105–148. doi: 10.1007/s10887-015-9115-2.

Arellano, M., and S. Bond. 1991. "Some Tests of Specification for Panel Data: Monte Carlo Evidence and an Application to Employment Equation." *The Review of Economic Studies* 58 (2):277–298. doi: 10.2307/2297968.

Assa, J. 2012. "Financialization and Its Consequences: The OECD Experience." *Finance Research* 1 (1):34–39.

Basu, S., R. Inklaar, and J. C. Wang. 2011. "The Value of Risk: Measuring the Service Output of U.S. Commercial Banks." *Economic Inquiry* 49 (1):226–245. doi: 10.1111/j.1465-7295.2010.00304.x.

Becker, J., J. Jager, B. Leubolt, and R. Weissenbacher. 2010. "Peripheral Financialization and Vulnerability to Crisis: A Regulationist Perspective." *Competition & Change* 14 (3–4):225–247. doi: 10.1179/102452910X12837703615337.

Bivens, J., and L. Mishel. 2013. "The Pay of Corporate Executives and Financial Professionals as Evidence of Rents in Top 1 Percent Incomes." *Journal of Economic Perspectives* 27 (3):57–78. doi: 10.1257/jep.27.3.57.

Blundell, R., and S. Bond. 1998. "Initial Conditions and Moment Restrictions in Dynamic Panel Data Models." *Journal of Econometrics* 87 (1):115–143. doi: 10.1016/S0304-4076(98)00009-8.

Bonizzi, B. 2013. "Financialization in Developing and Emerging Countries." *International Journal of Political Economy* 42 (4):83–107. doi: 10.2753/IJP0891-1916420405.

Boustanifar, H., E. Grant, and A. Reshef. 2018. "Wages and Human Capital in Finance: International Evidence, 1970–2011." *Review of Finance* 22 (2):699–745. doi: 10.1093/rof/rfx011.

Crotty, J., and K.-K. Lee. 2005. "The Causes and Consequences of Neoliberal Restructuring in Post-Crisis Korea." In *Financialization and the World Economy*, edited by G. Epstein. Cheltenham, UK: Northampton, MA: Edward Elgar.

De Vita, G., and Y. Luo. 2020. "Financialization, Household Debt and Income Inequality: Empirical Evidence." *International Journal of Finance and Economics* 2020:1–21. doi: 10.1002/ijfe.1886.

Demir, F. 2007. "The Rise of Rentier Capitalism and the Financialization of Real Sectors in Developing Countries." *Review of Radical Political Economics* 39 (3):351–359. doi: 10.1177/0486613407305283.

dos Santos, P. 2013. "A Cause for Policy Concern: The Expansion of Household Credit in Middle-Income Economies." *International Review of Applied Economics* 27 (3):316–338. doi: 10.1080/02692171.2012.721755.

Dumenil, G., and D. Levey. 2005. "Costs and Benefits of Neoliberalism." In *Financialization and the World Economy*, edited by G. Epstein. Cheltenham and Northampton: Edward Elgar.

Epstein, G. 2005. "Introduction: Financialization and the World Economy." In *Financialization and the World Economy*, edited by G. Epstein. Cheltenham and Northampton: Edward Elgar.

Epstein, G. 2018. "On the Social Efficiency of Finance." *Development and Change* 49 (2): 330–352. doi: 10.1111/dech.12386.

Epstein, G., and A. Jayadev. 2005. "The Rise of Rentier Incomes in OECD Countries: Financialization, Central Bank Policy and Labor Solidarity." In *Financialization and the World Economy*, edited by G. Epstein. Cheltenham and Northampton: Edward Elgar.

Epstein, G., and J. A. Montecino. 2016. *Overcharged: The High Cost of High Finance.* Roosevelt Institute: Reimagine the Rules.

Furceri, D., and P. Loungani. 2018. "The Distributional Effects of Capital account Liberalization." *Journal of Development Economics* 130:127–144. doi: 10.1016/j.jdeveco.2017.09.007.

Gutiérrez, G., and T. Philippon. 2017. "Investmentless Growth: An Empirical Investigation." *Brookings Papers on Economic Activity* 2017 (2):89–102. doi: 10.1353/eca.2017.0013.

Hein, E. 2015. "Finance-Dominated Capitalism and Redistribution of Income: A Kaleckian Perspective." *Cambridge Journal of Economics* 39 (3):907–934. doi: 10.1093/cje/bet038.

Hein, E. 2019. "Financialisation and Tendencies towards Stagnation: The Role of Macroeconomic Regime Changes in the Course of and after the Financial and Economic Crisis 2007–09." *Cambridge Journal of Economics* 43 (4):975–999. doi: 10.1093/cje/bez022.

Huber, E., B. Petrova, and J. D. Stephens. 2020. "Financialization, Labor Market Institutions and Inequality." *Review of International Political Economy.* doi: 10.1080/09692290.2020.1808046.

International Labor Organization (ILO). 2020. "ILOSTAT." https://ilostat.ilo.org/data/ :https://www.ilo.org/shinyapps/bulkexplorer38/?lang=enandsegment=indicatorandid=ILR_TUMT_NOC_RT_A.

Jaumotte, F., S. Lall, and C. Papageorgiou. 2013. "Rising Income Inequality: Technology, or Trade and Financial Globalization." *IMF Economic Review* 61 (2):271–309. doi: 10.1057/imfer.2013.7.

Kaltenbrunner, A., and J. Painceira. 2015. "Developing Countries' Changing Nature of Financial Integration and New Forms of External Vulnerability: The Brazilian Experience." *Cambridge Journal of Economics* 39 (5):1281–1306. doi: 10.1093/cje/beu038.

Kaplan, S. N., and J. Rauh. 2010. "Wall Street and Main Street: What Contributes to the Rise in the Highest Incomes?" *Review of Financial Studies* 23 (3):1004–1303. doi: 10.1093/rfs/hhp006.

Khan, M. 2000. "Rents, Efficiency and Growth." In *Rents, Rent-Seeking and Economic Development*, edited by M. Khan and K. Jomo. Cambridge: CUP.

Kotz, D. M. 2015. *The Rise and Fall of Neoliberal Capitalism.* Cambridge, MA: Harvard University Press.

Krippner, G. 2005. "The Financialization of the American Economy." *Socio-Economic Review* 3 (2):173–208. doi: 10.1093/SER/mwi008.

Kus, B. 2012. "Financialization and Income Inequality in OECD Nations: 1995–2007." *The Economic and Social Review* 43 (4):477–495.

Kuznets, S. 1955. "Economic Growth and Income Inequality." *American Economic Review* 45 (1):1–28.

Lane, P., and G. Milesi-Ferretti. 2017. "International Financial Integration in the Aftermath of the Global Financial Crisis." *IMF Working Papers* 17 (115):1. doi: 10.5089/9781484300336.001.

Lapavitsas, C. 2011. "Theorizing Financialization." *Work, Employment and Society* 25 (4):611–626. doi: 10.1177/0950017011419708.

Lapavitsas, C., and P. L. dos Santos. 2008. "Globalization and Contemporary Banking: On the Impact of New Technology." *Contributions to Political Economy* 27 (1):31–56. doi: 10.1093/cpe/bzn005.

Lavoie, M., and E. Stockhammer. 2013. *Wage-Led Growth: An Equitable Strategy for Economic Recovery* (M. Lavoie, and E. Stockhammer, Eds). New York, NY, The US: Palgrave MacMillan.

Lee, K.-K. 2014. "Globalization, Income Inequality and Poverty: Theory and Empirics." *Social Systems Studies* 28:109–134.

Lin, K.-H., and D. Tomaskovic-Devey. 2013. "Financialization and US Income Inequality, 1970–2008." *American Journal of Sociology* 118 (5):1284–1329. doi: 10.1086/669499.

Maestri, V., and A. Roventini. 2012. "Inequality and Macroeconomic Factors: A Time-Series Analysis for a Set of OECD Countries." Laboratory of Economics and Management (LEM) Working Paper Series, No. 2012/21.

Milanovic, B. 2015. "Global Inequality of Opportunity: How Much of Our Income is Determined by Where We Live?" *Review of Economics and Statistics* 97 (2):452–460. doi: 10.1162/REST_a_00432.

Onaran, O., E. Stockhammer, and L. Grafl. 2011. "Financialization, Income Distribution and Aggregate Demand in the USA." *Cambridge Journal of Economics* 35 (4):637–661. doi: 10.1093/cje/beq045.

Orhangazi, O. 2008. "Financialization and Capital Accumulation in the Non-Financial Corporate Sector: A Theoretical and Empirical Investigation of the US Economy, 1973–2004." *Cambridge Journal of Economics* 32 (6):863–886. doi: 10.1093/cje/ben009.

Pariboni, R., and P. Tridico. 2019. "Labour Share Decline, Financialisation and Structural Change." *Cambridge Journal of Economics* 43 (4):1073–1102. doi: 10.1093/cje/bez025.

Philippon, T. 2012. "Has the U.S. Finance Industry Become Less Efficient? On the Theory and Measurement of Financial Intermediation." NBER Working Paper Series 18077.

Philippon, T., and A. Reshef. 2012. "Wages and Human Capital in the U.S. Finance Industry: 1909–2006." *Quarterly Journal of Economics* 127 (4):1551–1609. doi: 10.1093/qje/qjs030.

Pi, J., and P. Zhang. 2018. "Skill-Biased Technological Change and Wage Inequality in Developing Countries." *International Review of Economics & Finance* 56:347–362. doi: 10.1016/j.iref.2017.11.004.

Piketty, T. 2020. *Capital and Ideology* (A. Goldhammer, Trans.). Cambridge: The Belknap Press of Harvard University Press.

Pollin, R. 2007. "The Resurrection of the Rentier." *New Left Review* 46:140–153.

Pontusson, J. 2013. "Unionization, Inequality and Redistribution." *British Journal of Industrial Relations* 51 (4):797–825. doi: 10.1111/bjir.12045.

Shin, H., and K. Lee. 2019. "Impact of Financialization and Financial Development on Inequality: Panel Cointegration Results Using OECD Data." *Asian Economic Papers* 18 (1):69–98. doi: 10.1162/asep_a_00659.

Solt, F. 2020. "Measuring Income Inequality Across Countries and Over Time: The Standardized World Income Inequality Database." *Social Science Quarterly* 101 (3): 1183–1199. Standardized World Income Inequality Database. https://fsolt.org/swiid

Stiglitz, J. E. 2015. "The Origins of Inequality and Policies to Contain It." *National Tax Journal* 68 (2):425–448. doi: 10.17310/ntj.2015.2.09.

Stiglitz, J. E. 2016. "Inequality and Economic Growth." *The Political Quarterly* 86 (S1): 134–155.

Stockhammer, E. 2004. "Financialization and the Slowdown of Accumulation." *Cambridge Journal of Economics* 28 (5):719–741. doi: 10.1093/cje/beh032.

Stockhammer, E. 2010. "Financialization and the Global Economy." Political Economy Research Institute Working Paper Series 240.

Tori, D., and O. Onaran. 2018. "Financialization, Financial Development and Investment. Evidence from European Non-Financial Corporations." *Socio-Economic Review*: 1–43. doi: 10.1093/ser/mwy044.

Wang, C. 2011. "What is the Value Added of Banks?" VoxEU, CEPR. https://voxeu.org/article/what-value-added-banks

World Bank. 2019. "Global Financial Development Database." https://www.worldbank.org/en/publication/gfdr/data/global-financial-development-database

World Bank. 2020. "World Development Indicators." https://databank.worldbank.org/source/world-development-indicators

World Inequality Database (WID). 2020. "World Inequality Database." https://wid.world/data/

Zhang, J. Y. 2017. "The Rise of Market Concentration and Rent Seeking in the Financial Sector." The Harvard John M. Olin Fellow's Discussion Paper Series No. 72.

Income inequality: past, present and future in a political economy perspective

Pascal Mickael Petit

ABSTRACT

In order to interpret the levels and evolution of income distribution, we need to take into account the variety of capitalism modes considered and their respective capacity to maintain an effective social contract. This makes it possible to assess the importance of the social crises that these countries are going through as well as their capacity to respond to the new challenges posed by environmental degradation. The question is all the more difficult because this response must be coordinated on a global scale and implies a profound questioning of the management of globalization over the past three decades.

Income inequality as a symptom of disruption

The issue of rising income inequality began to attract the attention of economists in the 1980s as the neo-liberal turn took hold in the developed economies. Income inequality had not previously been an economic policy objective in itself, as had the pursuit of full employment, income growth or lower inflation. This is not a marginal remark. Its explanation helps to set out the perspective we take to consider the place of income inequality in a given society. Inequality is a multidimensional notion. Beyond income inequality exist wealth inequality, access to public services inequalities and the likes. One should not think that the inequality issue in a society matters along time in the same manner. Clearly the importance of the issue and of its various dimensions vary with the changes in institutional context which characterize each phase of development of a given country. Thus the fact that such and such dimension of inequality is or not an issue in the political debates and in the policy measures does matter.

To capture this conditional and evolutionary nature of the question we shall retain the framework of analysis of the institutionalist approach of development proposed by the French Regulation school (see for instance Petit 1999). In this approach the institutional context of an economy is featured as composed of five interacting structural forms, namely (1) the State apparatus (justice, police and army), (2) money as an institution, (3) the organization of international relations. To these regalian functions two other forms have been added in the course of development (4) the regulation of trading activities for example the forms of competition and (5) the functioning of the labor market and of the work organization. These two last forms are more recent history as their development accompanied respectively the emergence of market regulations and of wage labor relations. This sequence recalls that at a given period in time a society gives a central importance to the development of one form. This prevalence can be seen as the basis of the social contract of the society under view at a given period. It does not imply that everyone agrees with any development of this form but that it is at the core of the political debates. It can be conflictual but it is legitimate and leads to institutional changes and policies, featuring the social contract of the society under view as a broad accord on objectives.

The development of the western world at the end of World War II with its "full employment acts" of various kinds gives a good illustration of the primacy given in the social contracts of these societies to the wage labor relationships. If full employment was a major objective, so was the fact that wages should increase with productivity gains. This last objective was more the result of expected good management practices in the various sectors of activities than of a central wage policy. By and large the combination of these two objectives has been viewed as a proper effective way to reduce income inequality. This reduction was not an upfront policy objective of these welfare states in construction but the outcome of a process combining productivity gains, wages rises all, boosted by demand policies. Indeed these Fordist Growth regimes were from the start associated with country specific schemes of redistribution by means of taxes and transfers, all reasons for which the period where these regimes were experienced have been referred to as the Golden Years of Capitalism (see Marglin and Shor 1992). Still these processes were vulnerable, being also based on arrangements regarding money and international relations (the second and third structural forms) which were bound to require some adjustments for the growth regimes to be sustainable.

Two major arrangements failed at the turn of the 1970s, (1) the relative stability of the exchange rates in dollar terms, a dominant currency itself based on a gold standard and (2) the coordinated set of trade restrictions and duties moderating external competition among countries of various levels of development. When these arrangements blew up first with the end of the gold exchange standard in 1971 (following the deficits of the US balance of payments due to the load of external conflicts, of which the

Vietnam war), soon followed by the development of a free exchange rate market and liberalization of trade flows, increasing on each growth regime the pressure of external price competition.

The crisis of the 1970s where the battle against price inflation and its disastrous effect on external competition became the major target, seemed to open a transition toward a consumer oriented society. The theme entered the political debates (see Ralph Nader one of the leaders of the consumerist movement in the US, running four times for the US presidential elections) and attempts to measure wellbeing flourished to go beyond the GDP per head which prevailed as a proxy of wellbeing measure in the previous period. All suggested a transition to a new growth regime centered around forms of competition favoring consumerism. Indeed the liberalization of trade boosted the purchasing power of consumers. All kinds of goods, including status goods as cars and housing equipment became more affordable. But the price to pay for this potential growth in wellbeing was a loss of jobs in the competition with low wages countries.

Moreover the neo-liberal order proned by Reagan and Thatcher in the early 1980s, reinforced at the turn of the 1990s by the demise of the communist bloc, had also a major impact on the internationalization of financial activities, fueling a credit based expansion of durable goods and real estates. This rather uncontrolled development of a debt economy led the whole global system open to major financial crises, of which the 1997 ASEAN Crisis, soon followed by the dot.com crisis of 2001, to echo the expansion of uncontrolled internet international transactions, all ending with the global financial crisis of 2008, fueled by this internationalization of financial activities in a rather uncontrolled debt economy. By that time it had become clear that the transition from the "Fordist" period was far to lead to a new growth regime centered on some kind of consumerist social contract. The prevalence of financial criteria, be it in the management of firms or in pushing citizens indebtment, made it clear that it was more a finance led than consumerist growth regime and even more a pseudo growth regime as it was impossible to associate it to any social contract. The fact that this neo-liberal "regime" had been, from its start, associated with a rise in income inequality in all developed economies active in this globalized world economy is one strong sign of this failure, largely confirmed by the general finance bashing which accompanied this rising importance of financial activities. The financialised growth regime turned out to be unable to answer the rise of critics against the continuous rise of income inequality.

Some major actors of the previous social compromise of the Fordist growth regimes, for example, the trade unions, were not anymore in position to address this issue, being strongly weakened by the competition of low wage countries. No new social arrangement has been developed that could have countered this trend increasing income inequality. Unemployment allowances could only mildly soften the blow. Expanding public services, which could have been a palliative, was against the neo-liberal principles as were tax increases at the required levels to counter the rise in income inequalities. As we shall see in most cases the redistributive schemes of taxes and transfers were unable to react and meet the challenge of growing income inequalities. Despite all these evidences on the deterioration of the social situations, income inequality has never played in the last three decades the role of an explicit objective to be followed and negotiated with the social partners, as unemployment and inflation rates had been in their time.

The generalized increase in income inequality was therefore seen as symptom of a dysfunction the importance and durability of which needed to be assessed. This elucidation seemed all the more necessary as this growth in income inequality affected not only developed countries but also developing ones, while the growth of their gross national product benefited from the liberalization of international trade and investment flows, which was further increased after the creation of the World Trade Organization in 1995. The same symptom was thus found in most countries even though trade and investment liberalization found their limits in a series of financial crises affecting both developed and developing countries, first the Asian crisis of 1997 and then some ten years later with the great global financial crisis of 2008. A decade later, even as the world faces a global health crisis, there is no guarantee that this phenomenon of growing income inequality will disappear. It is true that this phenomenon is not as simple as it seems, in the sense that it does not read the same way in all countries, while at the same time it is a source of significant change everywhere. Despite the abundance of data and the large body of interesting literature on the subject, the subject remains all the more open because all our societies are facing major environmental and social challenges. This abundance of questions is reflected in the various statistical and analytical studies that have been carried out since 2011 on the initiative of Thomas Piketty and his colleagues in Paris and Berkeley, providing an impressive statistical picture of income inequality for more than 80 countries over a period from 1980 to 2016 (see https://wid.world/world-inequality-lab/).

Nevertheless, these symptoms are difficult to interpret, as their impact on democracy or more precisely on the way societies build their social contracts is not obvious. This does not mean that these symptoms are a kind of white noise, they do manifest some deterioration of the social contracts, but in order to appreciate their lasting or reversible nature, one needs to confront them with the prevailing political and ideological situations.

Piketty has followed a similar path of questioning, starting in his book of 2014 (see Piketty 2014) with a statistical assessment of the changes in income inequalities, enlarging his quest to the ideological and political contexts in his 2019 book (see Piketty 2019) as well as in the collective work of 2021 (see Gethin, Martinez-Toledano, and Piketty, 2021).

In a more synthetic way, and starting from the fact that these rises of income inequalities have never been the object of direct reduction policies, we shall try to assess these evolutions as resulting from the confrontation of the specific past growth regimes of the various countries under view with the evolutions of their conditions of international exchange and financing.

On the hazardous transitions impulsed by the neo-liberal reaction to the crises of the 1970s

Let us come back on the follow up of the crisis which in 1971 put an end to the Bretton Woods system and led by 1973 to a mixture of fixed and fluctuating exchange rates and by the turn of the 1980s to a full neo-liberal turn. It led by and large to an expansion of world trade faster than world GDP. Thus the share of exports in world GDP rose from 9.2% in 1971 to 26.2% in 2008. Low wage countries benefited strongly from this liberalization of trade, all of which helped to reduce the inequality of development levels among countries.

Milanovic (2016) among others (see Tridico (2020) for an update), stressed that this reduction in inequality among countries coincided with the expansion of income inequality within countries. This observation came to be seen as the result of a tradeoff between reductions of inequality between countries and within countries. This presentation is misleading as the shift from inequality of development levels between countries to income inequality within countries is more the outcome of the crisis of the Bretton woods system than a general will to set up a new world order reducing inequalities among countries. The new state of trade and exchange rates did effectively benefit to some less developed countries but nothing implied that it would also lead to reduce income inequalities within these countries. On the contrary, in many cases of countries exporting raw materials, rises in exports have been fueling income inequalities (a case often referred to as extractivism). Much depends in fact on the social relations prevailing in the country under view. and how it has been impacted by the trade liberalization.

Moreover the neoliberal ideology, as expressed in the "Washington consensus" was strictly supporting market led developments and opposed to any planning and extension of public services. This neoliberalism also limited how countries which had belonged to the Bretton Woods system could accommodate the structural changes and rises in unemployment often implied by this trade liberalization. The erosion of the welfare states induced by this new context weakened the role that trade unions could play to support them and the consumer surpluses generated by the lower prices of imported goods could not fill the gap and by the 1990s the idea of a transition to a "consumerist model" petered out, acknowledging that welfare states had entered a long period of slow growth and social crisis. If the picture was rosier for some developing countries, many uncertainties remained.

The creation of the World Trade Organization in 1995 did give an institutional basis to arbitrate trade conflicts, with a specific status for developing countries, while the Washington consensus became progressively obsolete. Still this was not enough to give a sound support to the less developed countries while the rise of financial activities increased the risks of global financial crises that the rising process of regionalization (of which the EU was a leading example) could not counter. The world economy at the turn of the 21st century did seem to be stuck in a dead end, well featured in the trilemma suggested by Dany Rodrik (2011), whereby the world economy could not enjoy democracy if it could not choose clearly between its globalization process and its nation states empowerment.

As time went on, globalization of finance did push the development of global value chains, locating parts of the production process in low-wage countries but also optimizing the distribution of skilled production centers between various territories. There is no need to describe these structural developments in detail, but it should be stressed that the three decades from 1990 to 2020 have seen profound changes in national production structures, combining a certain de-industrialization of developed countries and, on the other hand, a notable industrialization of developing countries. These developments were quickly anticipated by the players and the financial sector was quick to speculate on this movement, which, it should be noted, was more subject to hazards than expected. The rules of the game have clearly changed between the thirty years following the Second World War (Steve Marglin and Juliet Shor's golden years of capitalism) and the thirty years of the 1990–2020 period, which have seen income inequalities increase.

The managerial elites have played a big role in these transformations. To highlight this difference in the way capitalism operates, we will speak of type 1 a Taylorian managerial capitalism for the 'Fordist' period where scientific organizations of the labor processes were major drivers of economic growth and type 2 a financial managerial capitalism for the following period where financial criteria (and share values) were key in the organization of productive activities. The influence of the financial sector in the regulation of production processes in this second phase of managerial capitalism will directly play a role in the development of wage structures and of income inequalities (see Duménil and Lévy 2015, 2018). The wages of CEOs will thus be related to share values, while CEOs wages in a Fordist perspective were seen in relation to the intra firm distribution of wages. But this management driven by a globalized financial sector, giving to its interventions an unprecedented mobility, will also be a source of financial crises, from the so-called Asian crisis in 1997 to the great global financial crisis of 2008.

Emerging from this great financial crisis will imply for most economies an increase in public indebtedness, leading in the second decade of the 21st century to unusual austerity policies. These measures will, in turn, lead to changes in the production and distribution of public services, as will be be seen in the health crisis, where certain health systems will prove unable to meet the demands of the pandemic. Though, even when following broadly similar means of interventions in a globalized world economy, countries differ in their recent experiences of social crises, a diversity which again refers to their specific institutional and historical contexts and which has to be taken into account to assess the impacts of income in inequality.

The diversity of countries and their growth patterns

It now remains for us to see in broad terms how the neoliberal wave presiding over the globalization of the world economy has impacted the growth strategies of countries and how this informs us about the importance for the social contract of the drift in income inequalities that can be observed. The first thing that was noticed in this second period of the 1990s–2020s was precisely the diversity of capitalisms at the beginning of the 21st century. While a number of countries had been living under fairly similar rules of capitalist market economies since the end of the Second World War, analyses of the characteristics of structural forms, i.e. institutions organizing the role of the state, wage relations or trade relations, revealed significant differences[1]. Beyond the dichotomy between capitalisms that are more or less regulated mainly by the market (a dichotomy stressed by Hall and Soskice 2001), we will retain five types of capitalisms to better define our approach (see Amable and Petit 2001; Amable 2003):

- T1) Anglo-Saxon capitalisms (the United States and the United Kingdom) where regulation by the market tends to prevail, as the most legitimate mode of organization with an open reluctance vis à vis public services.

- T2) social-democratic capitalisms with reference to the specificities of the fairly egalitarian social contracts of Scandinavian countries
- T3) continental European capitalisms, to evoke a still rather important role of the states in the social contract as in Germany and France
- T4) Mediterranean capitalisms where regional and family structures play a relatively important role in the regulation of economies
- T5) Meso-corporate capitalisms where companies play a particular role in the regulation of the social contract as in Japan and Korea.

This diversity of capitalisms should in principle allow us to anticipate the different ways in which, all things being equal, countries can react to the impacts on income distribution induced by the trade and exchange rates liberalization, and hence to what extent the social contract is seriously affected by the regulation of type 2 (financial managerial capitalism), bound to prevail after the neo-liberal turn of the 1980s boosted by the information and communication technological revolution.

Indeed, the impact of a structural evolution that would increase primary income inequalities could a priori be compensated by changes in the redistribution scheme attached to each type of capitalism if it strongly affected the essence of its social contract. The state in question could create and increase social transfers, enact new tax rules or change the nature of the free benefits and access to public services it provides.

For type 1 countries, where the legitimacy of market mechanisms prevails, the evolution of income inequalities should adjust by itself, with a marked resistance toward any new public intervention. If the duration or the size of the gaps were to be deemed too great, a major crisis would arise. This is the warning that comes through in Obama's quote about growing income inequality being a major challenge for American society, as noted by Joseph Stiglitz (2012) who speaks of a society approaching its level of dysfunction. Obama's health care reform was an attempt, strongly limited by the republicans under Trump, to address this dysfunction. The issue is less acute in the UK, which has a much celebrated national health system and a national education system, both limiting the disruptive effects of the erosion induced by the neo-liberalist turn on the primary distribution of income.

For type 2 capitalist countries, given the strong support to highly institutionalized and very inclusive wage labor relations enjoyed in these Scandinavian countries, one expects that the income inequalities that may arise will be moderated by adequate adjustments of taxes and transfers of public services, in order to properly reduce the risk of social fractures.

For type 3 countries, like France and Germany, where government policies retain a social protection mission associated with employment objectives, their public debt after the financial crises of the first decade of the 21st century have greatly strained their social situation. The yellow waistcoat crisis in France, triggered by the first tax measures taken to accompany the energy transition, shows this fragility. Various social movements, often described as "populist", will bear witness to the general nature of this social divide.

For type 4 countries, for example, the Mediterranean capitalisms, the situation is similar, except that the States are less committed to ensure social protection and to search for full employment. Regional differences may matter, helping to counter along with family solidarity, the erosion of the wage labor status induced by the diffusion of the neo-liberalist ideology. The changes in income distribution are therefore more difficult to offset. Public debt also clearly reinforced austerity policies after 2008, accentuating social fracturing and regional differences.

Finally, for type 5 countries, like Japan and South Korea, we can assume that large companies will tend to moderate downwards pressures on wages, leaving open the issue in small and medium entreprises.

The general extension of inequalities between labor incomes also has sectoral dimensions. The magnitude of the upwards and downwards pressures on the wage distributions depends on the degree and modalities of internationalization of the sectors considered. It has already been pointed out that the financial sector was one of the quickest to benefit from the liberalization of capital movements to raise the levels of high wages. The importance of this sector in an economy and its degree of internationalization are factors which, all other things being equal, contribute to increase inequality of labor incomes. Let us try to see how the various types of capitalism considered above effectively position themselves with regard to the extension of income inequalities considered.

Transformations in the distribution of income according to the types of capitalism

To concretize the evolution of income distribution, a common practice is to compare the evolutions of top and bottom national income shares. Table 1 compares the evolutions of top 10% shares of pretax national income with those of bottom 50% shares of national income for the sub-set of countries we retain to characterize the five types of capitalism identified at the turn of the XXI first century. The period under view 1990–2019 corresponds to three decades of fully fledge neo-liberalism in the world economy. With successive financial crises, including the global financial crisis (GFC) of 2008.

Table 1. Changes in the distribution of pretax national income over 1990–2019.

1	2	3	4	5	6	7	8
Type of capitalism	Countries	Income per head PPP Euro 2019	Ratio 2019/1990	Share 10% 2019	Ratio 2019/ 1990	Share 50% 2019	Ratio 2019/ 1990
1	U-States	52604	1.52	45	1.2	14	0.8
1	UK	34874	1.58	35	1.1	22	1.1
2	Denmark	47642	1.59	32	1.2	23	0.9
2	Sweden	44189	1.71	29	1.1	26	0.9
3	France	37249	1.23	32	1.1	22	0.9
3	Germany	40110	1.2	37	1.2	19	0.8
3	Netherlands	46331	1.46	30	1.1	23	0.9
4	Italy	30056	1.02	32	1.2	21	0.9
4	Spain	31763	1.34	34	0.9	22	1.2
5	Japan	30209	1.15	43	1.1	20	0.9
5	Korea	28632	2.25	45	1.3	19	0.8

Nota bene: Source: https://wid.world/data/
Column 3: income per head pretax in PPP Euro 2019; Column 4 ratio incomes per head 2019/1990.
Column 5: Pretax national income top 10% share; Column 6 ratio top10%shares 2019/1990.

Table 1 shows the general nature of the rise in income inequality over the period with an increase in the share of national income of the richest 10% (column 6) and a decrease in the share of the lowest 50% (column 8). It is noticeable that the levels and trends in these shares of the 10% richest are particularly high in the US. However, it is surprising that among the few exceptions, one finds the United Kingdom, where the share of the richest 10% (column 6) has indeed grown like the average but where the share of the poorest 50% (column 8) has also increased, returning in 2019 to levels close to those observed in the rest of the European countries shown in Table 1. We can also see that in the Scandinavian countries, the levels of the richest 10% and the poorest 50% have evolved like the average while maintaining their relative advantage, where the share of the rich is slightly smaller and that of the poor slightly higher than elsewhere in Europe. In fact, beyond the long-term trends that seem to be reflected in Table 1, political variations within each country can alter or accelerate the movement. As Fortunato (2021) points out, income inequality in the United Kingdom rose sharply under Margaret Thatcher's government (from May 1979 to November 1990) and then slowed down thereafter, which would explain why the share of the lowest 50% of income earners rose over the period 1990–2019. Similarly, it may be surprising to find in Sweden developments that are quite similar to those observed in other European countries, but the rise of the 'populist' Sweden Democrats party in the last decade accounts for a certain erosion of the social contract. In Table 1, the case of Spain, where the share of high incomes has fallen and that of low incomes has risen, appears curious, but this is likely due to the fall in property prices over the last decade in a country where the number of homeowners is high (see Anghel et al. 2018). The result is a bit fuzzy, as our expectations

Table 2. Cash Transfers by modes of capitalism 2014.

1	2	3	4	6	7
Type of Capita- lism	Countries	Spending Cash transfers %GDP 2014	Share of cash benefits income or means-tested 2012	Ratio Cash benefits to t poorest 20%	Ratio Cash benefits to richest 20%
1	U-States	9	26.6	20	18
1	UK	11	25.9	25	8
2	Denmark	14	5.2	34	8
2	Sweden	13	2.9	28	12
3	France	18	9.6	17	28
3	Germany	14	6.8	20	20
3	Netherlands	13	12.0	28	12
4	Italy	19	5.3	8	35
4	Spain	17	15.9	10	25
5	Japan	12	27.6	12	18
5	Korea	4	19.0	26	26

Source: White ford P. (2015). Data: OECD Social Expenditure database.

regarding changes in the distribution of incomes, based on our typology of capitalisms, have been only partly verified, with various unexpected changes for the UK, Sweden and Spain.

It is difficult though to see, in the impacts recalled in Table 1, the signs of drastic erosions of the wage-labor nexus. Many causes can impact the evolution of the primary distribution of income, adding to or moderating the impact of the liberalization of trade and capital movements. In developed countries, the changes in production systems driven by a largely globalized financial sector contribute to a growing dualism between managerial and subordinate jobs. It is interesting in this respect to see how countries react to reduce the impact of this dualism on income distribution through taxes and social benefits. Rousselon and Viennot (2020) point out that in Europe type 2 and 3 capitalisms tend to use social benefits and type 4 capitalisms (Mediterranean but also Eastern European) tend to use taxes. In fact, in order to better appreciate the impact of the changes in the distribution of earned incomes that the contemporary phase of globalization is impelling, it is necessary to characterize precisely the modes of adaptation of the various types of capitalism.

We thus tried to check whether or not the redistributive schemes of each form of capitalism have been moderating the effects of the neo-liberal turn. The figures presented in Table 2 underlined that these redistributive schemes are more complex and diversified than first thought of with transfers concerning both low and high incomes groups for different reasons.

This diversity of redistribution schemes explains that inequality of income distribution is not a sufficient indicator of the well-being of the societies under view. Still some figures are consistent with the typology of modes of capitalism we retained. In the first place the amount of spending cash transfers do show a reduced figure for capitalism of type 1 while the amount is in nearly all the other types of capitalism between 13 and 19%

Table 3. Human Development Index: impact of inequality by modes of capitalism 2019.

1 Type of Capita lism	2 Countries	3 HDI Value 2019	4 HDI value adjusted for inequalities	5 Overall loss	6 Difference From HDI rank
1	U-States	0.926	0.808	12.7	−11
1	UK	0 ;932	0.856	8.1	−3
2	Denmark	0.940	0.883	6.1	4
2	Sweden	0.945	0.882	6.6	0
3	France	0.901	0.820	9.0	2
3	Germany	0.947	0.869	8.2	−4
3	Netherlands	0.944	0.878	7.0	0
4	Italy	0.892	0.783	12.2	−7
4	Spain	0.904	0.783	13.4	−13
5	Japan	0.919	0.843	8.3	1
5	Korea	0.916	0.815	11	−2

Source: UNDP Human Development Report 2020 Overview.
Definitions: Human Development Index (HDI): A composite index measuring average achievement in three basic
  dimensions of human development—a long and healthy life, knowledge, and a decent standard of living. See
  Technical note 1 at http://hdr.undp.org/sites/default/files/hdr2020_technical_notes.pdf for details on how the
  HDI is calculated.
Inequality-adjusted HDI (IHDI): HDI value adjusted for inequalities in the three basic dimensions of human
  development.
See *Technical note 2* at http://hdr.undp.org/sites/default/files/hdr2020_technical_notes.pdf for details on how the
  IHDI is calculated.
Overall loss: Percentage difference between the IHDI value and the HDI value.
Difference from HDI rank: Difference in ranks on the IHDI and the HDI, calculated only for countries for which
  an IHDI value is calculated.

of GDP. Moreover when looking at the receivers of these transfers (columns 6 and 7 of Table 2) one can see that a sizeable share benefits the richest. Various reasons can explain that the transfers are not simply focused on the corrections of primary distributions of income, favoring the poorest. This diversity may stem from specific schemes of retirement or of public services, notwithstanding transfers accompanying some investments. This diversity is also found within each type of capitalism, especially regarding types 3, 4, and 5. Similar internal puzzling diversity would stem when looking at the structure of taxes. Therefore to complete our assessment it seems useful to compare directly the observations of Table 1 on rising inequality in the distribution of income with a synthetic index of well-being. The human development index (HDI) developed by the UNDP gives us such opportunity (see Table 3).

The indices in Table 3 stress that the adjustments for inequalities affect noticeably economies of type 1 while it hardly touched the economies of type 2 under view. Economies of type 4 (for example Italy and Spain) have also been severely affected which was not so expected. Meanwhile Human Development indices of economies of type 3 and 5 have been little affected if any.

But these assessments, however precise and partly in accord with the typology of types of capitalism, remain too broad to help to define the policy objective that each type could follow. Moreover the ways in which countries have been affected by the great financial crisis of 2008, and have launched in reaction austerity policies and increased public debts may have been determinant, if only as it led to further internationalization of productive processes. Similarly the global health crisis that began in 2020 may have changed the situation, making many of the previous rules of financial management obsolete. Many economies have been left very vulnerable to the pandemic, as their health systems did not have the autonomy to cope with the crisis situation. Many relocations of activities have been envisaged, which is not without effects on national production organizations and consumption patterns, especially as the ecological crisis is imposing its share of major transformations. The lessons to be drawn from the first two decades of the 21st century have to take into account this drastic change of context, which could for instance lead to some extension of transfers or of public services.

Income inequalities and capacities to overcome the health and environmental crisis

The global health crisis has in fact completely reopened the question of the future of the economies that have developed in the neoliberal era of the last three decades. In most economies, social movements, more or less intense, have manifested discontent (to use the term of Stiglitz (2003)) calling for institutional and organizational adjustments that the various types of capitalism were more or less able to make. The attachment of the Anglo-Saxon models, to market mechanisms, has been questioned and we saw in the previous section that certain modes had more capacity to adjust their modes of social protection by playing on social transfers or tax levies to attenuate the impacts on income distribution of the neo-liberal globalization. Esping-Andersen (1999, 2002) had clearly underlined the importance of these adjustment possibilities for the postwar welfare states to find their modus vivendi. The rise of discontent, often crudely described as populist, clearly showed that this adjustment was only very partial and led to situations that were less and less accepted by the populations.

The arrival of the global health crisis in this context of an already well eroded wage labor relationship forced major revisions of the financial austerity rules that had prevailed in the previous decade. This was quickly evident in the case of the European Union where the idea of a very Keynesian stimulus package of 750 billion euros was accepted by the end of the first half of 2020. The situation has long appeared more uncertain in the United States, but the victory of Joe Biden in the American presidential election, however narrow, has made it possible, in the context of the dysfunctional state of the American economy (as Stiglitz (2012) pointed out), for a recovery plan of 2250 billion dollars (1918 billion euros) as announced in March 2021.[2] Beyond the scale of the American plan, which puts the European Union's effort into perspective, we are also surprised by the social objectives of the American plan. While one-third of the plan concerns traditional infrastructure (roads, bridges, public transport), the other two-thirds are almost entirely allocated to social investments, targeting in particular disadvantaged communities. Interestingly though for our topic, in this reflation plan Biden had to drop the project of doubling the minimum wage per hour (from 7.5 dollars up to 15 dollars) to accommodate a specifically strong opposition of the Republicans. In addition nevertheless, the policy of raising corporate taxes still holds as well as a willingness to cooperate internationally to limit tax evasion by large multinational companies.

This may be a real turning point for the core model of market capitalism or at least a clear move to correct the dysfunction of the US social model that Stiglitz (2012) stigmatized. The way in which the budgets are used will be revealing, depending on whether they result in cash transfers to citizens/consumers or an extension of non-market services in the fields of housing, health, education and transport. The lack of emphasis on environmental issues raises concerns that the US plan could rely too heavily on market-based stimulus mechanisms to address the social issue of rising inequality in that country. This environmental issue is much more present in the European Union's (admittedly more modest) recovery plan, but the criteria for these "green deals" are still largely under debate.

On the other hand, the health crisis has highlighted the extent of inequalities in the capacity of the various social classes to cope with the hazards of the pandemic and environmental degradation, even though the collective nature of the scourges in question clearly requires the development of solidarity. Also, although the internal dysfunctions are less acute than in the United States, European countries feel more directly concerned by inequalities since the health crisis and their reduction may become an objective like the search for full employment was at a time. Still in the general drive toward more sustainable modes of development, inequality may be defined in a broader context than income distribution, targeting more a full citizenship, with easy access to public services and involvement in collective activities.

The great unknown in this forced "reset" of the modes of capitalism that we are outlining will be the way in which these adjustments will be articulated at global level. In fact, the challenges facing our societies are global, whether in terms of the environment or health, and national solutions must lead to globally sustainable results. As inequalities between countries remain high, achieving such solutions requires specific aid or cooperation regimes. It has now become clear in the international arena that market mechanisms, such as a carbon tax, cannot guarantee the emergence of such solutions. The levels and intensities of cooperation mechanisms to move rapidly enough toward a sustainable world remain largely to be invented. In other words the challenge for the global community is to find ways to overcome Rodrik's trilemma, building an international accord, global in its environmental scope, reasonably compatible with the specificities of national social contracts and democratic enough for everyone to feel as a responsible citizen of this global federation of states. The solidarities that the deterioration of our environment will fuel can make this new "great transformation" feasible. The preludes can be seen in the fabric of international, governmental or associative, organizations that participate in negotiations on the various issues of preserving our environment and health. The ongoing IPCC negotiations are one of the reference structures of this movement to coordinate efforts, and the role played by the scientific communities is one of the characteristics of this gestation. This positive development, which should favor to be effective, the spread of full and equal citizenship, runs the risk of being dangerously slowed down if not blocked by a confrontation between the United States and China that other countries could not mediate. Beyond this pitfall, the management of this ecological transition should also convert the financial world to fully support new "fair and sustainable" development objectives. This would involve restrictions on property rights and asset controls which are particularly unevenly distributed.

But the change in context that has taken place over the last five years with an increased awareness of the imperatives of the fight against environmental degradation, suddenly amplified by a global health crisis, should favor a reorientation of the management of our societies, implying an increased empowerment of civic virtues. This would put income inequalities in a different perspective if states, in order to ensure this accountability, guaranteed citizens access to a number of goods and services. The introduction of various universal income systems or free access to certain goods and services could facilitate this change. The big question remains whether this major transition will succeed in being established before environmental degradation precipitates a large part of the world into fairly irreversible catastrophic situations. An important factor for citizen mobilization to achieve this goal depends on the ability of the most unequal states to reduce relatively quickly enough the resentment of those they have greatly devalued. This is not an easy task and should be one of the major objectives of the expected transition management.

Disclosure statement

No potential conflict of interest was reported by the author(s).

Notes

1. On the diversity of capitalism, see Hall and Soskice(2001), assessing a lasting dichotomy between fully market led economies and others, Amable and Petit(2001) and Amable (2003) distinguishing five type of capitalisms and Boyer, Uemura and Isaogai (2012), specifying the types of Asian capitalisms.
2. For sure to be spent over 8 years, but following a budget of 1900 billions dollars of transfers to be distributed along the year 2021.

References

Amable, Bruno. 2003. *The Diversity of Modern Capitalism*. Oxford: Oxford University Press.

Amable, Bruno, and Pascal Petit. 2001. The Diversity of Social Systems of Innovation and Production during the 1990s working paper CEPREMAP N° 2001–15 http://www.cepremap.cnrs.fr.

Anghel, Brindusa, Henrique Basso, Olympia Bover, José María Casado, Laura Hospido, Mario Izquierdo, Ivan A. Kataryniuk, Aitor Lacuesta, José Manuel Montero, and Elena Vozmediano. 2018. "Income, Consumption and Wealth Inequality in Spain." *SERIEs* 9(4):351–387. doi:10.1007/s13209-018-0185-1.

Boyer, Robert, Hiroyasu Uemura and Akinori Isogai, eds. 2012. *Diversity and Transformation of Asian Capitalism*. Abingdon/New York: Routledge/Taylor and Francis Group.

Duménil, Gérard, and Dominique Lévy. 2015. "Neoliberal Managerial Capitalism: Another Reading of the Piketty, Saez and Zucman Data." *International Journal of Political Economy* 44 (2):71–89. doi:10.1080/08911916.2015.1060823.

Duménil, Gérard, and Dominique Lévy. 2018. "Managerial Capitalism: Ownership." *Management, & the Coming New Mode of Production*. Londres: Pluto Press.

Esping-Andersen, Gosta. 1999. *Social Foundations of Postindustrial Economies*. Oxford: Oxford University Press.

Esping-Andersen, Gosta. 2002. *Why We Need a New Welfare State*. Oxford: Oxford University Press.

Fortunato, Piergiuseppe. 2021. Inequalities and democratic corrosion, Social Europe March 4th https://www.socialeurope.eu/inequalities-and-democratic-corrosion

Gethin, Amory, Clara Martinez-Toledano, and Thomas Piketty. 2021. *Political Cleavages and Social Inequalities*. Harvard University. https://www.hup.harvard.edu/catalog.php?isbn=9780674248427

Hall, Peter, and David Soskice. 2001. *Varieties of Capitalism*. Oxford: Oxford University Press.

Marglin, Steve and Juliet Shor, eds. 1992. *The Golden Age of Capitalism: Reinterpreting the Post War Experience*, 340. Oxford: Clarendon Press.

Milanovic, Branko. 2016. *Global Inequality: A New Approach for the Age of Globalization*. Cambridge, MA: Harvard University Press.

Petit, Pascal. 1999. "Structural Forms and Growth Regimes of the Post Fordist Era" *Review of Social Economy* 57 (2):220–243. doi:10.1080/00346769900000037.

Piketty, Thomas. 2014. *Capital in the Twenty-First Century*, Harvard University Press, Cambridge, MA.

Piketty, Thomas. 2019. *Capital et idéologie*. Paris: Editions du Seuil Paris.

Rodrik, Dany. 2011. *The Globalization Paradox: Democracy and the Future of the World Economy*. New York: W.W.Norton & Company.

Rousselon, Julien, and Mathilde Viennot. 2020. « Inégalités, redistribution: une comparaison européenne », *Document de travail de France Stratégie*, n°17, décembre 2020.

Stiglitz, Joseph. 2003. *Globalization and its discontents*, 304. New York: W.W. Norton & Company.

Stiglitz, Joseph. 2012. *The Price of Inequality. How Todays' Divided Society Endangers Our Future WW*, 560. New York: Norton & Company.

Tridico, Pasquale. 2020. Global Inequality: Is there a Trade-Off? *Panoeconomicus*, LXVII/5

Whiteford, Peter. 2015. The Tax-Transfer System, Progressivity and Redistribution: How Progressive is the Australian Transfer System? https://www.austaxpolicy.com/the-tax-transfer-system-progressivity-and-redistribution-part-1-how-progressive-is-the-australian-transfer-system/

Transformation of the class structure in contemporary Japan

Kenji Hashimoto

ABSTRACT

Japan had experienced a rapid increase in economic disparity since the early 1980s. This article attempts to quantitatively clarify the structure of economic disparity and its social consequences in contemporary Japan from the perspective of Marxian class theory. Based on the analysis of government statistics and questionnaire survey data, the following facts were revealed. First, the class categories based on Marxian class theory had strong explanatory power for income and social consciousness. Second, in Japanese society, there is an exploitation relationship in which the three classes located in the capitalist mode of production exploit the old middle class located in simple commodity production. Within the capitalist mode of production, the capitalist class and the new middle class are the exploiting classes and the working class is the exploited class, however the central targets of exploitation are the underclass and female workers. Thirdly, the underclass is fundamentally different from the other classes in terms of income, life course, consciousness and living conditions. From the above, we can conclude that Japanese society today is a new class society that includes the underclass as an important element at the bottom of class structure.

Introduction: Expanding disparity and emergence of *"kakusa shakai"*

Expansion of economic disparity in Japan

In 2006, the term *kakusa* shakai became a buzzword in Japan. The Japanese term *kakusa* means disparity, whereas shakai means society, combined *kakusa* shakai is translated to disparity society. The term gained extreme popularity within a short time, and became firmly established as an everyday expression. Until approximately 2010, most of the Japanese has recognized that Japan is a socially divided society with increasing economic disparity.

At first, it would be useful to provide a brief overview of economic disparity in Japan after World War II. Figure 1 demonstrates the two forms

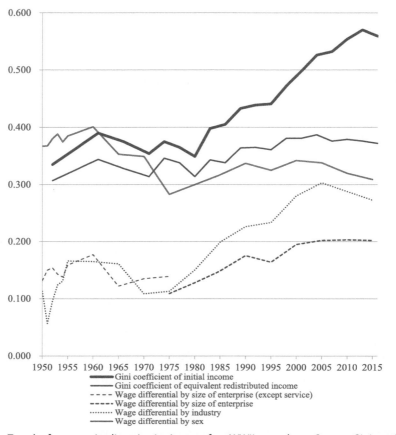

Figure 1. Trend of economic disparity in Japan after WWII *near here. Source.* Gini coefficient : Ministry of Welfare and Labor, Income redistribution survey Wage differential : Ministry of Welfare and Labor, Monthly Labor Survey *Note.* Index of wage differential is (max-min) / (max+min). Initial income is a concept similar to market income, but slightly different in that it includes private benefits. Redistributed income is initial income minus taxes, plus government transfers.

of Gini coefficients on household income and three indicators of wage differentials. Focusing on the Gini coefficient of initial income, which initially significantly increased from 1952 (0.335) to 1960 (0.390), and followed a downward trend and reached the bottom in 1980 (0.349). Since then, it continued to rise sharply for three decades and reach the peak at 2013 (0.570), which slightly declined in 2016 (0.559). The Gini coefficient of redistributed income shows roughly the same trend, which changed within a relatively small range and reached the peak a little earlier than initial income.

The three indices of wage differentials—size of enterprise, industry, and sex—also illustrate the same trend. Especially, wage differential by industry rose sharply from 1975 (0.113) to 2005 (0.303), which was deemed to contribute to the rise in the Gini coefficient. Wage differential between men and women since 1980 has remained below the peak in 1960, but the reason for this trend is that the wage differential in sex was extremely large from the 1950s to the 1960s. The fact that it continued to rise from 1975 to 2000 implies the seriousness of the gender gap in Japan.

In fact, economic disparity in Japan in the mid-1970s was small compared with most industrialized countries in the west (Sawyer 1976). However, economic disparity began to expand in the early 1980s, more than 20 years before *kakusa shakai* became a popular word. According to OECD Income Distribution Database (Accessed January 21, 2021.), the Gini coefficient of the initial income, the Gini coefficient of disposable income, and the poverty rate in Japan are the 10th, 11th, and 10th highest, respectively, among the 36 OECD countries excluding Colombia, which joined the OECD in 2020. Many countries that rank high in these indices are emerging economies, such as Chile, Mexico, and Turkey, and Japan is one of the countries with the greatest disparity when compared only with advanced Western countries.

Kakusa shakai and the class society

Considering these facts, Japan certainly deserves the name of *kakusa shakai*. However, *kakusa* is merely a term describing a state of unequal distribution of social resources, and the term *kakusa shakai* has no more meaning than simply "a society with large disparities". These are non-analytical terms that do not refer to the causes of disparity nor to its structure. We should elucidate the social mechanisms behind the generation and further expansion of such disparities and to do so, we need more social scientific terms. Needless to say, the concept of "class" meets this requirement.

I would like to summarize the theoretical importance of the concept of class as follows.

One of the basic propositions of Marxian social theory is that the mode of production is determinative of other social structures and processes. However, what is the mechanism through which the mode of production determines other social structures and processes? Class is a fundamental concept to give an answer to this question. The mode of production constitutes people into several different groupings, namely, classes, and creates common and conflicting interests. These interests trigger various social behaviors, which in turn determine other social structures and processes.

Thus, the concept of class, while starting from an economic concept, provides a basis for the analysis of more complex and concrete social phenomena and mediates between the economic realm and those of society and politics. In this sense, class is a fundamental concept that ensures that Marxian social theory is not just an economic theory, but a comprehensive social theory.

From a sociological perspective, the concept of class is an essential unit of analysis for the study of social phenomena. Sociology deals with much more diverse and complex social phenomena compared to economics. For this reason, sociology requires a unit of analysis at the intermediate level, in addition to a unit of analysis at the micro-level, such as the individual or household, or at the macro-level, such as the national economy. Such intermediate units of analysis are various concepts such as class, social groups, ethnicity, and gender. However, class is the most important unit of analysis among these intermediate units, at least in capitalist society. This is because, ethnicity and gender do not exist independently of class, they often become important by determining one's class location or creating divisions within a class (Hartman 1981; Westergaard 1993; Mann 1986), and social groups are often formed on the basis of classes.

From this perspective, class is the basis of various disparities, and *kakusa shakai* is nothing but a society in which people are divided into various classes, that is, the appearance form of a class society. The purpose of this study is to empirically analyze the current state of Japanese society, which has come to be known as *kakusa shakai*, from this perspective.

Class structure in contemporary capitalism

Scheme of class structure

To analyze the current state of Japanese society in relation to class structure, it is necessary to establish a scheme of class structure and to develop procedures for operationalizing the concept of class and measuring the class locations of the respondents. In essence, this study is adopting an appropriate combination of several schemes of class structure and methods of empirical research that have been proposed in the 1970s and 1980s. Such methods were formulated from the perspective of structuralist and analytical Marxism.

Class theories since the mid-1970s are best represented by Nicos Poulantzas, Erik Olin Wright, and John Roemer. First, Poulantzas (1974) developed the ideas of Althusser and Balibar in the mid-1970s. Based on the differentiation of levels of structure, multi-dimensional concept of possession, and coexistence/articulation of multiple modes of production, he established a scheme of class structure of contemporary capitalist society, which consists of four classes, namely, the bourgeoisie, new petit bourgeoisie that consists of managers and profesionals, old petit bourgeoisie that consist of self-employed, and proletariat.

Wright (1978, 1979) criticized Poulantzas' class theory from the aspects of theoretical conformity and data-based verification. However, the fundamentals of Poulantzas' theory, multi-dimensional concept of possession, and coexistence/articulation of multiple modes of production were maintained. In addition, Wright situated the bourgeoisie and proletariat in the capitalist mode of production (CMP) and the petit bourgeoisie in simple commodity production (SCP), which is another mode of production originating in the feudal mode of production.

Furthermore, Wright introduced a new concept of "contradictory class locations."

He argued that there are "contradictory class locations" between the bourgeoisie and proletariat, and here located managers, technocrats and supervisors, who are employed and not involved in the legal ownership of the means of production as well as proletariat, and are involved in the effective control of the means of production as well as bourgeoisie. Thus, Wright formulated the class structure of contemporary capitalist society. In addition, he used employment status, control of the labor process, company size, and other variables to operationalize this concept of class. Moreover, he conducted quantitative analysis based on survey data and proved that the explanatory power of class categories is stronger than the occupational status scale commonly used in sociology (Wright 1978, 1979).

Although Wright argued that "contradictory class positions" exist between the bourgeoisie and petit bourgeoisie and between the petit bourgeoisie and proletariat at the outset, he later retracted this idea. In other words, he eventually arrived at a four-class scheme.

Furthermore, later on, Wright proposed another scheme of class structure that consists of 12 classes, based on Roemer's theory that in capitalist society, there exists not only exploitation based on the means of production, but also exploitation based on organization and skill (Wright 1985, Roemer 1982). However, this scheme can be further reduced to the four-class scheme by integrating the categories.

The four-class scheme consists of the bourgeoisie (capitalist class), new petit bourgeoisie (new middle class), proletariat (working class), and old petit bourgeoisie (old middle class). By the 1990s, it was seen as a common element of or at least compatible with most class structure schemes (Waters 1991; Edgell 1993).

Based on the discussion so far, I postulate the following schemes of class structure. In capitalist society, production activities are conducted in two modes of production, namely, capitalist mode of production and simple commodity production, which coexist and are articulated mutually. A difference is observed in the organic composition of capital between the two modes of production. That is, such a difference is higher and lower for the capitalist mode of production and simple commodity production, respectively, which creates economic disparity between the two modes of

Table 1. Criteria for identification of class locations.

	Effective control of the means of production	Capitalist exploitation	Organic composition of capital
Capitalist class	+	Exploiting	High
New middle class	min.~+	Exploiting mildly or Exploited mildly	
Working class	0	Exploited	
Old middle class	min.~+	Not relevant	Low

production because, as Roemer (1982) has demonstrated, exploitation relations are generated between sectors with different organic compositions of capital.

The ownership of the means of production consists of ownership in the legal sense and the power to dispose or utilize the means of production. Although Roemer and Wright argued that the status in the organization and skills of employees are the basis for exploitation independent of the means of production, in fact these are considered to be the basis for exploitation through the disposition and utilization of the means of production. Therefore, ownership in the legal sense and the power to dispose or utilize the means of production can be collectively called "effective control of the means of production." Those located in the capitalist mode of production belong to the capitalist class, new middle class, and the working class. These classes are designated according to the degree of involvement in the effective control of the means of production and occupy different locations in the capitalist relations of exploitation. Those situated in simple commodity production constitute the old middle class and are not involved in the capitalist relation of exploitation.

Table 1 presents the criteria for the identification of class position. Figure 2 depicts the basic scheme of the class structure of the contemporary capitalist society.

Emergence of the underclass

The four-class scheme shown above is considered a class structure scheme that is commonly applicable to contemporary capitalist societies. However, significant changes have occurred in the working class recently. This is because there has been a significant increase in low-wage non-regular workers within the working class, and it seems increasingly difficult to see the working class as a single, internally homogeneous class.

Table 2 indicates the changes in economic conditions between 2005 and 2015, dividing the working class into regular workers and non-regular workers. Part-time housewife workers (female non-regular workers with spouse), who often work to complement their household income only for a short time each week, are excluded. We also limited the age of the

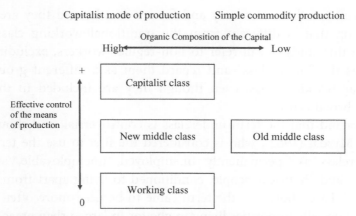

Figure 2. Scheme of class structure in contemporary capitalist society.

Table 2. Divided Working class.

	2005	2015	Δ
Individual income(1000 yen)			
Regular worker	3615	3745	130
Non-regular worker	1914	1865	−49
Household income(1000 yen)			
Regular worker	6098	6448	350
Non-regular worker	4092	3427	−665
Poverty rate			
Regular worker	8.6	6.3	−2.3
Non-regular worker	40.0	38.7	−1.3

Source. 2015 SSM Survey data
Notes. household income is the sum of the incomes of all family members who share the same livelihood.

respondents to under 60 years old so that pension income would not be included.

There is a large disparity between regular and non-regular workers in terms of both individual and household income, but the direction of change is opposite. In the decade since 2005, the annual individual income of regular workers has increased by 130,000 yen, while that of non-regular workers has decreased by 49,000 yen. The annual household income of regular workers increased by 350,000 yen, while that of non-regular workers decreased by 665,000 yen. There has also been a change in the poverty rate. The poverty rate for regular workers has decreased by 2.3% to 6.3%, and they are now almost free from poverty. In contrast, the poverty rate for non-regular workers, although slightly decreased, is still high at 38.7%, more than six times the rate for regular workers.

The working class is considered the lower and largest exploited class in capitalist society. However, regular workers, who constitute the majority of the working class, have been ensured relatively stable employment, especially in the manufacturing industry. In contrast, the rapidly increasing non-regular workers have precarious employment, and their wages are much lower than those of regular workers. In addition, as we will see later, it is difficult for them to marry and form a family, and they are constituting a group that is different from the traditional working class. For this reason, in this study, I will refer to non-regular workers, excluding married women, as the "underclass" and regard them as a different grouping from the regular working class, even though they are included in the working class in a broad sense.

I understand that the term underclass is controversial, and should be used carefully. Myrdal (1962), who is considered the first to use the term, defined the underclass as "permanently unemployed, unemployable, and under-employed" and "hopeless people, conditioned to living apart from the rest of the nation". Later, however, the term came to be used more often to refer to the poor, especially minorities living in ghettos in large urban areas, emphasizing the unique culture and behavioral patterns that cause deviance, immorality, and poverty, rather than the objective economic conditions. Therefore, under-class has been understood as a contentious concept with discriminatory nuances.

However, in the sociological studies of class and stratification, the under-class has been understood as a more general grouping.

Crompton argued, the underclass is "those in persistent poverty", and the existence of the underclass is "normal in a competitive capitalist society" (Crompton 1993, 158). Similarly, Edgell (1993) argued, the underclass is "the underemployed and unemployed fraction of the working class", and its existence is "regular feature of the class structure of advanced capitalist societies"(Edgell 1993, 80).

The existence of such a lower class has been commonly acknowledged in many countries, but it is called by various terms according to different countries and authors. Esping-Andersen (1999) argues that "there are signs that some losers are forming into long-term socially excluded strata" in many countries, and that the current situation is called by different names in different countries, such as the 'A-team and B-team', the 'two-third society', the 'two-speed society', and the 'underclass'. However, among these terms, the "underclass" seems to most accurately describe and give a clear picture of the reality of this class.

So how can the underclass be located in the class structure scheme described above? Theoretically, it could be considered as follows.

The working class is a subordinate class in capitalist society, and the continued existence of this class is an essential condition for the continued existence of capitalism. The prerequisite for this is that labor power can be sold at a price equal to its value, so that labor power can be reproduced daily, and that the working class can have and raise children, so that the working class can be reproduced on a generational basis.

Recently, however, the increasing influence of neoliberalism and the decline of labor unions have upset the balance of power between labor and capital, increasing the number of workers who are paid less than the value of their labor power. More specifically, for certain segments of workers, the reproduction of labor power has been redefined in a way that excludes the generational reproduction. The wages they receive barely allow them to survive and continue to work, but are insufficient to form a family and have and raise children. Thus, they become workers without the next generation. Marx argued " the maintenance and reproduction of the working-class is, and must ever be, a necessary condition to the reproduction of capital. But the capitalist may safely leave its fulfillment to the labourer's instincts of self-preservation and of propagation" (Marx 1867, Kap.21, Marx and Engels 1887, chap.23). However, as regards the contemporary underclass, such a condition is not fulfilled. This faction of the working class is emerging as non-regular workers other than part-time housewives.

More generally, the underclass can be defined as a grouping of people who are particularly impoverished among the lower classes of a society because they lack some of the minimum requirements of the lower classes. Contemporary non-regular workers are part of the working class, but they are impoverished because they do not meet the essential requirements of the working class in the sense that they are unable to sell their labor power consistently, and even when they do, their wages are far below the value of their labor power. From this viewpoint, the underclass is not limited to the non-regular working class. For example, the urban miscellaneous self-employed workers and tenant farmers in modern Japan were part of the old middle class, but they were impoverished because they owned few means of production or rented means of production from others.

With the emergence of the underclass, the class structure in contemporary Japan is significantly transforming. This is because the traditional four-class structure has been transformed into a de facto five-class structure by the formation of dividing lines within the working class. I will call this society with new class structure "the new class society".

Operationalization of class categories

After establishing the scheme of class structure, it is necessary to translate the theoretical class categories into operational ones that can be applied on empirical data. The study of Ohashi (1959, 1971) is useful for this purpose.

In postwar Japan, class studies have been developed as "class composition studies" primarily conducted by Ohashi (1959). He developed a simple method to translate class categories into operationalized ones by reconstructing the cross-tabulation tables of employment status and occupation in the Population Census. Based on this method, this study employs a new method of operationalization by adding two additional elements, namely, the size of employment and gender segregation of classes (for further details, see Hashimoto 2003).

The size of employment is a criterion used to differentiate between the capitalist class and old middle class. People whose employment status is employer, executive, or self-employed can be regarded as belonging to the capitalist class, or old middle class if their employment size is five or more and four or less, respectively.

I set the boundary between the capitalist class and the old middle class in this manner because most of the statistical surveys on enterprises cover enterprises with not less than five employees, and the common notion of "enterprise" generally refers to businesses with five or more employees, and the data show that income and living conditions of business owners and self-employed people change greatly beyond this boundary. According to data from the 2015 SSM survey, in companies with 2–4 employees, the annual income of the manager and employee is not significantly different, at 2972 and 2071 thousand yen, respectively. However, when the number of employees increases to 5–9, the difference is about twice as large, at 4224 and 2289 thousand yen, and the difference becomes larger as the size of the company increases up to 299 employees. This suggests that the proportion of the surplus-value in managers' income changes significantly after the five-employee size.

The gender segregation within occupational grouping is important for the classification of employees. Depending on the occupation, employees can be classified as new middle class or working class. However, class location may vary by gender even for people in the same occupation. This problem is especially important for clerical jobs because male clerical workers typically hold expertise and authority and are more likely to be promoted to managerial positions. In contrast, until recently in Japan, female clerical workers are less likely to hold expertise and authority, then are less likely promoted. For this reason, male and female regular clerical workers are classified as new middle class and working class, respectively. However, non-regular clerical workers are classified as working class, regardless of gender.

Table 3 presents the composition of class categories. Various quantitative analyses (see Hashimoto 2000, 2003 for details) have confirmed the validity of this class category.

To distinguish the underclass from the regular working class, the following method is applied. Although the majority of non-regular employees are classified as underclass, most of the female non-regular employees with spouses are not vulnerable to poverty because their husbands usually work

Table 3. Making of class categories.

	Regular employees	Non-regular employees	employers, executives or self-employed
Professional	New middle class		Enterprises with 5 workers
Managerial			or more: Capitalist class
Clerical	Male: New middle class	Working class	Enterprises with 4 workers
	Female: Working class		or less: Old middle class
Others	Working class		
Unknown	Excluded or working class		

Note: People whose occupation is unknown should be excluded from the analysis, but in recent surveys the number of respondents who do not answer their occupation has increased. Since it is unlikely that the actual occupation of respondents who do not answer their occupation are professional, managerial, or clerical, we will classify them into working class categories when we analyze the recent data, if appropriate.

as regular employees and support their livelihood. For this reason, only male or single female non-regular workers are classified as underclass, whereas female non-regular workers with a spouse are classified as part-time housewife workers.

Data

In this study, I employ government statistics and two questionnaire survey data. These are, Employment Status Survey, SSM survey and Tokyo Metropolitan Area Residents Survey.

Employment Status Survey is a large-scale government survey. The most fundamental population survey in Japan is the National Census, but because it is an extremely large scale survey covering all people living in Japan, the questionnaire length is limited. In order to analyze the class structure, it is necessary to distinguish between the size of companies and the marital status of non-regular workers, but it is not possible to distinguish these on the basis of the National Census. For this reason, this study uses the publicized tabulations of the Employment Status Survey.

SSM Survey is a large-scale survey conducted every ten years since 1955 by a group of sociologists specializing in the study of class and stratification, and is officially called the National Survey on Social Stratification and Social Mobility. The 2015 survey was funded by Japan Society for the Promotion of Science KAKENHI, grant no. 25000001, and targeted people aged 20–79 nationwide, with 7,817 valid responses. Permission to use the data was obtained from the Data Management Committee of the 2015 SSM Survey. The data used were February 27, 2017 version (version 070).

Tokyo Metropolitan Area Residents Survey, conducted in 2016, is characterized by a large number of questions on health conditions, worries, depression and stress in order to clarify the impact of disparity and poverty on people. The survey targeted people aged 20–69 living within 50 km of central Tokyo, with 2351 valid responses. The survey was supported by

Table 4. Annual individual income of 4 classes (1000 yen).

Capitalist mode of production (CMP)	
Capitalist class	6044
New middle class	4992
Working class	2626
Mean of CMP	3575
Simple commodity production (SCP)	
Old middle class	3029
Total	3493

Source. 2015 SSM Survey data

Japan Society for the Promotion of Science KAKENHI, grant no. 15H01970.

Class structure and economic disparities

Economic disparities and exploitation relations

Table 4 shows the disparity in individual income among the four major classes. Comparing the four classes, the capitalist class has the highest income (6044 thousand yen), the second is the new middle class (4992 thousand yen), the third is the old middle class (3029 thousand yen), and the lowest is the working class (2626 thousand yen). The average annual personal income of the three classes in the CMP is 3575 thousand yen.

It might be questioned whether average individual income of the about 6 million yen, or roughly $57,000, is high enough to deserve the name of the capitalist class. However, this amount is reasonable because the vast majority of the capitalist class are small capitalists, and Japanese economy has not grown at all in the last 20 years.

Let us simplify the mechanism of exploitation and focus only on the exploitation relations between classes as expressed in the income distribution among individuals. Assuming that the working hours of each class are roughly the same, the location of each class in the exploitation relations can be evaluated by comparing the amount of the average individual income of each class and the average individual income of the whole. The average annual individual income of the three classes located in the CMP (3575 thousand yen) is higher than the average of the four classes (3493 thousand yen) and the old middle class (3029 thousand yen).This fact suggests the existence of an exploitation relation through unequal exchange between the two modes of production, based on differences in the organic composition of capital. Comparing the three classes located in the CMP, the average individual income of the capitalist class and the new middle class is higher than the CMP average, while only the working class is lower than the CMP average. This suggests that within the CMP, the capitalist class and the new middle class are the exploiting classes, while only the working class is the exploited class.

Table 5. Annual individual income of 4 classes by sex (1000 yen).

	Total	Male	Female	F/M
Capitalist mode of production (CMP)				
Capitalist class	6044	7805	2957	0.379
New middle class	4992	5964	3381	0.567
Working class	2626	3656	1844	0.504
Mean of CMP	3575	4883	2249	0.461
Simple commodity production (SCP)				
Old middle class	3029	3839	1745	0.454
Total	3493	4699	2189	0.466

Source. 2015 SSM Survey data

However, gender disparity is as important as the class disparity in economic disparity in Japan. This is because Japan is one of the countries in the highly industrialized world where the income disparity between men and women is the largest. Table 5 shows the average annual personal income by class and by gender. As can be seen at a glance, the economic disparity between male and female is extremely large. The disparity between male and female is greatest in the capitalist class because in many small businesses in Japan, the wives of business owners are often nominally executives, however receive little or no remuneration. Similarly, in the old middle class, wives often work as family employees but receive little compensation. This increases the gender disparity in the old middle class.

However, in reality, the gender disparity in individual income is not so serious with regard to these two classes. This is because almost small businesses and self-employed businesses are family businesses, and husbands and wives share their bussinesses and livelihoods, and their incomes are combined and utilized for consumption. The gender disparity is more serious in the classes of employed people.

The gender disparity is also large for the employed classes, the new middle class and the working class. Looking at the individual incomes of the three classes located in the CMP by gender, the incomes of males in all classes are above the CMP average, while the incomes of females in all classes are below the CMP average. This fact suggests that Japanese capitalism is characterized more by the exploitation of female by male than by the exploitation between classes.

As mentioned previously, the working class is increasingly divided into regular workers and non-regular workers. In addition, married female non-regular workers, who make up a large portion of non-regular workers, often work as short-time workers to supplement the household while being financially supported by their husbands who work as regular workers. Then, dividing the working class into three categories: regular workers, non-regular workers (i.e., underclass), and part-time housewife workers, Table 6 shows their individual and household annual incomes, and the

Table 6. Annual individual and household income of 4 classes (1000 yen).

	Individual income	Household income	Poverty rate (%)
Capitalist mode of production (CMP)			
Capitalist class	6044	10,598	4.2
New middle class	4992	7981	2.6
Working class (total)	2626	5645	12.2
Regular worker	3698	6303	7.0
Non-regular worker: Underclass	2269	3908	27.5
Part-time housewife workers	1161	6001	8.3
Mean of CMP	3575	6766	8.6
Simple commodity production (SCP)			
Old middle class	3029	5875	17.2
Total	3493	6634	9.8

Source. 2015 SSM Survey data.

poverty rate as an indicator of whether the household income ensures a minimum standard of living.

The annual personal income of part-time housewife workers (1,161,000 yen) is extremely low, but this is mainly due to their short annual working hours. Their annual household income (6001 thousand yen), including their husbands' income, is slightly lower than that of regular workers, but is sufficient to live on, and the poverty rate is only 8.3%. Their wage rates are very low, so there is no doubt that these housewives are exploited as individuals, but their husbands, who often stand on the side of the exploiters, probably get a good portion of their exploited share back. In contrast, the annual individual income of the underclass (2269 thousand yen) is only about 0.6 times that of regular workers, the annual household income (3908 thousand yen) is also extremely low, and their poverty rate is extremely high at 27.5%. The annual individual income of regular workers (3698 thousand yen) is not only much higher than the underclass, but also slightly higher than the CMP average and the overall average. Household income is slightly below the CMP average and the overall average, although the poverty rate is not high at 7.0%. This suggests that it is the underclass that is most exploited in Japanese capitalism, and that regular workers are rather neutral in the exploitation relations, and male regular workers are often located on the side of the exploiters. More precisely, with the increase of non-regular workers, the status as regular worker has now become relatively scarce asset, which allows regular workers to exploit the underclass on the basis of their status, while being exploited on the basis of the means of production. Thus, they came to occupy the intermediate position in the exploitation relationships.

From the above examination, we can conclude that it is essential to distinguish between the regular working class and the underclass when examining class disparity in Japanese society. As for part-time housewife workers, their class location as non-regular workers does not determine their standard of living, and it is inappropriate to always regard them as

Table 7. Changes in class composition 1992–2017.

	1992	1997	2002	2007	2012	2017
Capitalist class	396.5	371.6	334.8	313.2	254.4	219.4
	(6.2%)	(5.7%)	(5.3%)	(4.9%)	(4.1%)	(3.5%)
New middle class	1170.7	1232.8	1220.5	1267.2	1285.5	1449.6
	(18.3%)	(18.9%)	(19.4%)	(19.8%)	(20.6%)	(22.8%)
Working class (Total)	3628.7	3782.6	3730.5	3903.5	3905.9	3933.4
	(56.6%)	(58.1%)	(59.2%)	(60.9%)	(62.5%)	(61.9%)
Regular working class	2636.8	2650.0	2322.3	2314.3	2192.5	2194.1
	(41.1%)	(40.7%)	(36.8%)	(36.1%)	(35.1%)	(34.5%)
Underclass	392.5	493.1	709.8	846.7	928.7	913.4
	(6.1%)	(7.6%)	(11.3%)	(13.2%)	(14.9%)	(14.4%)
Part-time housewife workers	599.4	639.4	698.3	742.5	784.8	825.9
	(9.3%)	(9.8%)	(11.1%)	(11.6%)	(12.6%)	(13.0%)
Old middle class	1215.0	1126.4	1020.1	927.6	806.0	629.7
	(19.0%)	(17.3%)	(16.2%)	(14.5%)	(12.9%)	(9.9%)
Total	6410.9	6513.5	6305.9	6411.5	6251.8	6353.7
	(100.0%)	(100.0%)	(100.0%)	(100.0%)	(100.0%)	(100.0%)

Source. Statistics Bureau of Japan, Employment Status Survey.

having their own class location. Therefore, in analyzing the disparity between classes, I will use the four-class scheme as a basis and use the five-class scheme, which divides the working class into regular workers and underclass and excludes part-time housewife workers, in combination.

The class composition

Table 7 is a class composition table from 1992 to 2017, which distinguishes the working class into three fractions: the regular working class, the underclass, and part-time housewife workers.

The capitalist class and the old middle class have been consistently decreasing, while the working class has been increasing. Over the past 25 years, the class structure of Japan as a whole has shown a typical progression of capitalist purification and proletarianization, with the decomposition of the capitalist class and the old middle class, and the expansion of the working class. However, with the recent rapid increase in the number of professionals in the health care and nursing care sectors, the new middle class grew considerably between 2012 and 2017, while the proportion of the working class declined slightly. The underclass, which accounted for only 6.1% of the working population in 1992, grew rapidly since then, especially between 1997 and 2007, and by 2012 accounted for 14.9%, exceeding the old middle class, which accounted for 12.9%. It can be argued that the underclass is already one of the major elements of Japan's class structure, albeit with a slight decline in 2017. In contrast, the number of part-time housewife workers has been increasing, but the change has been slow, and they have ceded their place in the mainstream of non-regular workers to the underclass.

Table 8. Multiple regression for effects on indivudual income.

	Adjusted R^2	Increment in R^2
Male		
Only basic variables	0.134	—
Basic + Occupational categories	0.228	0.094
Basic + Class categories (4 classes)	0.232	0.098
Basic + Class categories (5 classes)	0.258	0.124
Female		
Only basic variables	0.102	—
Basic + Occupational categories	0.134	0.032
Basic + Class categories (4 classes)	0.154	0.052
Basic + Class categories (5 classes)	0.184	0.082

Source. 2015 SSM Survey data.
Note. Employed except part-time housewife workers. Basic variables are age, age squared, years of schooling. Occupational categories are professional, adminitral, clerical, sales, service, security, agricultural/forestry/fisheries, manual.

Explanatory power of class categories

Next, I will examine the extent to which the five-class scheme can explain economic disparity, using multiple regression analysis. Table 8 presents the results of the multiple regression analysis of individual annual income. First, only the basic variables (age, age squared, and years of education) were used as independent variables, and then the eight occupational categories, the four class categories, and the five class categories (four class categories with the underclass added) were added as dummy variables, and the coefficients of determination (R2) were compared. As mentioned earlier, the income levels of males and females differ significantly, so the analysis is conducted separately by gender.

When only basic variables are used, R2 is 0.134 for males and 0.102 for females. In other words, age and years of education account for 13.4% of the variance in income for male and 10.2% for female. When eight occupational categories are added, R2 increases by 0.094–0.228 for male and by 0.032–0.134 for female. In contrast, when four class categories are added, R2 increases by 0.099–0.232 for male and by 0.052–0.154 for female. Compared to the eight occupational categories, the four class categories showed a larger increment in R2 and better explanatory power, even though the number of categories was smaller. Furthermore, when five class categories with underclass were used, R2 increased to 0.258 for male and 0.184 for female, indicating superb results.

To what extent is the disparity between classes reflected in people's consciousness? Table 9 shows the results of the same multiple regression analysis using subjective status identity as the dependent variable. When only the basic variables are used, R2 is small, 0.079 for male and 0.054 for female, but when the class categories are added, the explanatory power increases remarkably. The increment of R2 is larger for the 5 class categories (male: 0.058, female: 0.057) than for the 4 class categories (Male: 0.044, Female: 0.036). In contrast, when the eight occupational categories were

Table 9. Multiple regression for effects on subjective status identification.

	Adjusted R^2	Increment in R^2
Male		
Only basic variables	0.079	—
Basic + Occupational categories	0.108	0.029
Basic + Class categories (4 classes)	0.123	0.044
Basic + Class categories (5 classes)	0.137	0.058
Female		
Only basic variables	0.054	—
Basic + Occupational categories	0.073	0.019
Basic + Class categories (4 classes)	0.090	0.036
Basic + Class categories (5 classes)	0.107	0.053
Male under 59 years old		
Only basic variables	0.098	—
Basic + Occupational categories	0.127	0.029
Basic + Class categories (4 classes)	0.142	0.044
Basic + Class categories (5 classes)	0.172	0.074

Source. 2015 SSM Survey data.
Note. Employed except part-time housewife workers. See Table 5 for variables. Subjective status identification is measured in five levels: upper, upper-middle, middle-middle, lower-middle and lower.

added, the increment of R2 was small (Male: 0.029, Female: 0.019), and the superiority of the class categories in terms of explanatory power is clear.

Table 9 also shows the result of another analysis. In Japan, many male regular employees work as non-regular workers after retirement. This is because they want to earn an income to supplement their insufficient pensions, but because they have worked as regular employees for many years, they often have some assets, and even though their wages as non-regular workers are small, their lives are relatively stable and they tend to consider their level of living to be "middle" or higher. If these people are included in the underclass, the difference between the underclass and the other classes is likely to become unclear. Therefore, in order to exclude these people, a multiple regression analysis was conducted only for men under 59 years old, and the results are shown in the bottom part of Table 9. When the class categories are added, R2 are even larger, especially when 5 class categories are added, reaches 0.175.

Characteristics and internal composition of the underclass

Table 10 compares the various characteristics and economic conditions of the underclass with the other classes. There is not much difference in the proportion of female. In terms of age, the underclass has a significantly higher proportion of elderly people, with 48.5% of the population in their 60 s or older. This is because, as mentioned earlier, many of them are reemployed after retirement. The difference between the elderly and the young in the underclass will be examined in detail later. In terms of education, the proportion of higher-educated persons is relatively small, with a relatively high proportion of secondary school graduates (17.0%).

Table 10. Characteristics of the underclass.

	Underlass (%)	Other classes (%)
Proprtions of female	40.2	38.4
Age		
20s	15.3	10.9
30s	12.7	19.9
40s	12.1	25.2
50s	11.2	21.9
60s	37.6	14.5
70s	10.9	7.5
Education		
Received only compulsory education	17.0	7.3
Received higher education	23.1	41.6
Occupation		
Professional	0.0	25.1
Administrative	0.0	3.8
clerical	17.6	19.7
Sales	12.7	11.2
Service	18.4	7.8
Security	3.6	1.0
Agricultural/forestry/fisheries	2.3	6.1
Manual	45.4	25.2
Marital status		
Unmarried	34.1	20.8
Married	37.5	71.7
Divorced or Widowed	28.4	7.5

Source. 2015 SSM Survey data. Note. Employed except part-time housewife workers. Other classes consist of capitalist, new middle, working and old middle classes.

In terms of occupation, nearly half of the respondents (45.4%) were in manual jobs, and a relatively large proportion (18.4%) were in service jobs. The occupational categories with a larger number of respondents were sales clerks (47 persons), office clerks (20), cooks (18), waiters (18), cleaners (15), cashiers (13), warehouse workers and transporters (12). Most of them are working in jobs that support people's lives and the business activities at the bottom. In terms of marital status, 34.1% of the respondents are unmarried, and 28.4% are divorced or widowed.

However, the underclass is not homogeneous and varies greatly by age and gender. In particular, the elderly male underclass aged 60 and above often have long careers as regular employees, and the majority are pensioners and often have a certain amount of financial asset. Figure 11 shows the characteristics of the four types of underclass based on age and gender (Table 11).

The average weekly working hours of male underclass under 60 year old is relatively long (38.3 h), and in reality, 57.1% (not shown in the table) of them work more than 40 h. In terms of occupation, manual workers account for nearly 60%, followed by service and sales workers. A striking feature is the exceptionally high proportion of unmarried (66.4%), which suggests that the majority of these people will never marry until they reach the age of 50, making them so-called "lifetime unmarrieds". Individual and household incomes are the only 2130 thousand yen and 3838 thousand

Table 11. Four types of the underclass.

	Male under 60 years old	Female under 60 years old	Male over 60 years old	Female over 60 years old
Proportion in total underclass	23.1%	28.4%	36.7%	11.8%
Average worktime per week (h)	38.3	34.6	31.0	24.2
Occupation				
Clerical	9.2%	24.6%	17.4%	17.9%
Sales	11.8%	23.5%	7.4%	5.1%
Service	16.4%	25.7%	7.0%	39.7%
Security	3.3%	0.5%	7.4%	0.0%
Agricultural/forestry/fisheries	1.3%	0.5%	4.5%	1.3%
Manual	57.9%	25.1%	56.2%	35.9%
Marital status				
Unmarried	66.4%	56.1%	5.0%	9.0%
Married	25.7%	0.0%	86.0%	0.0%
Divorced or Widowed	7.9%	43.9%	9.1%	91.0%
Economic conditions				
Annual individual income (1000 yen)	2130	1639	2931	1926
Annual household income (1000 yen)	3838	3028	4589	3115
Poverty rate	28.6%	48.5%	17.1%	24.0%
No financial asset	42.5%	41.7%	17.1%	30.6%
Proportion of pensioners	0.7%	6.6%	77.3%	85.3%
Satisfied with job (satisfied + more or less satisfied)	18.4%	32.8%	42.3%	49.4%
Satisfied with earned income (same as above)	5.9%	10.2%	20.9%	31.2%
Satisfied with life (same as above)	13.8%	22.5%	30.2%	32.1%

Source: 2015 SSM Survey data

yen, respectively. The poverty rate has reached 28.6%, and the proportion of households with no financial assets at all has reached 42.5%. Only 18.4% are satisfied with their jobs, only 5.9% are satisfied with their income from work, and only 13.8% are satisfied with their lives. In terms of both reality and consciousness, these people can be said to occupy the lowest strata of Japanese society.

The average weekly working hours of the female underclass under 60 years old is slightly shorter (34.6 h), however 45.9% still work 40 h or more. In terms of occupation, almost a quarter each work as clerical, sales, service, and manual workers. The majority of them (56.1%) are unmarried, while remaining 43.9% are divorced or widowed. Another important feature of this group is that it includes many single mothers, 40.1% of female underclass under 60 live with their children (not shown in the table). Their individual and household incomes are only 1603 thousand yen and 3,028 thousand yen, respectively, and the poverty rate is as high as 48.5%. This is the group with the worst economic conditions. However, 32.8% of them were satisfied with their jobs and 22.5% with their lives, both of which are nearly twice as high as the male underclass under 59.

In contrast, for the underclass aged 60 and over, individual income is 2931 thousand yen for men and 1926, thousand yen for women, which is considerably more than the underclass aged under 60 years old, and household income is also slightly higher, this is because about 80% of them are pensioners. The poverty rate is relatively low, and the proportion of people satisfied with their lives is not low. Therefore, these people over the age of 60 are not typical underclass who remain in the lower class throughout most of their lives. For this reason, in the next section, we will present the results of the analysis limiting the underclass to those under 60 years old.

Five classes, five life-worlds

Table 12 summarizes economic conditions, marital status, educational background, satisfaction with job and life, subjective happiness, rate of unionization and political support of five classes, including the underclass. The tabulation covers the entire working population except for part-time housewife workers and the underclass over 60 years old. This enables us to sketch the profiles of the five classes.

Capitalist class

The capitalist class is the dominant class in capitalist society, but it is also the smallest class. Needless to say, this is the richest class, however because it includes small business owners, the poverty rate is 4.2%, higher than the new middle class. Not only they earn the amount of income, they also own the amount assets, with total household assets of 48.633 million yen, including financial assets of 23.126 million yen, and the proportion of households with no assets is extremely low. The proportion of those with higher education (42.3%) is the second highest after the new middle class.

As might be expected, most of them are satisfied with their circumstances, and the proportion of those who are satisfied with their jobs and lives are 47.7% and 45.1%, respectively, the highest proportions among the five classes. The proportion of those who feel that they are happy also reached 67.9%.

Needless to say, this class is politically conservative, supporting for the conservative governing party, the Liberal Democrats Party, at 47.7%, well above the other classes. The proportion of those who do not support any political party is low (35.1%), which is about 10–30% lower than the other classes. It can be characterized as an economically privileged, contented, and politically conservative.

New middle class

The new middle class is the second most affluent class after the capitalist class. The poverty rate is the lowest at 2.6%, so it can be said that this class is almost free from poverty. However, the total amount of household asset is 23.53 million yen, of which the financial asset are 9.465 million yen,

Table 12. Characteristics of five classes.

	Capitalist class	New middle class	Regular working class	Underclass	Old middle class
Poverty rate	4.2%	2.6%	7.0%	38.7%	17.2%
Average amount of household assets (million yen)	48.63	23.53	14.28	11.19	29.17
Average amount of household financial assets (million yen)	23.13	9.46	5.72	5.36	11.13
No asset at all	3.5%	5.9%	14.5%	31.5%	11.1%
Received higher education	42.3%	61.4%	30.5%	27.7%	27.2%
Satisfied with job (satisfied + more or less satisfied)	47.7%	37.8%	32.3%	26.3%	41.4%
Satisfied with life (same as above)	45.1%	36.3%	35.6%	18.6%	32.5%
Subjective happiness	67.9%	64.1%	52.6%	38.4%	53.4%
Organized into labor unions	–	28.9%	38.9%	13.8%	–
Political party support					
LDP	47.4%	27.5%	24.1%	15.3%	35.5%
No party	35.1%	56.6%	61.3%	67.9%	46.0%

Source. 2015 SSM Survey data.
Notes. Employed except part-time housewife workers. The underclass is for under 60 years old only. All other classes are 20–79 years old. Subjective happiness is the proportion of people with a score of 7 or higher on a 10-point scale

which is lower than the old middle class. Their educational background is high, with 61.4% of them having higher education.

The proportion of those who are satisfied with their jobs and lives is the second highest after the capitalist class, but there is a fairly large difference from the capitalist class, about 10%. However, subjective happiness is much closer to the capitalist class, with 64.1% feeling they are happy.

Thus although the new middle class is certainly affluent and contented, it is not exactly politically conservative, with only 27.5% supporting for the LDP, the proportion of those who do not support any party is 56.6%, and 28.9% are members of labor unions.

Regular working class

The working class is the subordinate class in capitalist society. However, the income of the regular working class, which consists of workers with secure employment, is not low and exceeds that of the old middle class. So, they can be seen as rather neutral in the exploitation relations, as shown earlier. The poverty rate is 7.0%, which is not high. However, total household assets are small at 14.28 million yen, most of which are real estate such as their own house, and the amount of financial asset is only 5.72 million yen.

The degree of satisfaction with job and life is not low, and the difference from the new middle class is not large. However, the fact that the proportion of those who consider themselves happy is 52.6%, more than 10% lower than that of the new middle class, suggests the characteristics of this class as a lower class. Although the overall labor union organization rate in Japan is not high, the rate of regular working class is relatively high at 38.9%. Support for the LDP is 24.1%, the second lowest after the underclass, however this does not imply a clear rejection of the LDP, as support for opposition parties is low and support for no party is high at 61.3%. Although they are a subordinate class in capitalist society, they can be said to be a class that is satisfied with their lives to some extent, have a certain level of income and standard of living.

Underclass

The underclass is literally the lowest class in contemporary Japanese society. Both individual and household incomes are extremely low, and the poverty rate is extremely high at 38.7%, especially for women at 48.5%, and 63.2% for divorced or widowed women. The total amount of household asset is 11.19 million yen, which may not seem extremely low, but most of it consists of their owned houses, and only 3.15 million yen for those without owned houses. The proportion of people with no assets at all is 31.5%.

As noted earlier, the important characteristics are low marriage rates for males and high rates of divorced or widowed for females, which suggests that it is difficult for underclass males to marry, and that it is difficult for the underclass to form stable families, regardless of gender. All underclass women are not married by definition, but the proportion of these who are divorced or widowed increases with age, with 11.5% in the 20 s, 37.5% in the 30 s, 60.9% in the 40 s, and 80.0% in the 50 s. While many underclass women remain unmarried, married women are flowing into the underclass after divorce or bereavement.

The satisfaction with job and life is low, and compared to other classes, the difference is extremely large. Only 18.6% of them are satisfied with their lives, and 61.6% do not consider themselves happy. The support rate for the LDP was 15.3%, the lowest among the five classes. The proportion of respondents who do not support any political party is 67.9%, the highest among the five classes, while the support for parties other than the LDP is 16.8%, which is higher than the LDP only among the five classes, indicating a strong antipathy toward the LDP. The 2015 SSM survey has a question that asks respondents to rate their favorability of five political parties, including the LDP, on an 11-point scale from 0 to 100 in 10-degree increments. According to the results, the proportion of respondents who had a favorability rating of 60 degrees or higher for the LDP was 54.4% for the capitalist class, 37.9% for the new middle class, 31.9% for the working class, 23.8% for the underclass, and 41.0% for the old middle class, with the underclass being the lowest. The labor union membership rate is low at 13.8%, but has risen substantially from 3.7% in the 2005 SSM survey.

Old Middle class

Although the income level of the old middle class is slightly lower than that of the regular working class, the poverty rate is high at 17.2%, reflecting the fact that it includes many people whose family businesses are in a difficult financial condition. The total amount of household asset is 29.17 million yen, of which the financial asset are 11.13 million yen, both of which are the second highest after the capitalist class.

The proportion of those who are satisfied with their jobs is 41.4%, the second highest after the capitalist class, which is reasonable because they manage their own business and have much autonomy. In contrast, satisfaction with lives is not high, slightly below that of the regular working class.

The LDP support rate is high at 35.5%. However, the support for the LDP among the old middle class was previously at the same level as that of the capitalist class, reaching nearly 60% between 1965 and 1985, so we can say that it has declined considerably and has become increasingly different from the capitalist class. In fact, in terms of support for other political parties, support for the Democratic Party of Japan (DPJ) and the Japanese Communist Party (JCP) is at 6.8% and 3.3%, respectively, both the highest among the five classes. Although it is a traditional and conservative middle class, it has been changing its political character as it continues to decompose and shrink in size.

The misery of the underclass

The difficult circumstances of the underclass are even more revealed based on the 2016 Metropolitan Area Residents Survey data. Table 13 shows some results.

Nearly half of the underclass, 42.2%, are very worried about their future lives. This proportion is less than 20% for the capitalist class and the new middle class, and less than 30% for the regular working class, so the severity of the worries of the underclass is outstanding. The proportion of those who consider their health condition as bad is only slightly above 10% for the capitalist class and the new middle class, and only 15% for the regular working class, while it reaches 23.2% for the underclass.

The results on mental depression and depressive or other mental illnesses are striking. 28.2% of the underclass experience mental depression that interferes with their work and life, which is almost twice the rate of other classes. Futhermore, proportion of those who have been diagnosed or treated for depressive or other mental illnesses has reached 20%, nearly three times the proportion of the other classes. These results clearly show the misery of the underclass.

The new Japanese class society

In this study, based on the quantitative analysis of the differences and disparities among the five classes, we can draw the following conclusions.

First, the class categories based on Marxian class theory can explain the differences in income and social consciousness well, and their validity in empirical research has been confirmed. In particular, the explanatory power of the five class categories that divide the working class into two groups, the regular working class and the underclass, is high, and it is important to distinguish between them in empirical research.

Second, focusing on individual annual income, we can observe the following multiple mechanisms of exploitation in Japanese society. An exploitation relationship exists between the capitalist mode of production and

Table 13. Worry, Health conditions and depression.

	Capitalist class (%)	New middle class (%)	Regular working class (%)	Underclass (%)	Old middle class (%)
Very worried about future life	13.6	19.4	29.0	50.4	25.9
Bad health condition (Bad + more or less bad)	12.6	11.1	15.0	23.2	18.4
having been unable to work or do daily activities due to depression (always + almost always + sometimes)	13.8	14.1	16.7	28.2	16.1
Have been diagnosed or treated for clinical depression or other mental illness	7.5	8.0	7.2	20.0	8.7

Source. 2016 Tokyo Metropolitan area Resident Survey.

simple commodity production, and the classes located in the capitalist mode of production as a whole exploit the old middle class located in simple commodity production. Within the capitalist mode of production, the capitalist class and new middle class are exploiting classes, and the working class is exploited class. However, the regular working class, whose annual personal income is roughly equal to the overall average, is in a near-neutral location in the exploitation relations, and the main target of exploitation is the underclass.

Third, the underclass is fundamentally different from other classes in terms of its extremely low income, vulnerability to the risk of poverty, difficulties in marriage and family formation, and large differences from other classes in consciousness and living conditions. Therefore, from the perspective of whether or not it is possible to maintain the general standard of living, the class structure of contemporary Japan can be regarded as being divided into underclass and other classes.

These conclusions indicate that a class-based approach is extremely useful in analyzing contemporary Japanese society, and that the concept of the underclass is an important element in this approach. It is obvious that contemporary Japan is a class society, and a new class society that includes the underclass as a significant element. From this perspective, it is necessary to accumulate various studies based on class theory, which is a common platform that connects various social sciences.

Funding

The study was supported by JSPS KAKENHI Grant Number 15H01970 and JP25000001.

References

Crompton, R. 1993. *Class and Stratification.* Cambridge, UK: Polity Press.

Edgell, S. 1993. *Class.* London, UK: Routledge.

Esping-Andersen, G. 1999. *Social Foundations of Postindustrial Economies.* Oxford, UK: Oxford University Press.

Hartman, H. 1981. "The Unhappy Marriage of Marxism and Feminism: Towards a More Progressive Union." In *Women and Revolution: A Discussion of the Unhappy Marriage of Marxism and Feminism,* edited by L. Sargent. Boston, MA: South End Press.

Hashimoto, K. 2000. "Class Structure in Contemporary Japan." *International Journal of Sociology* 30 (1) :37–64. doi: 10.1080/15579336.2000.11770211.

Hashimoto, K. 2003. *Class Structure in Contemporary Japan.* Melbourne, Australia: Trans Pacific Press.

Mann, M. 1986. "A Crisis in Stratification Theory?" In *Gender and Stratification,* edited by R. Crompton and Michael Mann. London, UK: Polity Press.

Marx, K. 1867. *Das Kapital, Band I.* Hamburg, Germany: Verlag von Otto Meissner.

Marx, K., and Engels, F. (ed.), 1887. *Capital, Volume 1*. Moscow, USSR: Progress Publishers.

Myrdal, G. 1962. *Challenge to Affluence*. New York, NY: Pantheon Books.

Ohashi, R. 1959. *[The Significance and Limitations of Class Composition Table]*, *[Collected Papers on Economics on the 40th Anniversary of the Faculty of Economics of Kyoto University]*, Tokyo, Japan: Yuhikaku. (in Japanese)

Ohashi, R. 1971. *[Class Composition of Japan]*. Tokyo, Japan: Iwanami Shoten. (in Japanese)

Poulantzas, N. 1974. "Les Classes Sociales dans le Capitalisme Aujourd'hui." Seuil, France: Seuil., Fernbach, D.(tr.), 1978, *Classes in Contemporary Capitalism*. London, UK: Verso.

Roemer, John E. 1982. *A General Theory of Exploitation and Class*. Cambridge, UK: Harvard University Press.

Sawyer, M. 1976. *Income Distribution in OECD Countries, OECD Economic Outlook*. Paris, France: OECD.

Waters, M. 1991. "Collapse and Convergence in Class Theory." *Theory and Society* 20 (2): 141–172. doi:10.1007/BF00160181.

Westergaard, J. 1993. "Class in Britain since 1979: Facts, Theories and Ideologies." In *[Class in Britain]*, edited by M. Watanabe. Tokyo, Japan: Aoki Shoten.

Wright, E. O. 1978. *Class, Crisis and the State*. London, UK: New Left Books.

Wright, E. O. 1979. *Class Structure and Income Determination*. London, UK: Academic Press.

Wright, E. O. 1985. *Classes*. London, UK: Verso.

On the labor theory of value as the basis for the analysis of economic inequality in the capitalist economy

Naoki Yoshihara

ABSTRACT

In this paper, we review the *labor theory of value* as the basis for the analysis of economic inequality in a capitalist economy. According to the standard Marxian view, the system of labor values of individual commodities can serve as the center of gravity for long-term price fluctuations in a precapitalist economy with simple commodity-production, where no exploitative social relation emerges, while in a modern capitalist economy, the labor value system is replaced by prices of production associated with an equal positive rate of profits as the center of gravity, in which exploitative relation between the capitalist and the working classes is a generic and persistent feature of economic inequality. Some of the literature such as Michio Morishima criticized this view by showing that the labor values of individual commodities are no longer well-defined if a capitalist economy has joint production. Given these arguments, this paper firstly shows that the system of individual labor values can be still well-defined in a capitalist economy with joint production whenever the set of available production techniques is all-productive. Secondly, this paper shows that it is generally impossible to verify that labor-value pricing serves as the center of gravity for price fluctuations in precapitalist economies characterized by the full development of simple commodity-production.

Introduction

Recently, a vast literature has analyzed the persistent, and widening, inequalities in income and wealth observed in the vast majority of nations,[1] while some data show inequality in per-capita income between the richer developed countries and the poorer developing ones which has been expanding since 1820.[2] Thus, the issue of the long-run distributional feature of wealth and income in the capitalist economy should be at the heart of economic analysis, as Piketty (2014) emphasizes, and one of the central questions in economics should be to ask what the primary mechanism to generate such disparity persistently between the rich and the poor is.

To discuss such a mechanism in the modern capitalist economy, Karl Marx paid special attention to a particular form of inequality related to the systematic *underpayment* of labor in relation to their contribution to production, which is known as *exploitation as unequal exchange of labor* (UE-exploitation, hereafter). He then argued that an UE-exploitative relation between capitalists and workers is generic and persistent in the capitalist economy. Though the notion of UE-exploitation has been paid less attention in the mainstream economics, it should have been one of the prominent concepts relevant to capitalist economic systems, particularly in a number of debates and analyses of labor relations, especially focusing on the weakest segments of the labor force (see, e.g., ILO, 2005a, 2005b).

Unlike the case of UE-exploitation in the feudal society, the application of this notion to the capitalist economy involves a fundamental difficulty, as the division of a worker's labor into working for him/herself and working for a capitalist is not observable. Moreover, the market contract between buyers and sellers of labor power is simply observed as an equal exchange of labor. Therefore, the existence of UE-exploitation in a capitalist economy should be measured through economic analysis. To promote such an analysis, one of the central issues in Marxian exploitation theory is to stipulate a suitable operational method to measure the difference between the labor expended and the labor received by an individual via his/her income, which is to answer the question of what a proper formal definition of UE-exploitation is. Indeed, there have been many proposals for such a definition, like Okishio (1963), Morishima (1974), Roemer (1982), Duménil (1980), and Foley (1982).[3]

Remember that Marx (1867, 1976) himself defined the notion of UE-exploitation on the basis of the labor theory of value (LTV, hereafter), and in particular, by means of the labor value of labor power. However, the recent literature on analytical Marxian exploitation theory, like the above mentioned works, suggests that the role of LTV in Marxian economics is quite limited. As Morishima (1973) and Roemer (1981, 1982) emphasized, the notion of labor values is relevant only in the formal definition of UE-exploitation, since it requires a formal definition of the amount of labor time that the workers can 'receive' via their wage revenue. This is indeed defined as the socially necessary labor time for the production of a real wage commodity bundle, that is the only part to which LTV is relevant. Moreover, as Steedman (1975) and Morishima (1973, 1974) argued, the additive model of labor valuation fails in the case of economies with joint production. Thus, in economies with joint production, it is claimed that the formal definition of labor value of every individual commodity is not only unnecessary, but also generally impossible.

In this paper, we review such recognition of LTV in the literature. First, we will show that at least for some subclass of joint production economies, the standard claims of LTV and the basic theorems of UE-exploitation can be preserved. To do so, we introduce a specific notion of the productiveness of production techniques, called *all-productiveness*, due to Kurz and Salvadori (1995, 239). Then, we model an economy with joint production, in which every available production technique is assumed to be all-productive. In such an economy, the labor value of every individual commodity is well-defined; thus a system of individual labor values can be identified for each production technique. Then, every alternative form of UE-exploitation can be represented by means of such a labor-value system, as in the case of economies with simple Leontief techniques[4].

Second, in this paper, we discuss the issue of the so-called *law of value* in LTV. The law of value implies that, in the case of a modern industrial capitalist economy, a system of *production prices* associated with *an equal positive rate of profits* can serve as the center of gravity for price fluctuations over the long term. Fortunately, such a claim of the law of value can be verified, which is one of implications from the main results in Duménil and Levy (1985) and Dana et al. (1989). Then, with reference to the literature on the so-called Fundamental Marxian Theorem, this consequence would also imply that the UE-exploitation is generic and persistent in a capitalist economy. Thus, we examine in this paper that whether a labor-value system can serve as the center of gravity for price fluctuations in a *precapitalist economy*. That is, the verification of the law of value in a pre-capitalist economy. By examining such an issue, while UE-exploitation is generic and persistent in the capitalist economy, we discuss whether it is non-generic and non-persistent in non-capitalistic market economies such as a simple commodity-production economy.

Before going into a more detail argument, let me briefly review the background arguments relevant to this issue. Although a typical interpretation of the LTV is that it asserts value/price proportionality, Marx's own view was that in a capitalist economy the system of labor values of individual commodities regulates fluctuating market prices. It has been recognized that this view could be verified by showing firstly, the correlations between production prices and labor value magnitudes at the aggregate level, and secondly, that *prices of production* can serve as the center of gravity for price fluctuations over the long term (that is, the law of value holds). In these two subjects, though the first one is relevant to the so-called *Transformation Problem*,[5] it is the second issue that this paper would like to focus.

As Itoh (2021) properly pointed out, in any type of society, "the total quantity of social labor time must somehow be allocated to the various kinds of concrete productive activity. The social division of labor in general represents not only the social organization of qualitatively different varieties of concrete labor, but also the quantitative division of abstract labor into the necessary branches.... Marx makes clear that such a division of labor time into various necessary branches does exist under any form of production,... Thus, it appears that abstract human labor, together with its concrete character, constitutes the common material basis for all societies (Itoh 2021, 97)" In a capitalist economy, such an allocation of labor time is exercised through market exchanges under free competition.[6] It implies that free exchanging activities in competitive markets are ultimately regulated on the basis of efficient quantitative-allocation of (abstract) social labor time among the various necessary branches, which is what the law of value shows.[7]

Note that both David Ricardo (1821, 1951) and Marx recognized that the full development of the law of value presupposes a freely competitive market economy with large-scale industrial production, in other words modern bourgeois society.[8] However, in contrast, it has been argued, since the era of Engels,[9] that the law of value holds generally for the period of precapitalist societies where simple commodity-production is sufficiently developed. In market economies with *simple commodity-production*, unlike the case of the modern industrial capitalist economy, it has been recognized that the labor-value system serves as the center of gravity for the fluctuating market exchanges.

However, in this paper, we show that the system of labor values cannot be verified as the center of gravity for the long term price fluctuations, in that in any precapitalist economy with unequal private ownership of capital goods, an infinite set of equilibrium prices including labor-value pricing equilibrium is observed. It implies that the long-term equilibrium prices are generically indeterminate, and so none of the long term equilibrium prices, including the labor-value pricing equilibrium, can be verified as the center of gravity for price fluctuations.

Basic models

Assume that there are n types of physical commodities. There is a finite set, $\mathcal{P}$, of linear production techniques, or *techniques*, (B, A, L), where B is the $n \times n$ nonnegative matrix of produced outputs, A is the $n \times n$ nonnegative matrix of produced inputs, and L is the $1 \times n$ positive vector of labor inputs. Let us call $\mathcal{P}$ a *production set*. Let a_{ij} and L_j denote, respectively, the amounts of physical input i and labor used in the j-th production process of the production technique (B, A, L), while b_{ij} denotes the amount of good i produced in production process j of the technique (B, A, L). Let x be the $n \times 1$ vector denoting the aggregate level of activating the various techniques. The vector of aggregate net output by activating the technique (B, A, L) with x activity level is $y = (B-A)x$. If every process produces only one good (no joint production), then B is diagonal and activities can be normalized such that $B = I$, and can be simply denoted as (A, L). Let us call such an (A, L) a *simple Leontief technique*.

All-Productiveness of production techniques

It is natural to assume that all of n types of commodities can be produced as net outputs by means of the production set $\mathcal{P}$. This property would be formulated as follows: for any non-negative vector $y \in \mathbb{R}^n_+$, there exist a technique $(B, A, L) \in \mathcal{P}$ and a non-negative vector $x \in \mathbb{R}^n_+$ such that $(B-A)x \geqq y$.[10] If an economy is associated with a simple Leontief technique, so that $\mathcal{P} = \{(A, L)\}$, then this producibility condition can be reduced to the standard notion of productiveness: a *technique* (A, L) *is productive* if and only if there exists a positive vector $x \in \mathbb{R}^n_{++}$ such that $x > Ax$. Compared to this natural producibility condition, however, a much more stringent condition can be introduced as follows. A *technique* (B, A, L) *is all-productive* if and only if for any semi-positive vector $y \in \mathbb{R}^n_+$, there exists a non-negative vector $x \in \mathbb{R}^n_+$ such that $(B-A)x = y$ (Kurz and Salvadori 1995, 239). A *production set is all-productive* if and only if every technique available in this set is all-productive. In the rest of the paper, we assume that the production set $\mathcal{P}$ is all-productive.

To see how stringent the all-productiveness is, let us consider the simplest case: $n = 2$. Then, let

$$(B-A) = \begin{bmatrix} \alpha & \beta \\ \gamma & \delta \end{bmatrix}.$$

As argued by Kurz and Salvadori (1995, 239), if (B, A, L) is all-productive, then $(B-A)$ is semi-positive invertible: $(B-A)^{-1} \geq 0$. Since

$$(B-A)^{-1} = \frac{1}{\alpha\delta - \beta\gamma} \begin{bmatrix} \delta & -\beta \\ -\gamma & \alpha \end{bmatrix},$$

all-productiveness of (B, A, L) implies that

$$(B-A)^{-1} e_1 = \frac{1}{\alpha\delta - \beta\gamma} \begin{bmatrix} \delta & -\beta \\ -\gamma & \alpha \end{bmatrix} \begin{pmatrix} 1 \\ 0 \end{pmatrix} \geqq 0;$$

$$\text{and } (B-A)^{-1} e_2 = \frac{1}{\alpha\delta - \beta\gamma} \begin{bmatrix} \delta & -\beta \\ -\gamma & \alpha \end{bmatrix} \begin{pmatrix} 0 \\ 1 \end{pmatrix} \geqq 0.$$

From $(B-A)^{-1}e_1 \geq 0$, it follows that $\delta \geq 0$ and $\gamma \leq 0$ whenever $\alpha\delta-\beta\gamma>0$; and $\delta \leq 0$ and $\gamma \geq 0$ whenever $\alpha\delta-\beta\gamma<0$. From $(B-A)^{-1}e_2 \geq 0$, it follows that $\alpha \geq 0$ and $\beta \leq 0$ whenever $\alpha\delta-\beta\gamma>0$; and $\alpha \leq 0$ and $\beta \geq 0$ whenever $\alpha\delta-\beta\gamma<0$. Without loss of generality, let us consider the case of $\alpha\delta-\beta\gamma>0$. Then, $\alpha>0, \beta \leq 0, \gamma \leq 0$, and $\delta>0$. This implies that $b_{11}-a_{11}>0, b_{12}-a_{12} \leq 0, b_{21}-a_{21} \leq 0$, and $b_{22}-a_{22}>0$. Thus, the matrix $(B-A)$ satisfies the assumptions of the Hawkins-Simon theorem, and so the technique (B, A, L) is essentially equivalent to simple Leontief, even though the non-diagonal elements of B could be positive. In other words, even if the technique (B, A, L) admits joint production, it is essentially a simple Leontief in terms of net output production, since any jointly produced commodity of any process cannot be a positive net output by the activation of this process alone.

There are plenty of cases where a process admits joint production as a positive net output of by-product in the class of economies with joint production. Such a rich class of joint production cases would be excluded from consideration by the assumption of an all-productive production set. However, such a restriction allows us to define the system of labor values of individual commodities in economies with joint production, as will be discussed later.

Labor Values in economies with all-productive production sets

If (B, A, L) is all-productive, a system of labor values of individual commodities for a technique (B, A, L) can be defined as the solution to the following system of equations:

$$vB = vA + L. \tag{3.1}$$

Indeed the solution to (3.1) is a positive vector $v>0$ satisfying

$$v = L(B-A)^{-1}. \tag{3.2}$$

As the production set $\mathcal{P}$ is all-productive, we can find such a solution for any system of equations defined from any technique available in $\mathcal{P}$. Therefore, if a technique (B^*, A^*, L^*) is selected according to the cost minimization principle, then a system of labor values associated with this cost minimizing technique is well-defined as $v^* = L^*(B^*-A^*)^{-1}>0$. Correspondingly, a formal definition of UE-exploitation can be proposed by means of the labor-value system v^*.

Let us examine whether the labor values defined as the solution to (3.1) are appropriate. This could be deemed appropriate if this can regulate market exchanges of commodities in order to allocate the total quantity of social labor time efficiently and appropriately to meet various social demands for commodities.[11]

To see this, let $c>0$ be an aggregate demand vector of all commodities. Let $(B, A, L) \in \mathcal{P}$ be an optimal technique in terms of cost minimization, and x^c be the aggregate production activities that meets social demand in the market economy, which is defined as

$$x^c = (B-A)^{-1}c>0. \tag{3.3}$$

This implies that the *total living labor time* necessary to meet the demand c is $Lx^c>0$. Then, left multiplying both sides of Equations (3.3) by L, and then taking (3.2) into account, we reach the following equation:

$$Lx^c = vc. \tag{3.4}$$

As in the case of the labor-value system in economies with simple Leontief techniques, Equation (3.4) implies that total living labor time Lx^c is appropriately allocated to meet social demand c through market exchange of commodities in accordance with the labor-value exchanging rates: v.

Indeed, on the right hand side of the Equation (3.4), $v_i c_i>0$ for each commodity $i = 1, ..., n$ represents the *socially necessary labor time* for the production of this commodity to meet its social demand c_i. Therefore, Equation (3.4) implies that the total living labor time Lx^c is allocated to each commodity i's production, and it is the social necessary labor time $v_i c_i$ that is allocated to each commodity i's production in order to meet its social demand c_i. Note that the left hand side Lx^c of (3.4) is the aggregation of the labor time $L_i x_i^c$ expended in each production process $i = 1, ..., n$. As well recognized, each labor expenditure $L_i x_i^c$ is not necessarily identical to the socially necessary labor time to produce c_i.

To see this last point in more detail, assume that $n=2$. Then, (3.3) is represented as follows:

$$x^c = \begin{pmatrix} x_1^c \\ x_2^c \end{pmatrix} = \begin{pmatrix} \dfrac{b_{22}-a_{22}}{|B-A|}c_1 + \dfrac{-b_{12}+a_{12}}{|B-A|}c_2 \\ \dfrac{-b_{21}+a_{21}}{|B-A|}c_1 + \dfrac{b_{11}-a_{11}}{|B-A|}c_2 \end{pmatrix} >0.$$

Therefore, we have:

$$L_1 x_1^c = L_1 \frac{b_{22}-a_{22}}{|B-A|}c_1 + L_1 \frac{-b_{12}+a_{12}}{|B-A|}c_2;$$
$$L_2 x_2^c = L_2 \frac{-b_{21}+a_{21}}{|B-A|}c_1 + L_2 \frac{b_{11}-a_{11}}{|B-A|}c_2. \tag{3.5}$$

In contrast, it follows from (3.2) that

$$v_1 c_1 = L_1 \frac{b_{22}-a_{22}}{|\mathbf{B}-\mathbf{A}|} c_1 + L_2 \frac{-b_{21}+a_{21}}{|\mathbf{B}-\mathbf{A}|} c_1;$$

$$v_2 c_2 = L_1 \frac{-b_{12}+a_{12}}{|\mathbf{B}-\mathbf{A}|} c_2 + L_2 \frac{b_{11}-a_{11}}{|\mathbf{B}-\mathbf{A}|} c_2.$$

(3.6)

By comparing (3.5) and (3.6), we can observe that to meet the social demand c_1 for commodity 1, $L_1 \frac{b_{22}-a_{22}}{|\mathbf{B}-\mathbf{A}|} c_1$ amount of living labor time is allocated from process 1 while $L_2 \frac{-b_{21}+a_{21}}{|\mathbf{B}-\mathbf{A}|} c_1$ amount of living labor time is allocated from process 2. Likewise, to meet the social demand c_2 for commodity 2, $L_1 \frac{-b_{12}+a_{12}}{|\mathbf{B}-\mathbf{A}|} c_2$ amount of living labor time is allocated from process 1 while $L_2 \frac{b_{11}-a_{11}}{|\mathbf{B}-\mathbf{A}|} c_2$ amount of living labor time is allocated from process 2. In other words, for the production of commodity 1 to meet social demand c_1, $L_2 \frac{-b_{21}+a_{21}}{|\mathbf{B}-\mathbf{A}|} c_1$ portion of the total labor time $L_2 x_2^c$ expended in process 2 needs to be allocated, and for the production of commodity 2 to meet social demand c_2, $L_1 \frac{-b_{12}+a_{12}}{|\mathbf{B}-\mathbf{A}|} c_2$ portion of the total labor time $L_1 x_1^c$ expended in process 1 needs to be allocated. In this way, (3.6) represents the state that the socially necessary labor time for each commodity's production is appropriately identified in order to meet its social demand, as the result of appropriate allocation of each process's total labor expenditure which is mediated by market exchange of commodities in accordance with the labor-value pricing.

In this way, the Equation (3.4) represents the crucial condition that a proper formal definition of labor values should satisfy, and our proposal (3.1)–(3.2) is shown to pass this test. Thus, the well-known criticism against LTV developed by the Steedman-Morishima controversy no longer applies to the class of all-productive joint production economies.

One remark is given for the above argument. It is true that all-productiveness of joint production techniques is mathematically quite stringent. However, this condition could be still reasonable from the viewpoint of economics. For instance, suppose that joint production comes only from the existence of a non-negative square matrix $\mathbf{\Phi}$ of *fixed-capital input coefficients*, which is depreciated with a fixed ratio in each production period. This implies that $\mathbf{\Phi}$ appears at the beginning of one production period, while another non-negative square matrix $\mathbf{\Phi}'$ (with $\mathbf{\Phi}' \leq \mathbf{\Phi}$) of fixed-capital input coefficients appears at the end of this period. Here, $\mathbf{\Phi}-\mathbf{\Phi}'$ corresponds to a standard *depreciation matrix of fixed-capital goods*. Let $\mathbf{C}$ be the standard nonnegative square matrix of *circulating-capital input coefficients* which is productive, and define $\mathbf{B} \equiv \mathbf{I} + \mathbf{\Phi}'$ and $\mathbf{A} \equiv \mathbf{C} + \mathbf{\Phi}$. Then, such a technique $(\mathbf{B}, \mathbf{A}, \mathbf{L})$ satisfies the assumptions of the Hawkins-Simon theorem whenever the diagonal elements of $B-A$ are positive, which implies that it could be all-productive.

Remarks on alternative LTV initiated by TSSI

By the way, there is some recent literature to propose an alternative formal definition of labor values, such as the *Temporal Single System Interpretation* (**TSSI**, hereafter) (Kliman and McGlone 1999), which denies the value Equations (3.1). According to **TSSI**, given that the technique $(B, A, L) \in \mathcal{P}$ is used in period t, labor values are determined at the end of period t by:

$$\varepsilon_t v_t B = p_{t-1} A + \varepsilon_t L \qquad (3.7)$$

where $p_{t-1} \geqq 0$ is the vector of market prices prevailed at the end of period $t-1$, and is assumed to be historically given at the end of period t. Moreover, $\varepsilon_t > 0$ is the *monetary expression of labor time* (**MELT**) at period t, which is to transform the unit of time to the unit of money. Therefore, labor values are determined temporally in each period, depending on the given market prices of the previous period, and so they may vary across different periods, even though no technical change from the present technique (B, A, L) takes place.

In this short subsection, just one fundamental criticism is raised against the **TSSI** definition of labor values. That is, the **TSSI** system (3.7) of labor values cannot properly represent a profile of each commodity's socially necessary labor time as the allocation of the total living labor expenditure through competitive market exchanges of commodities, whenever such market exchanges are mediated in accordance with the **TSSI** labor-value pricing. This difficulty should not be regarded as the failure of competitive market exchanges, but rather be attributed to improperness of the **TSSI** system (3.7) of labor values, because it cannot meet the fundamental condition (3.4).

To see the last point, again let $c > 0$ be an aggregate demand vector of all commodities, $(B, A, L) \in \mathcal{P}$ be an optimal technique in terms of cost minimization, and x^c be the aggregate production activities derived as the solution to (3.3). Then, from (3.7) it follows that

$$\varepsilon_t v_t (B - A) = (p_{t-1} - \varepsilon_t v_t) A + \varepsilon_t L$$

$$\Longleftrightarrow \varepsilon_t v_t = (p_{t-1} - \varepsilon_t v_t) A (B - A)^{-1} + \varepsilon_t L (B - A)^{-1}$$

$$\Longleftrightarrow v_t = \left(\frac{p_{t-1}}{\varepsilon_t} - v_t \right) A (B - A)^{-1} + v$$

where v is the labor-value system defined by (3.2), whereas v_t is the **TSSI** labor-value system given by (3.7). As $\frac{p_{t-1}}{\varepsilon_t} \neq v_t$, $\left(\frac{p_{t-1}}{\varepsilon_t} - v_t \right) A (B - A)^{-1} \neq 0$ holds. Therefore, it follows from (3.4) that

$$v_t c = \left(\frac{p_{t-1}}{\varepsilon_t} - v_t\right) A(B-A)^{-1} c + vc = \left(\frac{p_{t-1}}{\varepsilon_t} - v_t\right) A(B-A)^{-1} c + Lx^c,$$

and thus

$$v_t c \neq Lx^c \iff \frac{p_{t-1}}{\varepsilon_t} \neq v_t.$$

In general, $\frac{p_{t-1}}{\varepsilon_t} \neq v_t$ holds, so that we conclude $v_t c \neq Lx^c$. Thus, the market exchange rate determined by the **TSSI** labor-value system cannot appropriately stipulate a profile of each commodity's socially necessary labor time as an allocation of the total living labor to meet each commodity's social demand.

In this sense, the **TSSI** definition (3.7) of labor values is conceptually flawed.

On the (in)validity of the law of value in a precapitalist economy

Definition of a precapitalist economy with simple commodity-production

As argued in section 1 of this paper, it seems to be a common view within the Marxian camp that the labor-value system serves as the center of gravity for price fluctuations in the case of precapitalist economies, where simple commodity-production is supposed to be sufficiently developed.[12] However, how should we characterize the basic features of precapitalist economies with simple commodity-production, setting aside the more fundamental question of *whether a simple commodity-production economy had ever historically existed.*

In this respect, again we may refer to Marx (1894, 1981), where he asked what would happen if all commodities in the various spheres of production were sold at their labor values. In this context, he supposed that "the workers are themselves in possession of their respective means of production and exchange their commodities with one another"(Marx (1894, 1981), 276). In this setting, Marx admitted *unequal private ownership of capital goods among private producers* by arguing that "If worker I has higher outlays, these are replaced by the greater portion of value of his commodities that replaces this 'constant' part, and he therefore again has a greater part of his product's total value to transform back into the material elements of this constant part, while II, if he receives less for this, has also that much less to transform back" (Ibid., 277).

Under such a setting, Marx (1894, 1981) discussed the exchange of commodities at their labor values, and observed that "since I and II each receive the value of the product of one working day, they therefore receive equal values, after deducting the value of the 'constant' elements advanced" (Ibid., 277) and thus, "Profit rates would also be very different for I and II"

(Ibid., 277) because of the different volumes of constant capital between them. However, "the difference in the profit rate would be a matter of indifference, … just as in international trade the differences in profit rates between different nations are completely immaterial as far as the exchange of their commodities is concerned" (Ibid., 277).

Given these observations, Marx (1894, 1981) concluded that "The exchange of commodities at their values, or at approximately these values, thus corresponds to a much lower stage of development than the exchange at prices of production, for which a definite degree of capitalist development is needed." (Ibid., 277) Moreover, by arguing that "it is also quite apposite to view the values of commodities not only as theoretically prior to the prices of production, but also as historically prior to them" (Ibid., 277) Marx characterized the basic elements of precapitalist economies by (1) the "conditions in which the means of production belong to the worker" like "peasant proprietors and handicraftsmen who work for themselves", and (2) the features that "the means of production involved in each-branch of production can be transferred from one sphere to another only with difficulty, and the different spheres of production therefore relate to one another, within certain limits, like foreign countries or communistic communities." (Ibid., 277) These two basic properties imply that neither labor nor capital is freely exchanged in markets. He also presumed the competitiveness of commodity markets by the three conditions specified in Marx (1894, 1981, 278–279).[13] In this way, Marx argued that, under precapitalist economies characterized by the competitive commodity markets and the basic properties (1) and (2), the law of value governs prices and their movements by taking the system of labor values as the center of gravity.

Taking the above arguments into consideration, in the next subsection, we provide, as a thought experiment, a simple model of precapitalist economy,[14] in which unequal private ownership of capital goods among private producers; no labor market nor credit market is observed while commodity markets are perfectly competitive; all agents have a common *leisure preference* in that they are primarily concerned with enjoyment of free hours (or leisure time), given that a common subsistence consumption bundle, necessary for their survival, is ensured. Note that leisure preference was ubiquitous in the pre-industrial society before the new time-discipline was imposed by the eighteenth century (see Thompson (1967), Cunningham (1980, 2014), and Kawakita (2010)).

With such a simple model, we examine whether the labor-value pricing equilibrium is established as the center of gravity for price fluctuations.

A Simple model of precapitalist economy with a simple Leontief technique

Consider an economy with a simple Leontief technique,[15] so that assume $\mathcal{P} = \{(A, L)\}$. Moreover, let A be productive and indecomposable. Let $\mathcal{N} \equiv \{N, S\}$ be the set of individuals, and the number of the types of commodities be $n = 2$. Let $b \in \mathbb{R}^2_{++}$ be the *subsistence consumption bundle*, which every individual must consume for his survival in one period of production, regardless of whether supplying labor or not. For the sake of simplicity, the maximal amount of labor supply by every agent is equal to unity and there is no difference in labor skills among agents. Let $\bar{\omega} \in \mathbb{R}^2_{++}$ be the social endowments of material capital goods at the beginning of the initial period of production. For the sake of simplicity, assume $\bar{\omega} \equiv A[I - A]^{-1}(2b)$. Every individual has the common consumption space $C \equiv \left\{ c \in \mathbb{R}^2_+ \,|\, c \geqq b \right\} \times [0, 1]$ with a generic element (c, l), where $c \in \left\{ c \in \mathbb{R}^2_+ \,|\, c \geqq b \right\}$ represents a consumption bundle and $l \in [0, 1]$ represents an amount of labor expended. Moreover, every individual has the common *leisure preference* which is represented by a utility function $u : C \to \mathbb{R}$ defined as: for each $(c, l) \in C$,

$$u(c, l) = 1 - l.$$

That is, every individual does not concern about the increase of consumption goods beyond the subsistence level b, but mainly concerns about the increase of free hours (leisure time), once the consumption of the subsistence bundle b is ensured.

An economy with a simple Leontief technique is specified by a profile $\langle \mathcal{N}, (A, L, b), \bar{\omega} \rangle$, which we may call a *precapitalist economy*. Denote each individual's capital endowments at period t by $\omega_t^N = (\omega_{1t}^N, \omega_{2t}^N) > (0, 0)$ and $\omega_t^S = (\omega_{1t}^S, \omega_{2t}^S) > (0, 0)$. Needless to say, assume that $\omega_t^N + \omega_t^S = \bar{\omega}$ holds.

We explicitly take the time structure of production. Hence, the capital goods available at the present period of production cannot exceed the amount of capital goods accumulated until the end of the preceding period of production. Moreover, the time structure of production is given as follows:

1. Given market prices $p_{t-1} = (p_{1t-1}, p_{2t-1}) \geq (0, 0)$ at the beginning of the period t, each agent $\nu = N, S$ purchases, under the constraint of wealth endowment $p_{t-1}\omega_t^\nu$, the capital goods Ax_t^ν as inputs for production in the present period, and the commodities δ_t^ν to sell, for a speculative purpose, at the end of the present period;

2. Each agent is engaged in the production activity of period t by inputting labor Lx_t^ν and the purchased capital goods Ax_t^ν;

3.   The production activity is completed and x_t^ν is produced as an output at the end of this period. Then, in goods markets with market prices $p_t \geq (0,0)$, each agent earns the revenue $p_t x_t^\nu + p_t \delta_t^\nu$ derived from the output x_t^ν and the speculative commodity bundle δ_t^ν, with which he purchases the bundle b for the consumption at the end of this period and the capital stock ω_{t+1}^ν for the production of the next period. Therefore, the wealth endowment carried over to the next period $t+1$ is $p_t \omega_{t+1}^\nu$.

Given a price system $\{p_{t-1}, p_t\}$ prevailed at the beginning of period t, each agent $\nu(= N, S)$ solves the following optimization program (MP_t^ν) :

$$\min_{x_t^\nu, \delta_t^\nu} l_t^\nu$$

$$\text{s.t. } p_t x_t^\nu + p_t \delta_t^\nu \geqq p_t b + p_t \omega_{t+1}^\nu;$$

$$l_t^\nu = Lx_t^\nu \leqq 1;$$

$$p_{t-1} \delta_t^\nu + p_{t-1} Ax_t^\nu \leqq p_{t-1} \omega_t^\nu, \text{ where } \delta_t^\nu \in \mathbb{R}_+^2;$$

$$p_t \omega_{t+1}^\nu \geqq p_{t-1} \omega_t^\nu.$$

Denote the set of solutions for the optimization program of each agent ν at period t by $O_t^\nu(\{p_{t-1}, p_t\})$.

For the sake of simplicity, let us focus on the case of stationary equilibrium prices (that is, $p_t = p_{t-1} = p^*$). In this case, for any optimal solution $(x_t^{*\nu}, \delta_t^{*\nu}) \in O_t^\nu(p^*)$, it follows that $\delta_t^{*\nu} = 0$ and $p^* x_t^{*\nu} - p^* Ax_t^{*\nu} = p^* b$.

Now, an equilibrium solution is ready to be introduced.

Definition 1: For a precapitalist economy $\langle \mathcal{N}, (A, L, b), (\omega_t^N, \omega_t^S) \rangle$ at period t, where $\omega_t^N + \omega_t^S = \bar{\omega}$, a *reproducible solution (RS) in this period* is a profile of a price system p^* and production activities $(x_t^{*\nu})_{\nu \in \mathcal{N}}$ satisfying the following conditions:

i. $(x_t^{*\nu}, 0) \in O_t^\nu(p^*)$ $(\forall \nu \in \mathcal{N})$; (each agent's individual optimization)
ii. $2b \leqq [I - A](x_t^{*N} + x_t^{*S})$; (the demand-supply matching at the end of period t)
iii. $A(x_t^{*N} + x_t^{*S}) \leqq \omega_t^N + \omega_t^S$. (social feasibility of production at the beginning of period t)

In addition to the above definition, let us focus on the following subset of RS: *A reproducible solution is imperfectly specialized* if and only if $x_t^{*\nu} > 0$ holds for each $\nu \in \mathcal{N}$.

By the property of imperfect specialization RS, it follows that $p^* \in \mathbb{R}_{++}^2$ and $[I - A](x_t^{*N} + x_t^{*S}) = 2b$. The latter equation implies $(x_t^{*N} + x_t^{*S}) = [I - A]^{-1}(2b)$, therefore, $A(x_t^{*N} + x_t^{*S}) = A[I - A]^{-1}(2b) = \bar{\omega} = \omega_t^N + \omega_t^S$ holds.

Let $\boldsymbol{e}_i$ be the i-th unit vector (only the i-th component is unity, and any other is zero). Though there is no labor market in this economy, each agent $\nu \in \mathcal{N}$ should have his own personal view about the reward for his labor expenditure. That is, each agent $\nu \in \mathcal{N}$ should have a specific real number $w_t^\nu \geqq 0$, which represents ν's view that if the reward for the production in process i by supplying one unit of labor is less than w_t^ν, ν would not like to engage in such production activity. Formally speaking, $\frac{p_i - \boldsymbol{pAe}_i}{L_i}$ represents the reward per unit of labor for the production activity in process i. Therefore, ν would not like to work in process i if $\frac{p_i - \boldsymbol{pAe}_i}{L_i} < w_t^\nu$. Moreover, ν would recognize that the production in process i is *profitable* if $\frac{p_i - \boldsymbol{pAe}_i}{L_i} \geqq w_t^\nu$, where the latter inequality is equivalent to $\frac{p_i - \boldsymbol{pAe}_i - w_t^\nu L_i}{\boldsymbol{pAe}_i} \geqq 0$. In this case, ν would also recognize that the production in process i is more *profitable* than the production in process j if and only if $\frac{p_i - \boldsymbol{pAe}_i - w_t^\nu L_i}{\boldsymbol{pAe}_i} > \frac{p_j - \boldsymbol{pAe}_j - w_t^\nu L_j}{\boldsymbol{pAe}_j}$. If so, then ν would like to be perfectly specialized in process i.

Given these arguments, we may say that, under the imperfectly specialized RS, where $\boldsymbol{x}_t^{*\nu} > \boldsymbol{0}$ holds for every $\nu \in \mathcal{N}$, there exists a suitable profile of personal views of labor rewards and return rates, $(w_t^{\nu*}, r_t^{\nu*})_{\nu \in \mathcal{N}}$, such that every agent is willing to work in both process 1 and process 2, in that $\frac{p_i - \boldsymbol{pAe}_i}{L_i} \geqq w_t^\nu$ holds for every process $i = 1$, 2 and every agent $\nu \in \mathcal{N}$. Moreover, for every agent, both production processes are *equally profitable*: that is, for every $\nu \in \mathcal{N}$, $r_t^\nu = \frac{p_i - \boldsymbol{pAe}_i - w_t^\nu L_i}{\boldsymbol{pAe}_i}$ holds for every process $i = 1$, 2.

In summary, under the imperfectly specialized RS $\langle \boldsymbol{p}^*; (\boldsymbol{x}_t^{*\nu})_{\nu \in \mathcal{N}} \rangle$, every agent $\nu \in \mathcal{N}$ has a profile of his personal view of labor reward and return rate, $(w_t^{\nu*}, r_t^{\nu*})$, such that

$$\boldsymbol{p}^* = (1 + r_t^{\nu*})\boldsymbol{p}^*\boldsymbol{A} + w_t^{\nu*}\boldsymbol{L} \tag{4.1}$$

holds.

It is well-known that, in the so-called neoclassical Heckscher-Ohlin model of international trade, the factor price equalization theorem and the Heckscher-Ohlin theorem hold. Even in the model of precapitalist economy presented herein, where neither labor nor credit market exists, we can verify the following two theorems:

Theorem 1 (Factor price equalization): For any precapitalist economy $\langle \mathcal{N}, (\boldsymbol{A}, \boldsymbol{L}, \boldsymbol{b}), (\omega_t^N, \omega_t^S) \rangle$ with $\omega_t^N + \omega_t^S = \bar{\omega}$, let $\langle \boldsymbol{p}^*; (w_t^{\nu*}, r_t^{\nu*})_{\nu \in \mathcal{N}}, (\boldsymbol{x}_t^{*\nu})_{\nu \in \mathcal{N}} \rangle$ be an imperfect specialization RS at period t. Then, if $\frac{\boldsymbol{p}^*\boldsymbol{Ae}_1}{L_1} \neq \frac{\boldsymbol{p}^*\boldsymbol{Ae}_2}{L_2}$, then $(w_t^{N*}, r_t^{N*}) = (w_t^{S*}, r_t^{S*})$ holds.

Proof. This follows from Yoshihara and Kaneko (2016; Theorem 1). ∎

Theorem 2 (Quasi-Heckscher-Ohlin theorem): For any precapitalist economy $\langle \mathcal{N}, (\boldsymbol{A}, \boldsymbol{L}, \boldsymbol{b}), (\omega_t^N, \omega_t^S) \rangle$ with $\omega_t^N + \omega_t^S = \bar{\omega}$, let $\langle \boldsymbol{p}^*; (w_t^*, r_t^*), (\boldsymbol{x}_t^{*\nu})_{\nu \in \mathcal{N}} \rangle$ be an imperfect specialization RS at period t with $\frac{\boldsymbol{p}^* \boldsymbol{A} \boldsymbol{e}_1}{L_1} > \frac{\boldsymbol{p}^* \boldsymbol{A} \boldsymbol{e}_2}{L_2}$. Then, if $\boldsymbol{p}^* \omega_t^N > \boldsymbol{p}^* \omega_t^S$, the wealthier agent, N, sells the more capital-intensive good, good 1, and purchases the more labor-intensive good, good 2. Correspondingly, the poorer agent, S, sells the more labor-intensive good 2 and purchases the more capital-intensive good 1.

Given an RS $\langle \boldsymbol{p}^*; (w_t^{\nu*}, r_t^{\nu*})_{\nu \in \mathcal{N}}, (\boldsymbol{x}_t^{*\nu})_{\nu \in \mathcal{N}} \rangle$ for an economy $\langle \mathcal{N}, (\boldsymbol{A}, \boldsymbol{L}, \boldsymbol{b}), \bar{\omega} \rangle$, the supply of labor hours to earn the revenue $\boldsymbol{p}^* \boldsymbol{b}$ for its own survival is $\boldsymbol{L} \boldsymbol{x}_t^{*\nu}$ for each agent $\nu = N, S$, while the amount of socially necessary labor for producing $\boldsymbol{b}$ as a net output is given by

$$\frac{1}{2} \boldsymbol{L} (\boldsymbol{x}_t^{*N} + \boldsymbol{x}_t^{*S}) = \boldsymbol{vb} = \boldsymbol{L}[\boldsymbol{I} - \boldsymbol{A}]^{-1} \boldsymbol{b}.$$

Then, the notion of UE-exploitation under precapitalist economies is formally defined as follows:

Definition 2 [Yoshihara and Kaneko (2016)]: For a precapitalist economy $\langle \mathcal{N}, (\boldsymbol{A}, \boldsymbol{L}, \boldsymbol{b}), \bar{\omega} \rangle$, let $\langle \boldsymbol{p}^*; (w_t^{\nu*}, r_t^{\nu*})_{\nu \in \mathcal{N}}, (\boldsymbol{x}_t^{*\nu})_{\nu \in \mathcal{N}} \rangle$ be an RS at period t. Then:

$$\nu \text{ is an } exploiting \text{ agent} \iff \boldsymbol{L} \boldsymbol{x}_t^{*\nu} < \boldsymbol{vb};$$
$$\nu \text{ is an } exploited \text{ agent} \iff \boldsymbol{L} \boldsymbol{x}_t^{*\nu} > \boldsymbol{vb}.$$

Under the presumption of Definition 2, the following theorem indicates that if the quasi-Hecksher-Ohlin type of social division of labor is generated in the market-exchange relation, it is characterized as an exploitative relation:

Theorem 3 (The generation of exploitative relations in precapitalist economies): For any precapitalist economy $\langle \mathcal{N}, (\boldsymbol{A}, \boldsymbol{L}, \boldsymbol{b}), (\omega_t^N, \omega_t^S) \rangle$ with $\omega_t^N + \omega_t^S = \bar{\omega}$, let $\langle \boldsymbol{p}^*; (w_t^*, r_t^*), (\boldsymbol{x}_t^{*\nu})_{\nu \in \mathcal{N}} \rangle$ be an imperfect specialization RS at period t with $\frac{\boldsymbol{p}^* \boldsymbol{A} \boldsymbol{e}_1}{L_1} > \frac{\boldsymbol{p}^* \boldsymbol{A} \boldsymbol{e}_2}{L_2}$. Then, if $r_t^* > 0$ and $\boldsymbol{p}_t^* \omega_t^N > \boldsymbol{p}^* \omega_t^S$, then the wealthier agent, N, is exploiting, and the poorer agent, S, is exploited, in terms of Definition 2. Conversely, if $r_t^* = 0$ or $\boldsymbol{p}^* \omega_t^N = \boldsymbol{p}^* \omega_t^S$ holds, then there is no exploitative relation.

Proof. This follows from Yoshihara and Kaneko (2016; Corollary 1). ∎

In the above Theorem 3, the inequality $\boldsymbol{L} \boldsymbol{x}_t^{*N} < \boldsymbol{vb} < \boldsymbol{L} \boldsymbol{x}_t^{*S}$ representing *unequal exchange of labor* definitely implies the *generation of exploitative* *relation.* In an RS for a precapitalist economy, both N and S earn the minimal income to purchase the subsistence bundle b. However, there is a difference between the two agents in terms of their labor supply, and agent N can enjoy more hours as freedom from the necessary labor for survival than agent S.

Given that $p_t^* \omega_t^N > p^* \omega_t^S$, Theorem 3 implies that an RS is UE-exploitative if and only if $r_t^* > 0$. It is well-known that equilibrium prices p^* are labor-value pricing if and only if $r_t^* = 0$. Therefore, the existence of UE-exploitation in this precapitalist economy implies that labor-value prices could not be the unique equilibrium prices, and so would not necessarily serve as the center of gravity for price fluctuations in the long term.

The last view is indeed verified by the following theorem:

Theorem 4 (The existence of the continuum of RSs): Consider a precapitalist economy $\langle \mathcal{N}, (A, L, b), \bar{\omega} \rangle$, such that the Leontief technique (A, L, b) is sufficiently productive: $vb < 1$ holds. Moreover, for the unique Frobenius row vector $q > 0$ of A, let L and q be linearly independent. Then, there exists a unique positive profit rate $\bar{r} > 0$ such that $L[I - (1 + \bar{r})A]^{-1} b = 1$ holds. Moreover, let us define a subset of the profit-wage curve as:

$$G_{\bar{r}} \equiv \left\{ (r, w) \in [0, \bar{r}] \times \left[1, \frac{1}{vb} \right] \middle| w = w(r) \equiv \frac{1}{L[I - (1 + r)A]^{-1} b} \text{ for any } r \in [0, \bar{r}] \right\}.$$

Then, there exists $\theta^S \in \left(0, \frac{1}{2} \right)$ such that for $(\omega_t^N, \omega_t^S) \equiv ((1 - \theta^S)\bar{\omega}, \theta^S \bar{\omega})$ and for any $(r, w(r)) \in G_{\bar{r}}$, the corresponding price vector $p(r) > 0$ is given by

$$p(r) \equiv w(r) L[I - (1 + r)A]^{-1},$$

and $(p(r), w(r), r)$ associated with a suitable profile of each agent's activities $(x^N(r), x^S(r))$ constitutes an imperfect specialization RS at period t.

Proof. First of all, given that L and q being linearly independent, it can be ensured from Yoshihara and Kaneko (2016) that for any $r \in [0, R)$, where $\frac{1}{1+R} > 0$ is the Frobenius eigenvalue of A, and for any $p^r \equiv L[I - (1 + r)A]^{-1} > 0$, the vectors $p^r[I - A]$ and $p^r A$ are linearly independent. Then, since $[I - (1 + r)A]^{-1}$ is continuous and strongly increasing with respect to r and every component of $[I - (1 + r)A]^{-1}$ is divergent to infinity as $r \to R$, we have $\lim_{r \to R} L[I - (1 + r)A]^{-1} b = \infty$. Then, it follows from $L[I - A]^{-1} b = vb < 1$ and the continuous and strong increasingness of $L[I - (1 + r)A]^{-1} b$ with respect to r that there exists $\bar{r} > 0$ such that $\bar{r} < R$ and $L[I - (1 + \bar{r})A]^{-1} b = 1$ holds. Let the simplex of commodity prices be given by $\triangle \equiv \left\{ p \in \mathbb{R}_+^2 \middle| pb = 1 \right\}$. Then, the wage rate $w(\bar{r}) =$

$\frac{1}{L[I-(1+\bar{r})A]^{-1}b} = 1$ holds, so that any propertyless worker must supply one unit of labor to purchase the subsistence consumption vector whenever $(p(\bar{r}), w(\bar{r}), \bar{r})$ prevails. This implies that for any $r > \bar{r}$ with $r < R$, $w(r) < 1$ holds, so that any propertyless worker cannot survive. Therefore, let us define the available class of profit rates as $[0, \bar{r}]$. Then, correspondingly, the class of available wage rates is given by $[1, \frac{1}{vb}]$, where $w(\bar{r}) = 1$ and $w(0) = \frac{1}{vb}$.

Define

$$G_{\bar{r}} \equiv \left\{ (r, w) \in [0, \bar{r}] \times \left[1, \frac{1}{vb}\right] \middle| w = w(r) \equiv \frac{1}{L[I - (1+r)A]^{-1}b} \text{ for any } r \in [0, \bar{r}] \right\},$$

and $p(r) \equiv w(r)L[I - (1 + r)A]^{-1}$. Then, consider the following problem: given any $(r, w(r)) \in G_{\bar{r}}$,

$$\min \theta \text{ s.t. } p(\mathrm{r})(I - A)x = p(\mathrm{r})b \& p(\mathrm{r})Ax = \theta p(\mathrm{r})\bar{\omega} \& Lx \leqq 1 \text{ for some } x > 0.$$

Note that for $x^b \equiv [I - A]^{-1}b > 0$, it follows that $p(r)(I - A)x^b = p(r)b$, $p(r)Ax^b = \frac{1}{2}p(r)\bar{\omega}$, and $Lx^b < 1$. At a fixed $(r, w(r)) \in G_{\bar{r}}$, decreasing θ continuously from $\theta = \frac{1}{2}$ leads $x(\theta; r) > 0$, which satisfies $p(r)(I - A)x(\theta; r) = p(r)b$ and $p(r)Ax(\theta; r) = \theta p(r)\bar{\omega}$, to increase $Lx(\theta; r)$ continuously. Therefore, the above problem is well-defined, and the solution $\theta(r) > 0$ should exist as $\theta(r) < \frac{1}{2}$ whenever $p(r)(I - A)$ and $p(r)A$ are linear independent, where the latter claim holds as confirmed above.

Next, consider

$$\max_{r \in [0, \bar{r}]} \theta(r)$$

and it has a unique solution, say θ^*, as $\theta(r)$ is continuous over $[0, \bar{r}]$. Note that $\theta^* < \frac{1}{2}$, as $\theta(r) < \frac{1}{2}$ for any given $(r, w(r)) \in G_{\bar{r}}$. As argued above, at any fixed $(r, w(r)) \in G_{\bar{r}}$, decreasing the value θ from $\theta = \theta^*$ implies increasing the value $Lx(\theta; r)$ from $Lx(\theta^*; r) < 1$ by keeping $Lx(\theta; r) < 1$, which implies that for any $(r, w(r)) \in G_{\bar{r}}$, $\theta(r) \leqq \theta^*$ and $Lx(\theta^*; r) \leqq Lx(\theta(r; r)) < 1$.

Now, let $\theta^S \equiv \theta^*$ and define $(\omega_t^N, \omega_t^S) \equiv ((1 - \theta^*)\bar{\omega}, \theta^*\bar{\omega})$. As $\theta^* < \frac{1}{2}$, we have $\omega_t^N > \omega_t^S$. Then, for each $(r, w(r)) \in G_{\bar{r}}$, let $x^S(r) \equiv x(\theta^*; r) > 0$, and $x^N(r) \equiv [I - A]^{-1}Nb - x^S(r) > 0$. As $p(r)(I - A)x^S(r) = p(r)b$ and $p(r)Ax^S(r) = p(r)\omega_t^S$ hold for $\omega_t^S = \theta^*\bar{\omega}$, we have $p(r)(I - A)x^N(r) = p(r)b$ and $p(r)Ax^N(r) = p(r)\omega_t^N$ hold for $\omega_t^N = (1 - \theta^*)\bar{\omega}$. Moreover, $Lx^S(r) > Lx^N(r) > 0$ holds for any $(r, w(r)) \in G_{\bar{r}}$, which implies $Lx^N(r) < 1$ for any $(r, w(r)) \in G_{\bar{r}}$.

Finally, by construction of $x^N(r)$, we have $Lx^S(r) + Lx^N(r) = vb$, $Ax^S(r) + Ax^N(r) = \bar{\omega}$, and $[I - A]x^S(r) + [I - A]x^N(r) = Nb$ for any $(r, w(r)) \in G_{\bar{r}}$. As $x^\nu(r)$ is an optimal solution for MP_t^ν at the price system

$(\boldsymbol{p}(r), w(r), r)$ for each $\nu = N, S$, we have $\boldsymbol{x}^\nu(r) \in \boldsymbol{O}_t^\nu(\boldsymbol{p}(r))$ for each $\nu = N, S$.

Thus, in summary, for each $(r, w(r)) \in G_{\bar{r}}$, a price system $(\boldsymbol{p}(r), w(r), r)$ associated with $(\boldsymbol{x}^N(r), \boldsymbol{x}^S(r))$ constitutes an imperfect specialization RS for the economy $\langle \mathcal{N}, (\boldsymbol{A}, \boldsymbol{L}, \boldsymbol{b}), (\omega_t^N, \omega_t^S) \rangle$ in period t. ∎

Note that in Theorem 4, an imperfect specialization RS $(\boldsymbol{p}(r), w(r), r)$ is continuous at every $r \in [0, \bar{r}]$, and so we can specify a continuum set of imperfect specialization RSs as follows:

$$\left\{ (\boldsymbol{p}(r), w(r), r) \middle| r \in [0, \bar{r}], \ w(r) = \frac{1}{\boldsymbol{L}[\boldsymbol{I} - (1+r)\boldsymbol{A}]^{-1}\boldsymbol{b}} \text{ and } \boldsymbol{p}(r) = w(r)\boldsymbol{L}[\boldsymbol{I} - (1+r)\boldsymbol{A}]^{-1} \right\},$$

which constitutes an one-dimensional equilibrium manifold. This equilibrium manifold also contains the *labor-value pricing equilibrium* $(\boldsymbol{p}(0), w(0), 0)$ where $w(0) = \frac{1}{\boldsymbol{v}\boldsymbol{b}}$ and $\frac{\boldsymbol{p}(0)}{w(0)} = \boldsymbol{v}$.

From Theorem 4, we can see that for any precapitalist economy $\langle \mathcal{N}, (\boldsymbol{A}, \boldsymbol{L}, \boldsymbol{b}), \bar{\omega} \rangle$, a continuum set of imperfect specialization RSs exists under some unequal initial distribution of capital goods $\bar{\omega}$. This continuum set contains the labor-value pricing equilibrium, but there are infinitely many RSs with positive profit rates. By Theorem 3, such RSs are UE-exploitative.

In conclusion, unlike the standard Marxian view, it is impossible to verify that in a precapitalist economy with simple commodity-production, the labor-value pricing equilibrium serves as the center of gravity for long terms price fluctuations. This is because, by Theorem 4, there are infinitely many candidate equilibrium prices which could serve as the center of gravity, and no intrinsic mechanism in precapitalist economy is found to select a unique labor-value pricing as the center of gravity. [16]

A final remark is given for what was wrong in Marx's (1894, 1981, Chapter 10) own arguments, from the viewpoint of main theorems in this section. Marx (1894, 1981, Chapter 10) presumed that even under the unequal private ownership of capital goods between workers I and II, they supply the same living labor time so that this purchase and consume the same consumption bundle, where their individual return rates (profit rates) differ. His argument is insufficient in that it lacks the analysis of the social division of labor between the two producers which market competition could generate.

In contrast, our analysis in this section shows that even if the two producers purchase and consume the same consumption bundle, the social division of labor between them emerges through market competition as Theorem 2 shows, and then it leads them to the inequality of the supply of living labor time, due to the unequal initial endowments of capital goods, as Theorem 3 shows. In such a situation, profit rates are equalized among all processes under the imperfect specialization RS, as Theorem 1 shows. A possibility of these three features was ignored by Marx (1894, 1981).

Conclusions

In this paper, we reviewed LTV as the basis for the analysis of economic inequality in the capitalist economy. According to the standard Marxian view, the system of labor values of individual commodities can serve as the center of gravity for long-term price fluctuations in a precapitalist economy with simple commodity-production, where no UE-exploitative social relation emerges, while in a modern capitalist economy, the labor value system is replaced by the prices of production associated with an equal positive rate of profits as the center of gravity, in which UE-exploitative relation between the capitalist and the working classes is a generic and persistent feature of economic inequality. Some of the literature such as Morishima (1973, 1974) criticized this view by showing that the labor values of individual commodities are no longer well-defined in a capitalist economy with joint production.

Given these arguments, this paper firstly shows that the system of individual labor values can be still well-defined in a capitalist economy with joint production whenever the set of available production techniques is all-productive. Under such a restricted class of joint production economies, the standard formal definition of individual labor values can be deemed appropriate, since the market exchanges of commodities in accordance with labor-value pricing can allocate the total quantity of the living labor time in order to meet social demands for each and every commodity. With the same criterion, the paper also shows that an alternative LTV instantiated by **TSSI** cannot be verified.

Secondly, this paper shows that it is generally impossible to verify that labor-value pricing serves as the center of gravity for price fluctuations in precapitalist economies characterized by the full development of simple commodity-production. Though labor-value pricing is just one candidate for the role of center of gravity, there are infinitely many other candidates, and no proper mechanism to uniquely select labor-value pricing can be found within a simple commodity production economy.

Notes

1. For example, see Piketty (2014).
2. For instance, see Maddison (2001).
3. The recent literature of axiomatic analysis of UE-exploitation, like Yoshihara (2010, 2017), Yoshihara and Veneziani (2009, 2018), and Veneziani and Yoshihara (2015,

2017a, 2017b), addresses this fundamental question. These works introduce *axioms* to represent some basic properties that any appropriate definition of UE-exploitation should have, and then examine whether each of the well-known formal definitions of UE-exploitation satisfies them.

4. Note that an economy with a simple Leontief technique is often called a *single product system* in the Sraffian literature, like Kurz and Salvadori (1995).

5. Regarding the recent literature on the Transformation Problem, Mohun and Veneziani (2017) provide a comprehensive survey.

6. Thus, in the case of capitalist economies, a system of labor values of individual commodities is the objectified expression of an efficient quantitative-allocation of abstract human labor among the necessary branches, where each allocated abstract labor is objectified as the socially necessary labor time for the production of each commodity.

7. Essentially the same view of the law of value is also developed by Sasaki (2021, 137–141).

8. Indeed, Marx (1859, 1970) argued that: "operation of the law depends on definite historical pre-conditions. He [Ricardo] says that the determination of value by labor-time applies to "such commodities only as can be increased in quantity by the exertion of human industry, and on the production of which competition operates without restraint."

9. For instance, see Engels, F., "*Supplement to Capital vol. III*" in Marx (1894, 1981), where Engels argues that "Marxian law of values hold general, as far as economic laws are valid at all, for the whole period of simple commodity-production, that is, up to the time when the latter suffers a modification through the appearance of the capitalist form of production. Up to that time prices gravitate toward the values fixed according to the Marxian law and oscillate around those values, so that the more fully simple commodity-production develops, the more the average prices over long periods uninterrupted by external violent disturbances coincide with values within a negligible margin" (Ibid., 1037).

10. Indeed, this condition is equivalent to the producibility of any nonnegative net outputs, formulated as **A5** in Roemer (1981, 36).

11. As argued in section 1, one of the essential claims of LTV is that, in any type of society, total living labor time must be appropriately distributed to various spheres of production in order to meet the social needs for these products, and in a modern capitalist society, the allocation of total labor is mediated through free competition in market exchanges, which results in the distribution of total labor time in proportion to the socially necessary labor time (labor value) of each commodity corresponding to its social needs. This claim is also explicitly represented by the following statements of Marx himself: "Every child knows, too, that the masses of products corresponding to the different needs required different and quantitatively determined masses of the total labor of society. That this necessity of the distribution of social labor in definite proportions cannot possibly be done away with by a particular form of social production but can only change the mode of its appearance, is self-evident. No natural laws can be done away with. What can change in historically different circumstances is only the form in which these laws assert themselves. And the form in which this proportional distribution of labor asserts itself, in the state of society where the interconnection of social labor is manifested in the private exchange of the individual products of labor, is precisely the exchange value of these products" (Marx (1868, 1988).

12. Indeed, when Marx (1867, 1976, 168) argued that "The production of commodities must be fully developed before the scientific conviction emerges, from experience itself, that all the different kinds of private labor (which are carried on independently of each other, and yet, as spontaneously developed branches of the social division of labor, are in a situation of all-round dependence on each other) are continually being reduced to the quantitative proportions in which society requires them. The reason for this reduction is that in the midst of the accidental and ever-fluctuating exchange relations between the products, the labor time socially necessary to produce them asserts itself as a regulative law of nature", it was under the supposition of fully developed commodity-production economy with the abstraction of capitalistic production.

13. "If the prices at which commodities exchange for one another are to correspond approximately to their values, nothing more is needed than (1) that the exchange of different commodities ceases to be purely accidental or merely occasional; (2) that, in so far as we are dealing with the direct exchange of commodities, these commodities are produced on both sides in relative quantities that approximately correspond to mutual need, something that is learned from the reciprocal experience of trading and which therefore arises precisely as a result of continuing exchange; and (3) that, as far as selling is concerned, no natural or artificial monopolies enable one of the contracting parties to sell above value, or force them to sell cheap, below value" (Ibid., 278–279).

14. Such a model has been discussed by Roemer (1982, Chapter 1) and Yoshihara and Kaneko (2016).

15. The following economic model is a simpler version of the model in Yoshihara and Kaneko (2016), though their interpretations are different. We will interpret the following model as a representation of the simple commodity production economy discussed in Marx (1894, 1981, 275–279), while Yoshihara and Kaneko (2016) regard it as a model of pre-industrial world economy with no international labor nor credit market. Among the main theorems presented below, Theorems 1 and 3 are taken from Yoshihara and Kaneko (2016), but Theorems 2 and 4 are the new results in this paper.

16. This criticism is particularly relevant if it is applied in the context of non-equilibrium price dynamics with no intertemporal structure. In contrast, if the issue of the center of gravity is considered in an intertemporal economy, it is Kaneko and Yoshihara (2019), among other works like Duménil and Levy (1985), Dana et al. (1989), and Veneziani (2007, 2013), which would provide us with the most relevant insights. In that paper where the intertemporal precapitalist economy with no labor nor credit market is considered, the path of intertemporal equilibrium labor allocations among nations converges to the egalitarian one, and so the UE-exploitation would tend to disappear in the infinite limit. However, *it does not necessarily imply that equilibrium prices converge to the labor-value pricing.* The egalitarian convergence of labor allocations takes place either because of the convergence of the prices to the labor values or because of the convergence of the wealth distributions to the egalitarian distribution.

Acknowledgments

I am grateful so much to the editor and the three anonymous referees for their suggestions toward the final revision of the paper. I am also thankful to Makoto Itoh and Takao Sasaki for discussions with them on the earlier version of the paper.

References

Cunningham, H. 1980. *Lecture in the Industrial Revolution: c.1780–c.1880*. New York: St. Martin's Press.

Cunningham, H. 2014. *Time, Work and Leisure: Life Changes in England since 1700*. Manchester, UK: Manchester University Press.

Dana, R.-A., M. Florenzano, C. Le Van, and D. Levy. 1989. "Production Prices and General Equilibrium Prices: A Long-Run Property of a Leontief Economy." *Journal of Mathematical Economics* 18 (3):263–280. doi:10.1016/0304-4068(89)90024-4.

Duménil, G. 1980. *De la Valeur aux Prix de Production*, Paris: Economica.

Duménil, G., and D. Levy. 1985. "The Classicals and the Neoclassicals, a Rejoinder to Frank Hahn." *Cambride Journal of Economics* 9:327–345.

Foley, D. K. 1982. "The Value of Money, the Value of Labor Power, and the Marxian Transformation Problem." *Review of Radical Political Economics* 14 (2):37–47. doi:10.1177/048661348201400204.

International Labour Office (ILO). 2005a. *Human Trafficking and Forced Labour Exploitation*. Geneva: International Labour Office.

International Labour Office (ILO). 2005b. *Forced Labour: Labour Exploitation and Human Trafficking in Europe*. Geneva; International Labour Office.

Itoh, M. 2021. *Value and Crisis, Essays on Marxian Economics in Japan* (2nd ed.). New York: Monthly Review Press.

Kaneko, S., and N. Yoshihara. 2019. "On the General Impossibility of Persistent Unequal Exchange Free Trade Equilibria in the Pre-industrial World Economy," Working Paper 2019-05, UMass Amherst Economics Papers.

Kawakita, M. 2010. *Lectures on Modern British History, (in Japanese) Gendai-Shinsho Series 2070*. Tokyo, Japan: Kodansha Ltd..

Kliman, A., and T. McGlone. 1999. "A Temporal Single-System Interpretation of Marx's Value Theory." *Review of Political Economy* 11 (1):33–59. doi:10.1080/095382599107165.

Kurz, H., and N. Salvadori. 1995. *Theory of Production: A Long-Period Analysis*. Cambridge, UK: Cambride University Press.

Maddison, A. 2001. *The World Economy*. Paris: OECD.

Marx, K. 1859, 1970. *A Contribution to the Critique of Political Economy*, trans. by S. W. Ryazanskaya. Moscow, UK: Progress Publishers.

Marx, K. 1867, 1976. *Capital. A Critique of Political Economy, Vol.I.*, trans. by B. Fowkes. Harmondsworth, UK: Penguin Books.

Marx, K. 1868, 1988. "Marx to Ludwig Kugelmann in Hanover: London, 11 July 1868." In *Marx-Engels Collected Works*, vol. 43, 68.

Marx, K. 1894, 1981. *Capital. A Critique of Political Economy, Vol.3*, trans. by D. Fernbach. Harmondsworth, UK: Penguin Books.

Morishima, M. 1973. *Marx's Economics*. Cambridge: Cambridge University Press.

Morishima, M. 1974. "Marx in the Light of Modern Economic Theory." *Econometrica* 42 (4):611–632. doi:10.2307/1913933.

Mohun, Simon, and Roberto Veneziani. 2017. "Value, Price, and Exploitation: The Logic of the Transformation Problem." *Journal of Economic Surveys* 31 (5):1387–1420. doi:10.1111/joes.12223.

Okishio, N. 1963. "A Mathematical Note on Marxian Theorems." *Weltwirtschaftliches Archiv* 91:287–299.

Piketty, T. 2014. *Capital in the Twenty-First Century*. Cambridge, MA: Harvard University Press.

Ricardo, D. 1951. "On the Principles of Political Economy and Taxation." in *The Works and Correspondence of David Ricardo*, edited by P. Sraffa, vol. I, Cambridge: Cambridge University Press.

Roemer, J. E. 1981. *Analytical Foundations of Marxian Economic Theory*. Cambridge, MA: Harvard University Press.

Roemer, J. E. 1982. *A General Theory of Exploitation and Class*. Cambridge, MA: Harvard University Press.

Sasaki, R. 2021. "Towards Understanding Marx's Theory of Equilibrium and Prices of Production." In *Marx-Engels-Jahrbuch 2019/20*, edited by Internationale Marx-Engels-Stiftung (IMES), 135–157. Berlin: Akademie Verlag | 2192-8207.

Steedman, I. 1975. "Positive Profits with Negative Surplus Values." *The Economic Journal* 85 (337):114–123. doi:10.2307/2230532.

Thompson, E. P. 1967. "Time, Work-Discipline, and Industrial Capitalism." *Past and Present* 38 (1):56–97. doi:10.1093/past/38.1.56.

Veneziani, R. 2007. "Exploitation and Time." *Journal of Economic Theory* 132 (1):189–207. doi:10.1016/j.jet.2005.07.001.

Veneziani, R. 2013. "Exploitation Inequality and Power." *Journal of Theoretical Politics* 25 (4):526–545. doi:10.1177/0951629813477275.

Veneziani, R., and N. Yoshihara. 2015. "Exploitation in Economies with Heterogeneous Preferences, Skills and Assets: An Axiomatic Approach." *Journal of Theoretical Politics* 27 (1):8–33. doi:10.1177/0951629814538911.

Veneziani, R., and N. Yoshihara. 2017a. "One Million Miles to Go: Taking the Axiomatic Road to Defining Exploitation." *Cambridge Journal of Economics* 41 (6) :1607–1626. doi:10.1093/cje/bew053.

Veneziani, R., and N. Yoshihara. 2017b. "Globalisation and Inequality in a Dynamic Economy: An Axiomatic Analysis of Unequal Exchange." *Social Choice and Welfare* 49 (3–4):445–468. doi:10.1007/s00355-017-1062-8.

Yoshihara, N. 2010. "Class and Exploitation in General Convex Cone Economies." *Journal of Economic Behavior & Organization* 75 (2):281–296. doi:10.1016/j.jebo.2010.03.007.

Yoshihara, N. 2017. "A Progress Report on Marxian Economic Theory: On the Controversies in Exploitation Theory since Okishio (1963)." *Journal of Economic Surveys* 31 (2):632–659. doi:10.1111/joes.12151.

Yoshihara, N., and S. Kaneko. 2016. "On the Existence and Characterization of Unequal Exchange in the Free Trade Equilibrium." *Metroeconomica* 67 (2):210–241. doi:10.1111/meca.12125.

Yoshihara, N., and R. Veneziani. 2009. "Exploitation as the Unequal Exchange of Labour: An Axiomatic Approach." *IER Discussion Paper Series A. No.524*, The Institute of Economic Research, Hitotsubashi University.

Yoshihara, N., and R. Veneziani. 2018. "The Theory of Exploitation as the Unequal Exchange of Labour." *Economics and Philosophy* 34 (3):381–409. doi:10.1017/S0266267118000238.

Index

Note: Page numbers followed by "n" denote endnotes.

Fischer, Andrew 37
five life-worlds 110
five-class structure 14
Fortunato, Piergiuseppe 83
four-class scheme 95, 96, 105
Freeman, A. 2
fundamental population survey 101

gender 94, 100, 103, 106, 108, 113; disparity 103
Gini coefficient 56, 62, 66, 92, 93
Gini index 30, 31
global health crisis 77, 86, 88
global inequality 29
globalization 2, 5, 57, 58, 64, 67, 79, 80, 84
great financial crisis 80, 86
green deals 87
Grimshaw, R. 24n5
growth patterns 80

Haberler, G. 16
Harrod, Roy 33, 39
Hashimoto, K. 13
hazardous transitions 78
health crisis 80, 87
Heckscher-Ohlin model 131
Hein, E. 51
Hickel, J. 2, 27, 31, 38
Hirsch, Fred 34
household income 92, 96, 97, 104, 108, 109, 112
household inequality 2, 6
Huber, E. 56

income distribution 14, 60, 65, 67, 68, 81, 82, 84–87
income inequality variable 61
individual commodities 17, 120, 123, 136
individual income 102, 103, 109
individual labor values 17, 120, 136
inequality: effect 56, 61, 64; evolution of 28, 33; measuring 31
inequality-income relationship 10
inflation 2, 35, 36
Inklaar, R. 53
international income inequality 2–5, 10–17, 20–22
international trade 14, 16, 17, 57, 77, 128, 131
Itoh, M. 121

Japan 11–13, 91, 93, 100, 101, 103, 105, 107, 112, 114
Japanese capitalism 103, 104
Jaumotte, F. 57
joint production 17, 119, 120, 122, 123, 125, 136

kakusa shakai 91, 93, 94
Kaneko, S. 14, 132, 138n15, 138n16
Kaplan, S. N. 55

Khan, M. 55
King, S. 2
Korzeniewicz, Patrici 30
Kregel, Jan 39
Kurz, H. 120, 122
Kus, B. 56, 61, 64, 69n12
Kuznets, S. 8, 10
Kuznets curve relationship 61, 64
Kvangraven, Ingrid 37

labor incomes 82
labor power 98, 99, 119
labor theory of value (LTV) 16, 118–120, 125
labor values 17, 119–121, 123, 125–128, 136
labor-value pricing equilibrium 121, 128, 135
labor-value system 17, 120, 121, 123, 124, 126, 127
Lall, S. 57
Lane, P. 61
Latin America 27, 28, 33, 35, 38, 42, 57
Lee, K. 56
Lee, Kang-Kook 9
Lerner index 59, 65, 67
Levey, D. 120
lifetime unmarrieds 108
living labor time 125, 135, 136
lower aggregate demand 55, 68
Luo, Y. 52, 56

market capitalism 87
Marx, Karl 119
Mediterranean capitalisms 81, 82
meso-corporate capitalisms 81
Milanovic, B. 2, 6, 29, 30, 41, 78
Milesi-Ferretti, G. 61
Mohun, Simon 137n5
Montecino, J. A. 53, 54
Moran, Timothy 30
Morishima, M. 119
Myrdal, G. 98

national income 7, 8, 82, 83
neoclassical theory 15, 16, 20, 23
neoliberal ideology 78
neoliberalism 3, 10, 33, 54, 78, 99
new Japanese class society 114
new middle class 95, 96, 100, 102, 103, 105, 110, 112–114, 116

Ocampo, Jose 34
occupation 100, 108, 109
Ohashi, R. 99
Okishio, N. 23
old middle class 14, 95, 96, 99, 100, 102, 103, 105, 112, 113, 116
Olin Wright, Erik 33
O'Rourke, Kevin 30

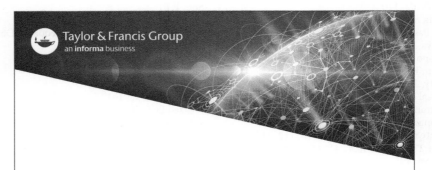

For Product Safety Concerns and Information please contact our
EU representative GPSR@taylorandfrancis.com Taylor & Francis
Verlag GmbH, Kaufingerstraße 24, 80331 München, Germany